HISTORICAL ATLAS OF WASHINGTON

HISTORICAL ATLAS OF WASHINGTON

By James W. Scott
and Roland L. De Lorme

Cartography by Ted R. Brandt
and Patrick S. Grant

University of Oklahoma Press   Norman and London

BY JAMES W. SCOTT

Social Science Research Handbook (with Raymond G. McInnis) (New York, 1974; 1984)
Pacific Northwest Themes (Bellingham, Wash., 1978)
Early Industries of Bellingham Bay and Whatcom County (Bellingham, Wash., 1980)
Historical Atlas of Washington (with Roland L. De Lorme) (Norman, 1988)

BY ROLAND L. DE LORME

Antidemocratic Trends in Twentieth-Century America (with Raymond G. McInnis) (Reading, Mass. 1969)
Of Man, Time, and the River (Bellingham, Wash., 1977)
Historical Atlas of Washington (with James W. Scott) (Norman, 1988)

Library of Congress Cataloging-in-Publication Data

Scott, James William, 1925–
    Historical atlas of Washington.

    Bibliography: p.
    Includes index.
    1. Washington (State)—Historical geography.
2. Washington (State)—Maps. 3. Northwest, Pacific—Historical geography. 4. Northwest, Pacific—Maps.
I. De Lorme, Roland L. (Roland Lawrence), 1937– .
II. Brandt, Theodore R., 1954– . III. Grant,
Patrick S. (Patrick Stephen), 1957– . IV. Title.
F891.S38 1988   911'.797   87-40557
ISBN 0-8061-2108-4

The paper in this book meets the guidelines for permanence and durability of the Committee on Production Guidelines for Book Longevity of the Council on Library Resources, Inc.

CONTENTS

PREFACE

Although the recorded history of the state of Washington is relatively brief compared to that of many other states, Washington's history has seldom been lacking in interest to residents or visitors.

From the time of the Spanish and British explorations of the 1770s—a series of events that helped draw the attention of the world to the Pacific Northwest—to the present day, Washington has become increasingly involved in the wider scene of international commerce and politics. Whereas in the eighteenth and early nineteenth centuries the region was little more than a pawn to be toyed with by authorities in London or Madrid or Washington, D.C., today Washington state is a major participant in national and international trade. Politically it also has steadily increased its national and international role and stature. The fur trade, the region's first developed natural resource, has been replaced by trading of an immensely more varied sort. Meanwhile, the political problems of resource allocation—notably of water and fish—and of environmental controls have become controversial issues of major concern to state and local officials and to businessmen on both sides of the Canadian-American border.

This atlas attempts to present graphically, with accompanying text, the progress of the state from prehistoric times through the twentieth century. It begins with a group of maps that cover the geographical bases—terrain, climate, vegetation, hydrography, and land use. Then subsequent sections of the atlas display and record the evolution of settlement, the development of the state's economy, and the progress of society and culture from Indian times to the present. Some of the maps cover major historical events or specific periods; others show present-day patterns of activity, and the historical background is dealt with in the adjacent commentary.

Bellingham, Washington   JAMES W. SCOTT
                                  ROLAND L. DE LORME

ACKNOWLEDGMENTS

Compiling an atlas is never an easy task. There are the often insidious choices to be made of what to include and what to leave out, what to emphasize and what to downplay, what authorities and agencies to consult, and what sources to track down and check. In the preparation, drafting, and writing of the atlas we have incurred many debts. We have had the willing cooperation of our colleagues in the Departments of History and of Geography and Regional Planning, as well as the backing of the College of Arts and Sciences, in Western Washington University. The dean of the Graduate School made available a full graduate assistantship during two quarters of one academic year, which greatly helped in the design and drafting of the maps; and the Bureau for Faculty Research was ever helpful in providing typing and proofreading services. To Dr. James W. Davis, Professor of Political Science and former Dean of Arts and Sciences; Dr. Sam Kelly, Dean of Graduate Studies and Research; Jane Clark, formerly Director, Bureau for Faculty Research; Eugene A. Hoerauf, Staff Cartographer, Department of Geography; and Mary Rudd, Administrative Secretary, Department of Geography and Regional Planning, all of Western Washington University, we are especially grateful; as we are also to Nancy Pryor, Librarian of the Washington Room, The State Library, Olympia, who has answered so many questions and provided constant interest and support. We would also like to acknowledge the helpful suggestions we have had from John N. Drayton, Editor-in-Chief, University of Oklahoma Press, and his staff, especially Sarah I. Morrison, Associate Editor, for her valiant efforts in shepherding this volume through the press.

In expressing our sincere thanks also to the following persons, we trust that we have not inadvertently omitted any names:

Terry Abraham, Manuscripts Librarian, Washington State University

Dr. Angelo Anastasio, Professor Emeritus of Anthropology, Western Washington University

John Bengvall, Washington State Department of Natural Resources

Galen Biery, local historian, Bellingham

R. M. Brown, Union Pacific Railroad, Omaha

Janet Collins, Map Curator, Department of Geography and Regional Planning, Western Washington University

Steve Craig, Washington State Energy Office

Dr. Howard J. Critchfield, Professor of Geography, Western Washington University, and State Climatologist

Roger Dierking, Bureau of Land Management, Portland

A. Thomas DiDomenico, Senior Planner, Makah Indian Reservation

Ken Earlywine, Hydropower Division, U.S. Army Corps of Engineers

Roy C. Ellis, Data Services Office, Bureau of the Census, Seattle

Tom Glenn, formerly Manager, Port of Bellingham

Dr. Garland Grabert, Professor of Anthropology, Western Washington University

Bill Haig, Washington State Archives, Olympia

Dr. James Hitchman, Professor of History, Western Washington University

Sidney F. McAlpin, State Archivist, Olympia

Professor Raymond G. McInnis, Head Reference Librarian, Western Washington University

Dr. Robert L. Monahan, Professor of Geography and Director, Canadian and Canadian-American Studies, Western Washington University

Dr. Debnath Mookherjee, Professor of Geography, Western Washington University

James D. Moore, Regional Archivist, Northwest Regional State Archives, Bellingham

Dale O'Dell, Burlington Northern Railroad

Bob Passey, Burlington Northern Railroad

Vance Reynolds, Georgia Pacific Company, Bellingham

Sarah Rhinehardt, Administrative Secretary, Department of History, Western Washington University

George Saito, Federal Aviation Administration

Alan Scott, Rail Division, Washington Utilities Commission

Professor William H. O. Scott, Documents Librarian, Western Washington University

Sue Shaw, Public Information Officer, Washington State Department of Fisheries

Dr. John C. Sherman, Professor of Geography, University of Washington

Dolores Sickles, Bureau for Faculty Research, Western Washington University

Dr. James Talbot, Academic Vice-President and Provost, Western Washington University

Dr. Herbert C. Taylor, Jr., Professor of Anthropology, Western Washington University

David G. Tremaine, Lake Stevens School District

Daniel E. Turbeville, Simon Fraser University, British Columbia

Ellis Vonheeder, Geologist, Department of Natural Resources, Olympia

Geri Walker, Bureau for Faculty Research, Western Washington University

Lawrence Weissner, Population Data Division, Office of Financial Management, State of Washington, Olympia

PART I

PHYSICAL ENVIRONMENT

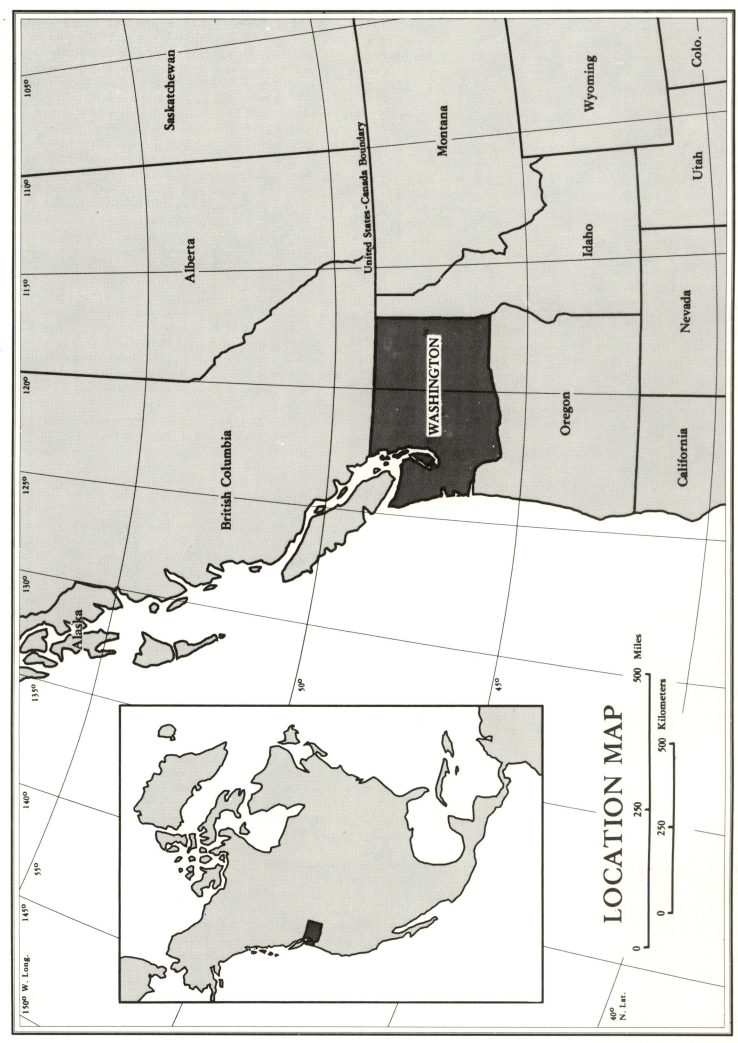

LOCATION MAP

1. LOCATION

Situated in the northwestern corner of the conterminous United States, the state of Washington extends from the forty-ninth to the forty-fifth parallel of north latitude, and longitudinally from 116° west to 124°40′ west. Washington extends from north to south approximately 275 miles (440 kilometers) and from east to west approximately 350 miles (560 kilometers).

North of the forty-ninth parallel Washington is bounded by the Canadian province of British Columbia. Idaho is on its eastern border, and Oregon on its southern border. On the west lies the Pacific Ocean and its associated inland waters—the Strait of Juan de Fuca, the Strait of Georgia, and Puget Sound. At comparable latitudes in Europe are France and the Swiss Alps; and in Asia, Manchuria and the island of Sakhalin. British Columbia and Alaska are the only regions in the Americas occupying the same meridians of longitude.

With an area of 68,192 square miles (174,592 square kilometers) Washington ranks twentieth among the United States, a little behind Missouri (69,686 square miles) (178,400 square kilometers) and Oklahoma (69,919 square miles) (179,008 square kilometers), but well ahead of Georgia (58,876 square miles) (150,720 square kilometers) and Florida (58,560 square miles (149,888 square kilometers). Its area, which amounts to slightly more than the combined areas of the six New England states, comprises 66,709 square miles (170,752 square kilometers) of land and 1,483 square miles (3,795 square kilometers) of water. This area is larger than that of more than eighty, or approximately one-half of the independent nations of the world.

Washington's location is geographically advantageous. On the rim of the world's largest ocean, the Pacific, the state in general benefits from a climate that is temperate and equable. (See Maps 4 and 5 for details.)

Historically, the state's location for a long time kept it remote from world events. During the first century and a half of European settlement in North America, the Pacific Northwest region was quite literally a terra incognita, and even after the visits of Spanish, English, Russian, and other explorers, in the late eighteenth century it remained remote and isolated from Euro-American influences. The tyranny of distance was too great to be overcome by the transportation of the day, and it was not until the later nineteenth century, when railroads were built across the continent, and steamship service was initiated, that the state of Washington ceased to be isolated.

From an economic standpoint the remoteness of the region resulted in slow growth and delayed exploitation of its mineral and other natural resources. Today Washington is advantageously placed for trade with the Orient, as well as Alaska and other parts of the Pacific rim. These and other aspects of Washington's location are presented cartographically and examined textually in the pages of this atlas.

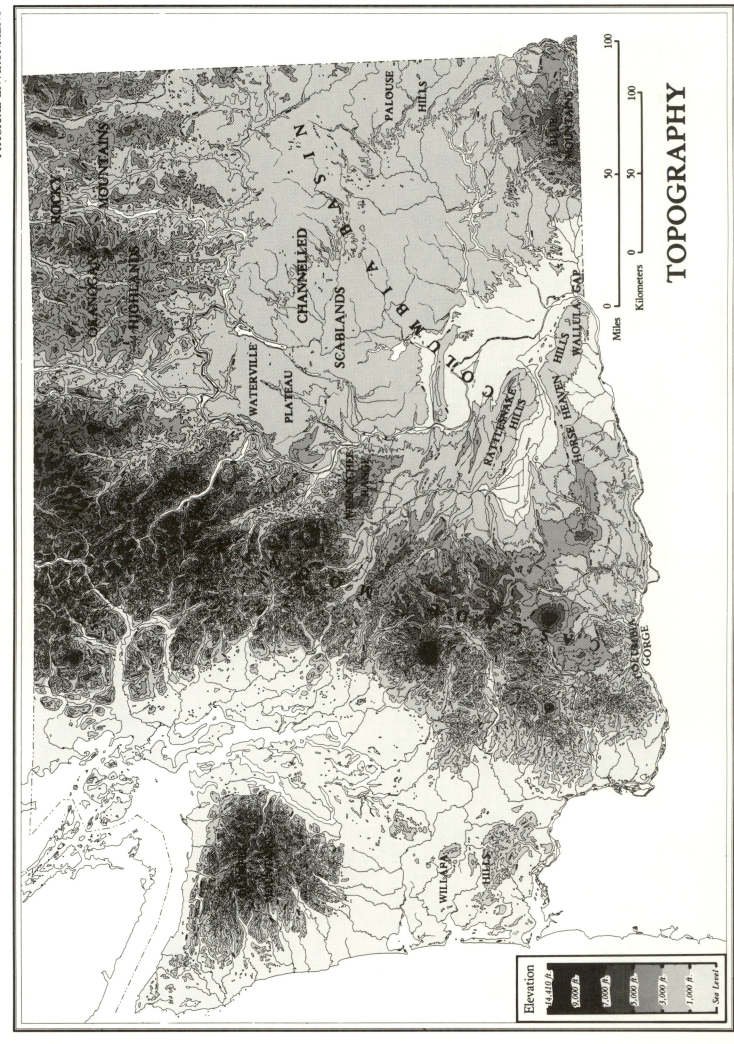

ROCKY MOUNTAINS

OKANOGAN HIGHLAND

COLUMBIA BASIN

WATERVILLE PLATEAU

CHANNELLED SCABLANDS

PALOUSE HILLS

BLUE MOUNTAINS

WENATCHEE

RATTLESNAKE HILLS

HORSE HEAVEN HILLS

WALLULA GAP

WILLAPA HILLS

COLUMBIA GORGE

TOPOGRAPHY

Elevation	
14,410 ft.	
9,000 ft.	
7,000 ft.	
5,000 ft.	
3,000 ft.	
1,000 ft.	
Sea Level	

Miles

Kilometers

0   50   100

0   50   100

© 1988 by the University of Oklahoma Press

2. TOPOGRAPHY

Although the mean altitude of the state of Washington—1,700 feet (517 meters) above sea level—is little more than half that of Oregon, its neighboring state on the south, and barely one-third the mean altitude of Idaho, its neighbor on the east, the relative relief of Washington is varied and often dramatic. The minimum altitude is found at sea level along the Pacific Coast, and the maximum at Mount Rainier, 14,410 feet (4,388 meters) above sea level. The Cascades, of which Mount Rainer is part, stand out as the highest mountain range in the state, with four other volcanic peaks rising to towering heights above the general level of the range. From north to south these are Mount Baker (10,778 feet) (3,282 meters), Glacier Peak (10,568 feet) (3,218 meters), and at approximately the same latitude but separated by about thirty-five miles (fifty-eight kilometers), Mount Saint Helens (8,365 feet*) (2,550 meters), and Mount Adams (12,276 feet) (3,738 meters). Less elevated, though often no less rugged or dramatic, are the Olympics (with Mount Olympus, at 7,965 feet, or 2,423 meters, the highest peak), the Okanogan Highlands (of which the highest peak, Mount Bonaparte, is 7,298 feet, or 2,222 meters), the Blue Mountains (of which the highest in Washington is 6,381 feet, or 1,943 meters), and the Rockies (of which highest in Washington is 7,309 feet, or 2,226 meters).

Lower-lying regions such as the Palouse Hills reach elevations of more than 3,500 feet (1,066 meters).

Relief, however, is not to be confused with altitude or elevation. Relief encompasses the myriad changes of gradient and elevation that occur in an area. In general, the more frequent the changes the more rugged the relief. It is in the mountain areas of Washington, therefore, that the relief is most dramatic, particularly in the mountain regions that have been affected by glaciation. Alpine (or valley) glaciation, which has affected virtually all the more elevated parts of the state, has produced in the Cascades and the Olympics in particular, and to a more limited extent in other mountain areas, relief features such as great U-shaped valleys with nearly sheer sides and the occasional hanging valley high above the valley floor, an abundance of dramatic cascades and waterfalls, and many pyramid peaks with deeply excavated cirques around their perimeter separated by knifelike ridges known as arêtes.

In contrast, the lowland areas around Puget Sound, and to a lesser extent the valley of the Lower Columbia, are without marked regional relief, although locally some small hills, an occasional escarpment, or a deeply incised river with steep valley walls, present relief of a moderately dramatic sort. Most of these lowland areas of western Washington are covered with layers of till or outwash gravels, sands, and silts, the products of Pleistocene glaciation derived from valley glaciers or the continental ice sheets. In covering much of the lowland areas, they frequently have masked, or totally buried, earlier relief features.

The Columbia Basin—known to early pioneers as the Great Columbia Plain—is, in fact, a basin-shaped plateau where the elevation varies from less than 1,000 feet (304 meters) to more than 3,000 feet (913 meters). Covered in large part by extensive flows of basaltic lava, the region has been deeply incised by rivers and glaciers. Deep canyons, gorges, and coulees provide many dramatic changes of relief, especially in the Channelled Scablands in the northeast part of the basin. In the southeast section wind-blown deposits of loess are aligned in an approximately southwest-northeast direction to form the unique Palouse Hills with their constantly changing gradients and generally smooth surfaces. Surrounding the Columbia Basin to the north, northeast, and south are mountains of greater elevation and more rugged relief than the Palouse Hills—the Okanogan Highlands, the Rockies, and the Blue Mountains.

In brief, the relief of the state of Washington is seldom subdued or monotonous. More often it is a constantly changing phenomenon, varied and frequently dramatic, an attraction to resident and visitor alike.

*The eruption of May 18, 1980, reduced Mount Saint Helen's height by approximately 1,300 feet.

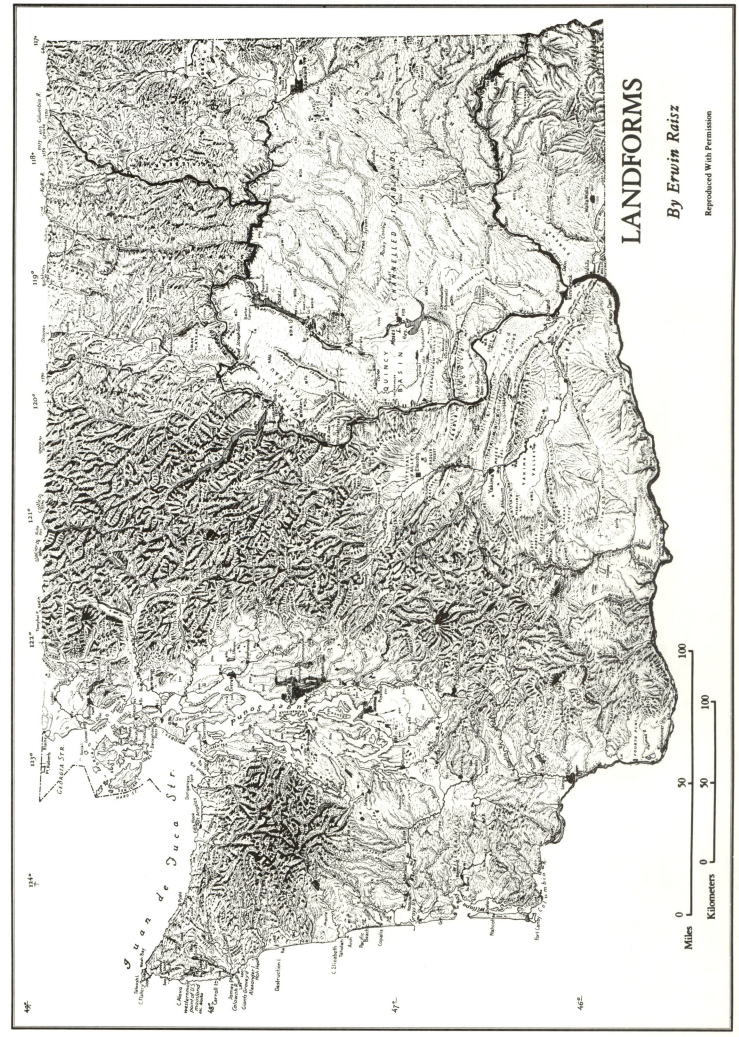

LANDFORMS

By Erwin Raisz

Reproduced With Permission

3. LANDFORMS

In the diversity and beauty of its regional landscapes Washington is surpassed by few other states. The basic ingredient of this diversity is Washington's extensive array of widely contrasting landforms. These range from towering volcanic peaks and symmetrical cinder cones to narrow canyons and chasmlike coulees; from flat deltaic lowlands to rugged, deeply eroded alpine uplands; from migratory sand dunes to sharply delineated basaltic buttes; and from broad, gently sloping river valleys to magnificent U-shaped glacial valleys.

The three mountain ranges shown in Map 2—the Olympics, the Cascades, and the Rockies—contain many of the state's best-known and most spectacular landforms. Lying between the Cascades and the Rockies is one of the largest extrusions of volcanic lava in the world, the Columbia Basin, or Plateau, and between the Cascades and the Olympics is the much-embayed Puget Sound lowland, where the sound itself is bejewelled with hundreds of small and large islands.

The Olympic Mountains and the lower-lying, less-rugged Willapa Hills form the western border of Washington. Sculpted by valley glaciers during the Pleistocene epoch, the Olympics display spectacular mountain scenery in individual peaks, such as Mount Olympus, and along the valleys of deeply incised rivers like the Hoh, the Elwha, and the Dosewallips. The coastal plain fringing the Pacific Ocean is a narrow strip of lowland that displays on the south extensive sand dunes, and on the north, low-but-steep-sided cliffs and isolated sea stacks rising precipitously from the surrounding waters. Penetrating this generally north-south coastline are two extensive, shallow bays—Willapa Bay and Grays Harbor.

The Puget Sound region, located east of the Olympic Mountains, is an extensive lowland that is covered for the most part with a thick mantle of glacial till and glacial-outwash gravels and silt. The landforms there in general are more subdued than those to the east or west, and only occasionally are they spectacular. The gradients are gentler than in the regions on the east, west, and south, but some scenic variety is provided by frequent changes in the shoreline, which is interrupted by countless bays and many headlands and peninsulas. Offshore lie hundreds of islands, which range in size from San Juan, Whidbey, and Bainbridge islands, many square miles in area, to tiny islets that show no more than a few square yards of exposed rock. The mountains that lie on the east and west provide a stunning backdrop to the landforms of Puget Sound when the visibility is good—perhaps no more than one day in four or five on average. Extending south as far as the Columbia River is the Cowlitz Corridor, an area of undulating lowland and low hills.

The Cascade Range effectively divides the state of Washington into two major climatic regions. Among its many scenic attractions are five magnificent volcanic peaks; most of the existing glaciers of the conterminous United States; glacial lakes that range in size from the huge, fiordlike Lake Chelan, Washington's largest natural lake, to tiny mountain tarns; alpine meadows strewn with glacial detritus; and river valleys replete with spectacular waterfalls of impressive height and volume. Geologists have long distinguished the North Cascades from the South Cascades, placing the dividing line across Snoqualmie Pass east of Seattle. The North Cascades is a more elevated and more rugged mountain region in which volcanic fire and glacial ice have been the principal forces responsible for the scenic diversity that exists, whereas the South Cascades is scenically a more subdued landscape, although its three volcanic peaks—Rainier, Adams and Saint Helens—dominate its skyline to a far greater degree than do Mount Baker and Glacier Peak in the North Cascades.

The Columbia Plateau is a huge basin-shaped region that forms an approximate triangle between the Cascades and the Rockies on the west and east, respectively, and the Blue Mountains on the south. Covered by extensive sheets of basaltic lava during the Tertiary era, the Columbia Plateau has been extensively eroded by glacial and river action in more recent times. Its northernmost parts were directly affected by ice sheets that moved southward form Canada during the Quaternary period. Glacial erratics, kame terraces, kettle holes, and other glacial landforms are visible in many parts. The catastrophic changes wrought by the rapid draining of glacial Lake Missoula, via the Spokane River valley, can be seen in the impressive series of northeast-southwest-trending coulees that form the Channeled Scablands of the northeast and center of the Columbia Basin. Most remarkable of the many regional landforms is Dry Falls, which is many times the breadth and height of Niagara Falls but today lacks even a trickle of water. Remarkable also are the steeply undulating and somewhat regularly distributed Palouse Hills, which were formed of wind-borne loessial deposits derived from glacio-fluvial materials deposited west and southwest of the region during the Quaternary ice age.

Forming the northern and northeastern borders of the Columbia Plateau are the Okanogan Highlands (shown in Map 2), an integral part of the Rocky Mountain system. The complex lithology and structure of the Okanogan Highlands is of greater interest to the geologist than to the lay observer, who is more likely to see the region as one of rounded hills (even though some are of considerable elevation), deep, often U-shaped valleys, and subdued rather than spectacular landforms. In contrast, the Blue Mountains on the southeastern border of the state provide, particularly in the Grande Ronde and Snake valleys, some spectacular vistas, including some impressive gorges that reveal with startling clarity the many, often brightly colored, lava flows that helped build up the region.

The most successful attempt to map the landforms of Washington is that of the late Erwin Raisz of Harvard University. Created originally in 1939 to accompany Wallace W. Atwood's *The Physiographic Provinces of the United States*, Raisz's map, redrawn and improved in subsequent editions, has been reproduced many times since. The Washington portion of the map is produced here by permission.

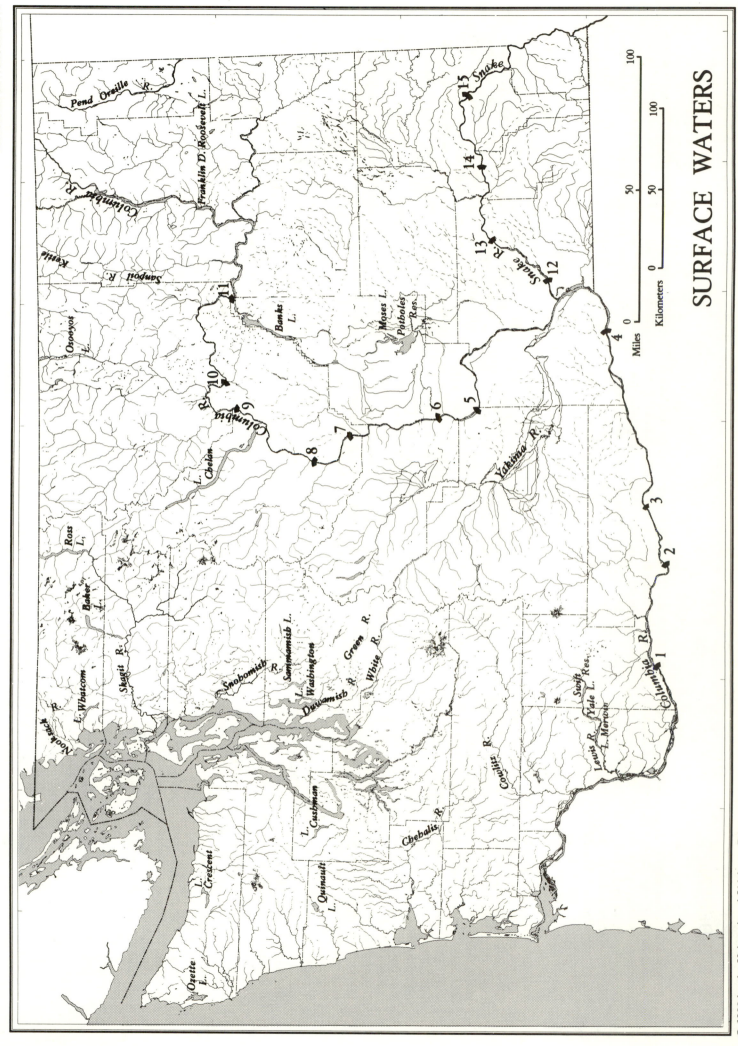

SURFACE WATERS

Miles
0   50   100

Kilometers
0   50   100

Among the Pacific states Washington is exceeded only by Alaska in the percentage of its total area covered by water, and only by Alaska and California in the actual area occupied by lakes and rivers. With 2.2 percent of Washington's area, or 1,529 square miles (3,914 square kilometers), in lakes and rivers, the state possesses a great variety of surface-water resources. The value of surface waters for such activities as fishing, navigation, hydroelectric production, irrigation, industry, and recreation has long been recognized, and efforts have been made to develop each activity to its fullest potential. Not all of these, however, are compatible uses. Conflicts have resulted, most notably between those interested in preserving the salmon runs and those interested in building dams for hydroelectricity and irrigation.

The total water supply available has been estimated to average 216 million acre-feet annually. However, less than half of this—approximately 92 million acre-feet—originates in the state, and more than two-thirds of these 92 million acre-feet are in western Washington, the result of the orographic effect of the Cascades. Hence it is the more than 120 million acre-feet that flow into the state from British Columbia, Idaho, and Montana that provide eastern Washington with the bulk of its water—water that for decades has been used for power generation and irrigation.

The construction of dams and the creation of reservoirs have done much to regulate the extreme variations of flow experienced on many of the rivers of Washington, and hence have reduced the effects of flooding and provided water for power generation and irrigation throughout the year. Note, for example, the fifteen dams on the Columbia River shown on the map. For planning purposes the state is divided into sixty-two Water Resource Inventory Areas, each of which is a distinct drainage basin. These areas can be grouped into three major *hydrologic regions* (or systems). The eighteen basins that constitute the Puget Sound System cover some 13,360 square miles (34,202 square kilometers) and collect a total average annual runoff of 39,299,000 acre-feet. The Coastal System, which stretches from the Strait of Juan de Fuca to the estuary of the Columbia River, comprises seven basins with a total area of 6,470 square miles (16,563 square kilometers) and an average annual runoff of 28,200,000 acre-feet. The remaining thirty-seven basins constitute the Columbia River System. Together they total some 67,750 square miles (173,440 square kilometers), although only 25,600,000 acre-feet of the more than 140 million acre-feet that flow through the Columbia River System are derived from runoff within the region.

Associated with these drainage basins and their many streams and rivers are thousands of lakes. Some of the lakes have no outlets. These include some saline lakes in small interior drainage basins in eastern Washington, and a few rock-basin lakes in the High Cascades.

In western Washington there are an estimated 3,887 lakes and reservoirs with a total surface area of 176,920 acres (71,595 hectares). Twenty-two of them are more than one thousand acres (404 hectares) in size, and seven of those are reservoirs. It should be noted also that some of the natural lakes have had their surface area and capacity enhanced by dams at their outlet. The latter include Lake Washington, the largest lake in the region (22,138 acres) (8,959 hectares), Lake Whatcom (5,127 acres) (2,075 hectares), Lake Cushman (4,003 acres) (1,620 hectares), and Upper Baker Lake (3,616 acres) (1,463 hectares). The largest of western Washington's reservoirs is Ross Lake (11,678 acres) (4,726 hectares). Other large reservoirs lie around the flanks of Mount Saint Helens: Swift Reservoir (4,588.8 acres) (1,857 hectares), Merwin Lake (4,089.6 acres) (1,655 hectares), and Yale Reservoir (3,801.6 acres) (1,538 hectares).

Eastern Washington's 4,051 lakes cover an area—436,662.1 acres (176,714 hectares)—more than twice that of western Washington's lakes. A high proportion of the largest eastern Washington lakes, however, are reservoirs; only ten of the thirty largest lakes are natural, and of the fifteen largest, only one is natural—Lake Chelan, which is the largest natural lake in the state (33,104 acres) (13,397 hectares). There are forty-one lakes that are more than 1,000 acres (404 hectares) in size or that have more than 1,000 acres in the state. Largest of these is Lake Franklin D. Roosevelt, the reservoir behind Grand Coulee Dam, which covers 79,000 acres (31,966 hectares) and stretches 151 miles upstream almost to the United States–Canadian border. Among the other larger reservoirs are Umatilla Lake, behind John Day Dam (52,000 acres in Washington) (21,044 hectares); Lake Wallula, behind McNary Dam (38,800 acres in Washington) (15,702 hectares); Potholes Reservoir, behind the O'Sullivan Dam (28,200 acres) (11,412 hectares); and Banks Lake (24,900 acres) (10,077 hectares). In addition to Lake Chelan, other large natural lakes in eastern Washington are Moses Lake (6,815 acres) (2,758 hectares), Osoyoos Lake (5,729 acres in Washington) (2,318 hectares), and Lake Wenatchee (2,445 acres) (989 hectares). As in western Washington, a good many natural lakes in eastern Washington have been increased in size by the construction of storage or stabilizing dams.

Although an estimated 80 million acre-feet of ground water exists in the state, supplies are unevenly distributed. They are scarce in the Cascade and Olympic mountains but are abundant in the basalt rocks of the Columbia Basin and in the unconsolidated rocks, sand, gravel, and the like of the Puget Sound region and the Yakima and Spokane rivers.

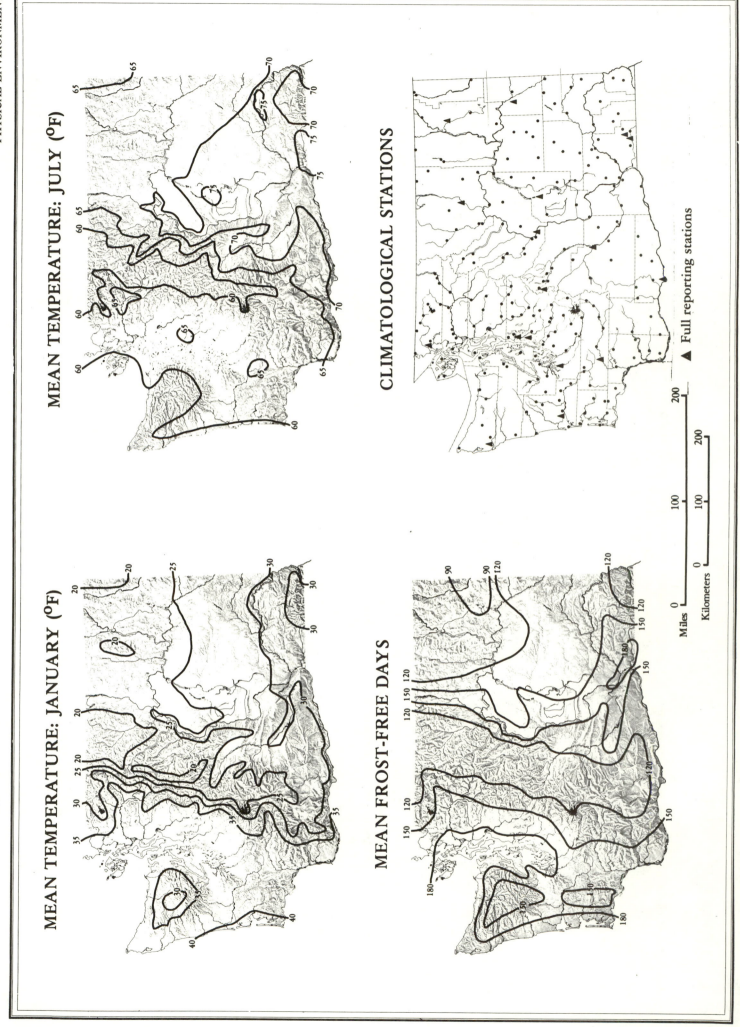

MEAN TEMPERATURE: JULY (°F)

MEAN TEMPERATURE: JANUARY (°F)

CLIMATOLOGICAL STATIONS

▲ Full reporting stations

MEAN FROST-FREE DAYS

Miles

Kilometers

5. CLIMATE

During most of the year the influence of an on-shore flow of moist air from the Pacific Ocean is felt throughout the state, despite the barrier of the Cascade Range. As a result the climate of western Washington is distinctly maritime, while that of eastern Washington is transitional between maritime and continental.

As shown by the two isothermal maps of mean temperature for January and July, the lowland areas west of the Cascades have mean January temperatures that are above 32°F (0°C) and in the vicinity of Willapa Bay above 40°F (4.4°C), while mean July temperatures exceed 65°F (18.3°C) only close to the Columbia River and inland in a few spots between the Columbia River and Puget Sound. By contrast, parts of eastern Washington experience mean January temperatures below 20°F (−6.6°C) and mean July temperatures above 75°F (24°C). In other words, the range of mean temperatures from winter to summer in western Washington seldom is more than 30°F (16.6°C), whereas in eastern Washington it may exceed 55°F (30.5°C). Hence the western region may be considered to have an equable climatic regime and the eastern a more extreme one.

Mention should be made of the considerable influence of elevation on temperature. This is best displayed in the upper left-hand map, where in the Olympics the mean temperature plunges below 30°F (−1°C), and in the higher reaches of the Cascades, where mean temperatures are below 20°F (−6.6°C).

Among the records kept by the weather stations located on the lower right-hand map are maximum and minimum temperatures. Summer temperatures of more than 100°F (37.7°C) are common in eastern Washington, but are seldom experienced west of the Cascades. Similarly, winter temperatures of less than 0°F (−17.7°C) are uncommon in western Washington, but frequently occur in some parts of eastern Washington. The high-

est official temperature ever recorded in the state was 118°F (47.7°C), recorded both at Wahluke on July 24, 1928, and at Ice Harbor Dam on the Snake River on August 3, 1961. The lowest temperature on record is −48°F (−44.4°C), registered at both Mazama and Winthrop in the Methow valley on December 30, 1965.

The following table provides average maximum and minimum temperatures for January and July for nine of the ten climatic regions into which the state is subdivided by the National Weather Service. Data for the Cascade Mountains are of limited range and value, and hence are omitted.

Table 1. Average maximum and minimum temperatures in the state of Washington

	January		July	
Climatic Region	Maximum	Minimum	Maximum	Minimum
West Olympic– Pacific Coast	43°–48°F 6°–9°C	32°–38°F 0°–3°C	70°–75°F 21°–24°C	50°F 10°C
N.E. Olympic– San Juan	40s 5°–6°C	lower 30s 0°–2°C	65°–75°F 18°–24°C	50°F 10°C
Puget Sound Lowland	41°–45°F 5°–7°C	28°–32°F −2°–0°C	73°–78°F 23°–25°C	50°F 10°C
East Olympic– Cascade Foothills	38°–45°F 3°–7°C	25°–32°F −4°–0°C	75°–80°F 24°–27°C	50°F 10°C
East Slope of Cascades	25°–35°F −4°–2°C	15°–25°F −9° to −4°C	79°–85°F 26°–30°C	45°–50°F 7°–10°C
Okanogan– Big Bend	28°–32°F −2 to 0°C	15°–20°F −9° to −7°C	85°–90°F 30°–32°C	lower 50s 10°–12°C
Central Basin	30°–40°F −1° to 4°C	15°–25°F −9° to −4°C	lower 90s 32°–34°C	upper 50s 13°–15°C
Northeast Washington	30°F −1°C	15°F −9°C	85°–90°F 30°–32°C	45°–50°F 7°–10°C
Palouse– Blue Mountain	34°–38°F 1°–3°C	20°–25°F −7° to −4°C	upper 80s 30°–32°C	mid 50s 12°–13°C

With respect to frost-free days, Washington appears to be well served by nature. Only one settled portion of the state—southern Pend Oreille and Stevens counties—has fewer than ninety frost-free days. With most field crops requiring a growing season of less than ninety days, limitations to agriculture due to frost would seem to be minimal. The frequent incidence of late spring frosts, however, and occasional early frosts in fall, made farming a particularly precarious activity in the pioneer period. The journals of the Reverend Elkanah Walker, an American Board missionary in northeast Washington between 1838 and 1847, contain frequent references to disastrous early and late frosts. Genetic improvements have tended to lessen the danger of frost on field crops, but in the fruit-growing districts near Wenatchee and in the Yakima and Okanogan valleys, the presence of smudgepots, electric blowers, and other devices attests to the continuing need to protect young fruit in the weeks after blossom time.

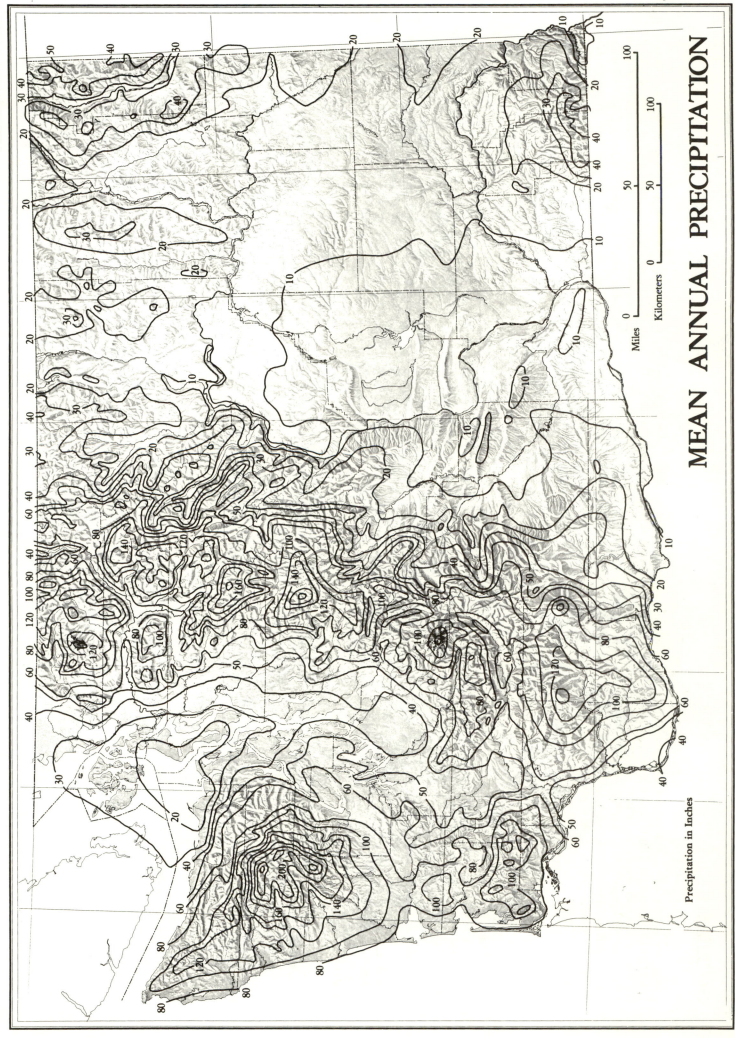

MEAN ANNUAL PRECIPTIATION

Precipitation in Inches

6. MEAN ANNUAL PRECIPITATION

No aspect of climate in Washington is so prone to regional variations and deviations from the norm, or the subject of so much comment, serious and jocular, as precipitation.

The seeming superabundance of rain in the western part of the state—a total of thirty-five inches in four days was recorded at the Quinault ranger station in January 1935—and its relative scarcity in eastern Washington have resulted in the popular perception of a wet west and a dry east, but as the map indicates, this is too simplistic a distinction. Isohyets—the lines of equal mean precipitation shown on the map—may be as low as twenty inches (50 cms) in western Washington and as high as fifty inches (127 cms) in eastern Washington.

Because the prevailing winds blow out of the west and carry with them moisture-laden air masses from the Pacific Ocean, it is the westward slopes of the Olympics and Cascades that receive the highest precipitation, an average of between 60 and 150 inches (152 and 381 centimeters). A record high for the state of 184 inches (467 centimeters) was recorded at Wynoochee Oxbow (elevation 600 feet) (185 meters) in the "rainforest" region of the Olympics. Mean totals of 80 inches (203 centimeters) and more are common from sections of the Pacific Coast eastward to just beyond the crest of the Olympics. Such high totals are replicated farther east across the Puget Sound lowland in the foothills and the higher elevations of the west Cascades. By contrast, the east-facing slopes of the Olympics and the Puget Sound lowland have mean totals of 50 inches (127 centimeters) or less. Indeed, in the "rain shadow" immediately northeast of Mount Olympus, stretching from the Sequim-Dungeness lowland to the San Juan Islands, precipitation falls below 20 inches (50 centimeters). This decline in precipitation in scarcely more than a dozen miles is one of the most pronounced in the world.

Precipitation in western Washington, though generally well distributed through the year, is heaviest in winter, especially in December and January, when rain (or snow) may fall on twenty to twenty-five days each month. During the summer, particularly in July and August, not even a shower may occur in a period of two to three weeks. Hail is an infrequent form of precipitation in western Washington. Snow, on the other hand, occurs over most of the region every year, increasing in amount rapidly with elevation. Snowfalls of 500 inches (1,270 centimeters) or more are received in some years in the higher elevations of the Olympics, while in the Cascades snowfalls of more than 1,000 inches (2,540 centimeters) have been recorded at the Mount Rainier–Paradise ranger station (elevation, 5,500 feet) (1,675 meters). The importance of the resulting snowpack in regulating the runoff on the Skagit and other western rivers cannot be overemphasized.

Shielded by the Cascades from the moisture-laden air masses that move in from the Pacific Ocean throughout the year, eastern Washington is markedly drier—and much less cloudy—than western Washington. As the air masses cross the mountains and descend the eastern slopes, they become both warmer and drier. The Cascades, in fact, create an effective rain shadow that extends eastward almost to the Blue Mountains and the foothills of the Rockies.

In eastern as well as western Washington, winter is the season with the highest precipitation, often in the form of snow. The summer, especially July and August, is the season with the lowest precipitation. Droughts four to eight weeks in duration are quite common. The lowest mean totals of between 7 and 9 inches of rain (18 and 23 centimeters) are found in an area between the confluence of the Columbia and Snake rivers and the confluence of the Columbia and Yakima rivers. Northwards and eastwards the totals slowly increase to about 45 inches (102 centimeters) in the higher reaches of the Blue Mountains of southeastern Washington, and about 50 inches (127 centimeters) in the foothills of the Rockies in extreme northeastern Washington. Rainfall is not only less in amount and more sporadic in eastern Washington, it is frequently more spectacular, arriving with thunderstorms that may dump inches of rain in an hour or less. Hailstorms are also quite common in summer.

The coincidence of little rainfall, low humidity, and much higher temperatures than usually occur in western Washington results in high evapotranspiration rates and high deficit water budgets throughout eastern Washington. The development of irrigation schemes and accompanying reclamation projects by the federal government has done much to offset the effects of these.

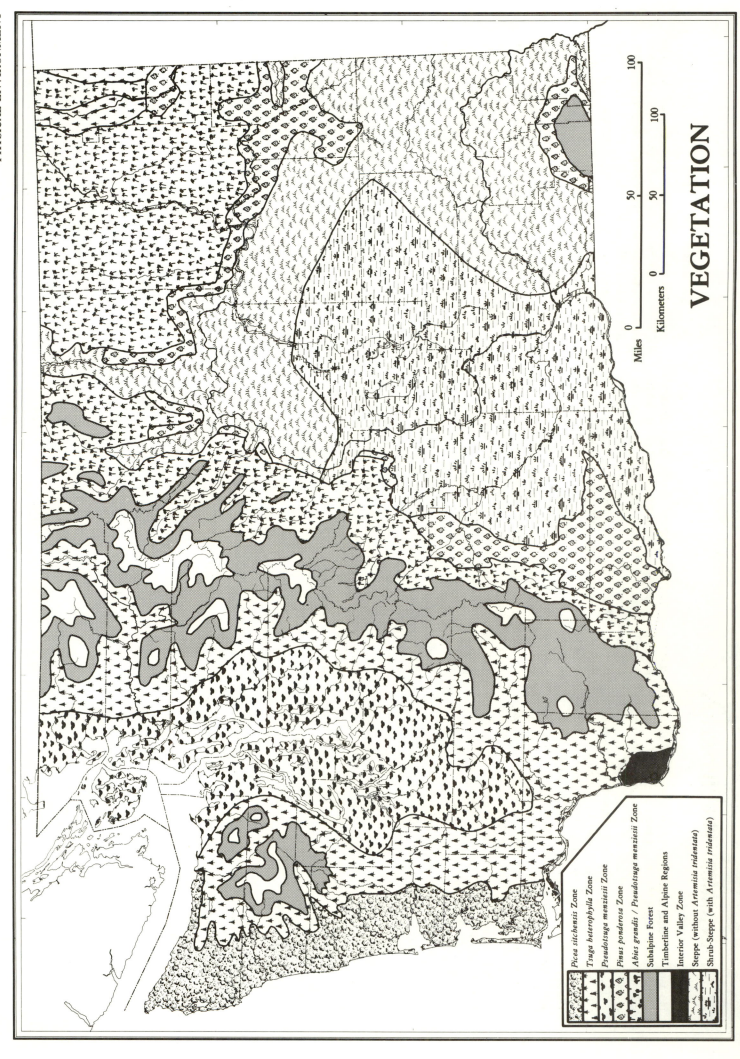

VEGETATION

Miles
0   50   100

Kilometers
0   50   100

Picea sitchensis Zone
Tsuga heterophylla Zone
Pseudotsuga menziesii Zone
Pinus ponderosa Zone
Abies grandis / Pseudotsuga menziesii Zone
Subalpine Forest
Timberline and Alpine Regions
Interior Valley Zone
Steppe (without Artemisia tridentata)
Shrub-Steppe (with Artemisia tridentata)

© 1988 by the University of Oklahoma Press

A number of environmental factors play important roles in the evolution of a region's vegetation. Among these are temperature; precipitation; wind; soil structure, chemistry, porosity, and drainage; terrain and aspect; gradient; and elevation. Another factor, formerly ignored, is fire, whether natural or man-induced, which today is recognized as a powerful force in determining a region's vegetation. In the Pacific Northwest the most significant factors are fire, precipitation, and elevation.

The concept of a *natural vegetation*—one that remains fixed and unchanging for long periods—has largely given way to an emphasis on *plant succession* and the evolution of *natural plant communities*. Plant succession may begin on a newly cleared plot or on one that has undergone a catastrophic change such as a volcanic eruption. The succession continues toward a *climax vegetation* in which one or more species dominate. In general, in western Washington and along the eastern slopes of the Cascades, as well as at higher elevations in the mountains of northeast and southeast Washington, a forest vegetation dominates the scene, whereas in the lower-lying regions east of the mountains a dry steppe vegetation, with or without shrubs, is widespread, except along moist river bottoms, where trees may again appear. The forests vary greatly in their species associations, dominant species, size and spacing of trees, and in understory vegetation. Seven distinct forest zones can be identified, as well as two steppe zones and an alpine zone.

Picea sitchensis Zone. Sitka spruce (*Picea sitchensis*) is the dominant tree in a narrow zone that parallels the coast on the Pacific side of the Olympic Peninsula. This is the region that has the mildest climate in the state, the highest average precipitation, and the greatest frequency of fog and low clouds. The zone widens here and there as it penetrates the lower reaches of rivers such as the Hoh and the Quinault. Among the other tree species are western hemlock, western red cedar, Douglas fir, grand fir, and Pacific silver fir. The lush understory vegetation includes a wide range of shrubs, ferns, and fungi.

Tsuga heterophylla Zone. This extensive zone stretches from the northern edge of the Olympic Peninsula to the Columbia River. It includes the lower elevations of the Olympic Mountains, and it continues north from the Columbia along the lower parts of the western side of the Cascades. Western hemlock (*Tsuga heterophylla*) and western red cedar (*Thuja plicata*) are the dominant species, with Douglas fir, grand fir, and—on glacial gravels—western white pine and lodgepole pine. With generally abundant rainfall, a luxurious forest biome has evolved in which there is a thick understory of shrubs, ferns, fungi, and wildflowers.

Pseudotsuga menziesii Zone. Lying partially in the rain shadow of the Olympic Mountains and the Willapa Hills, the Puget Sound lowland has a somewhat lower rainfall that ranges from thirty to thirty-five inches in the wetter parts to as little as fifteen inches. The region is regarded by many botanists as part of the western–hemlock zone, although it has features that make it somewhat distinct. Lodgepole pine and ponderosa pine are quite common, as is Garry oak. Douglas fir (*Pseudotsuga menziesii*) is the dominant species, although western hemlock and western red cedar are also widely distributed throughout the zone, as are many deciduous species. Clearcutting and the planting of Douglas fir by the United States Forest Service and timber companies has led to important changes in localized plant communities.

Pinus ponderosa Zone. This zone, characterized by the ponderosa pine, forms a rather narrow strip from ten to about twenty miles wide on the eastern flanks of the Cascades between 2,000 and 4,000 feet in elevation and at similar heights on the south-facing slopes of the Okanogan Highlands and the western slopes of the northern Rockies. The zone is widest east of Mount Adams and in the Spokane River valley. At its upper limits the forest grades into the *Abies grandis*/*Pseudotsuga menziesii* Zone, and at its lower limits into the steppe or shrub-steppe.

Abies grandis/*Pseudotsuga menziesii* Zone. This zone extends over much of the eastern slopes of the Cascades at elevations from 3,500 to 5,000 feet, as well as

throughout the Okanogan Highlands and the northern Rockies. The grand fir (*Abies grandis*) is found in association with ponderosa pine, lodgepole pine, western larch, and Douglas fir (*Pseudotsuga menziesii*), any one of which may dominate particular forest stands. The understory vegetation is sparse and includes many shrubs.

Subalpine Forest. This is the most elevated forested zone along the western slopes of the Cascades and the Olympics at heights upwards of 4,000 feet. Mountain hemlock (*Tsuga mertensia*) and subalpine fir (*Abies lasiocarpa*) are the major species, accompanied in most places by a variety of shrubs and herbacious plants.

Timberline and Alpine Regions. At timberline, which begins above 6,000 feet in the southern part of the Cascades and drops to under 5,000 feet farther north, trees are replaced by shrubs and plants in the alpine meadows that are found at higher elevations in the Olympics, the Cascades, the Okanogan Highlands, and the northern Rockies. Here are found the marvellous wildflowers that turn the high mountains into a riot of color in late spring and early summer, and that help provide some of the brilliant reds and yellows of fall.

Interior Valley Zone. A tiny portion of southern Washington immediately north of the Willamette valley of Oregon is an extension of the Interior Valley Zone of that state. Important species are Garry oak (*Quercus garryana*), madrone (*Arbutus Menziesii*), and a variety of conifers including Douglas fir.

Steppe (without *Artemisia tridentata*). With improved moisture available in the eastern section of the Columbia Basin, sagebrush (*Artemisia tridentata*) gradually disappears, and Idaho fescue (*Festuca Idahoensis*) joins the bluebunch wheatgrass (*Agropyron spicatum*) as a major ground cover.

Shrub-Steppe (with *Artemisia tridentata*). This is the driest of Washington's vegetation zones, although it is far from being a desert. Shrubs, particularly artemesia sagebrush, and various perennial grasses, particularly bluebunch wheatgrass (*Agropyron spicatum*), are mingled throughout the region. Low-lying bluegrass (*Poa*) and cheatgrass (*Bromus*) are also found.

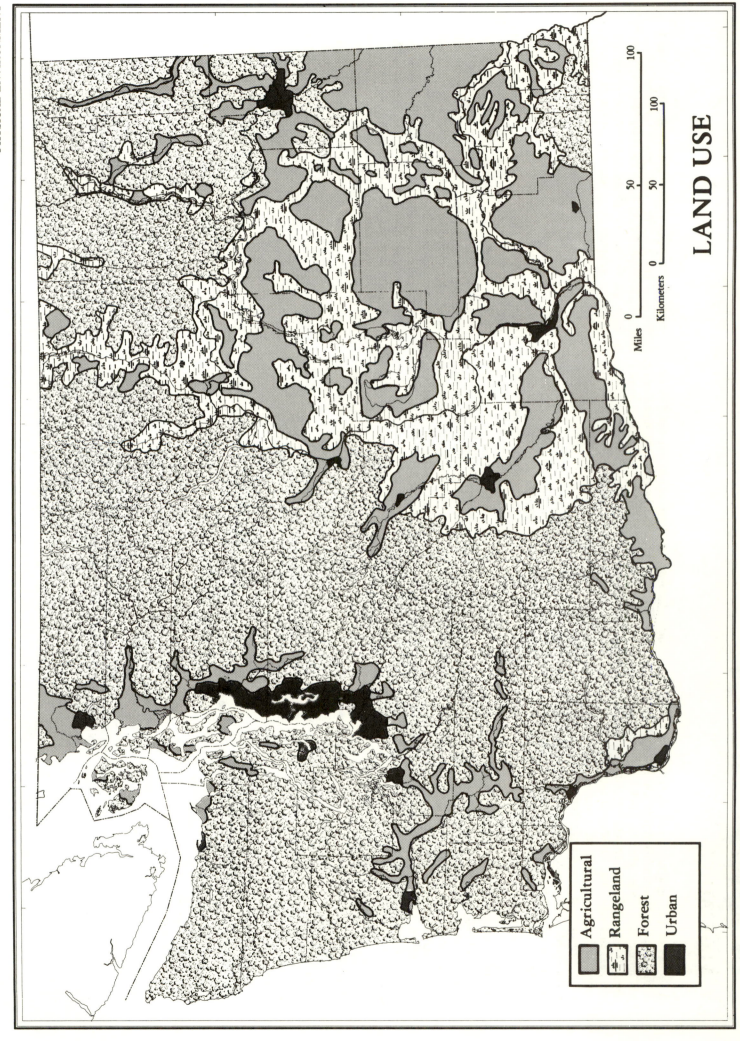

LAND USE

Miles

0   50   100

Kilometers

0   50   100

Agricultural
Rangeland
Forest
Urban

For thousands of years the uses to which the land of Washington was put underwent hardly perceptible change as environmental conditions improved—or in some places deteriorated—following the retreat northwards of the continental ice sheets. However, as population increases led to the spread of settlement, new demands were placed on the land and its resources. It is not too fanciful to suggest that when the first whites arrived in the Pacific Northwest the land looked little different from what it had looked a thousand, even five thousand, years before. There had been only some changes in plant associations, a few changes in the region's fauna, and here and there land had been cleared by burning to encourage food plants, such as camas.

In the past two hundred years, by contrast, and particularly since the late nineteenth century, the changes have been momentous, affecting every part of the state. Croplands and improved pastures have replaced virgin forest, irrigated fields have replaced parched steppelands, and large sprawling cities have replaced the small inconspicuous settlements of Indian bands and tribes.

Since the retreat of the ice sheets, forests have dominated the scene in most of western Washington. Even the open prairies noted by the first white visitors may have been burned-over or cut-over forest land. The same was true of a good deal of eastern Washington beyond the limits of the Columbia Basin. Although in 1980 more than 22 million acres of Washington forest remained, only in remote areas, amounting to only a

small percentage of the total forest area, could the forests be classified as first growth. Furthermore, much of Washington's forest has been cut over more than once in the past century, and its regeneration has in many parts been promoted by deliberate planting of desired species and removal of unwanted ones. Although today's forests might look little different to a visitor from the eighteenth century, it is argued by some that they are better managed and more productive than they were in the past. Timber harvesting is indisputably the forest's principal use, although it must be emphasized that over extensive tracts hunting and other forms of recreation, mineral exploitation, and some miscellaneous forest industries are of some significance.

Cropland, which occupies almost 8.4 million acres, is to be found in every part of the state, but with the largest concentrations in eastern Washington in the Palouse Hills and in the valleys of the Okanogan, Yakima, and Columbia rivers. Maps 54 through 56 in this volume show the distribution patterns of the major, and many of the minor, crops. Acreages devoted to each crop change annually; a few crops that were once grown, like flax, are no longer to be found, while others of little importance a century ago, such as grapes, have assumed importance in recent years.

Almost as impressive as the changes in cropland, but certainly less noticeable to the casual observer have been the changes in rangelands. Over wide areas the bunchgrass and sagebrush on these steppelands have

been replaced by improved eastern and European grasses (bunchgrass, in fact, has all but disappeared). The area of rangeland has been enormously increased as irrigation has made possible the expansion of settlement into hitherto unused and remote areas. And as the antelope and mustang were killed off, sheep, horses, and cattle took their place, first on the open range and then, in later years, on fenced pastures. In 1980 rangeland totalled approximately 8.2 million acres, most of it in the drier parts of eastern Washington.

The remaining 3.1 million acres of the state are put to several uses, particularly urban settlement, transportation routes, and recreation. Attempts to limit, or at least control, the loss of prime agricultural land to the developer have been notably ineffective, with the result that the amount of cropland in western Washington has declined in every census of the past forty years. Fortunately, the loss of this land to agriculture has been offset by increases in eastern Washington, where irrigation has been extended to areas hitherto too dry to cultivate.

Projections that have been made to the year 2020 indicate that there will be only limited overall loss of cropland—a shrinking from 8.4 to about 8.2 million acres—and a somewhat similar loss of rangeland— from about 8.2 to 8.0 million acres. In the same period, 1980 to 2020, the land devoted to other uses will increase from 3.1 to almost 3.8 million acres, most of the increase being to housing developments, transportation, and recreational facilities.

PART II
INDIAN HISTORY

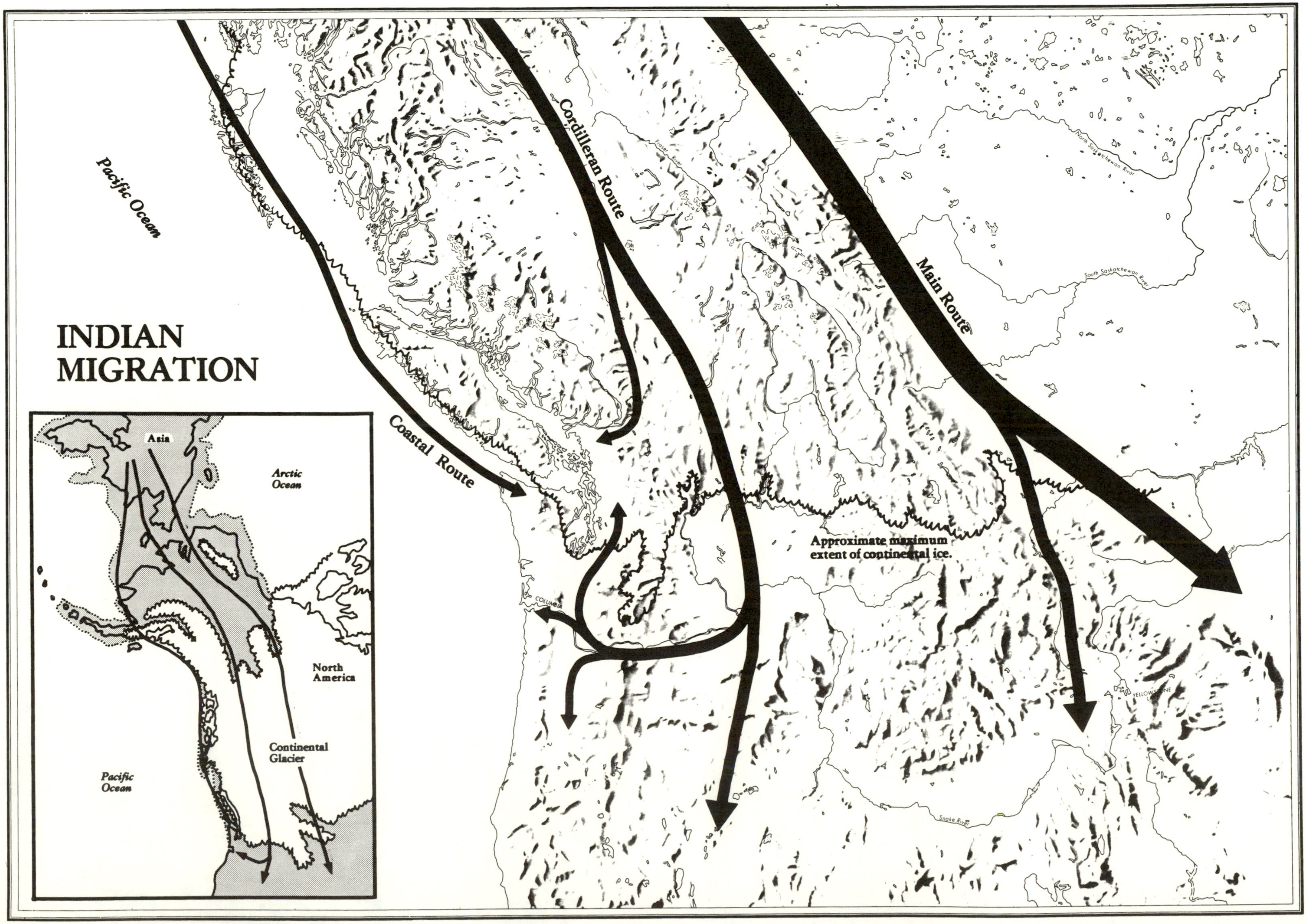
INDIAN MIGRATION
Pacific Ocean
Coastal Route
Cordilleran Route
Main Route
Fraser River
North Saskatchewan River
South Saskatchewan River
Approximate maximum extent of continental ice.
Columbia
Yellowstone
Snake River
Asia
Arctic Ocean
North America
Continental Glacier
Pacific Ocean

It has long been accepted by anthropologists that the native peoples of the Americas arrived more than 10,000 years ago—and perhaps as early as 40,000 years ago—from Asia via the Bering Strait, which at intervals during the Pleistocene epoch became a land bridge connecting the two continents. Using a variety of evidence, glacial geologists have estimated that this bridge, which they have named Beringia, was largely unglaciated dry land during the period from approximately 25,000 to 14,000 years ago, as well as for two briefer intervals in the ensuing 4,000 years.

Whether the date of the first migrations eventually turns out to be between 15,000 and 19,000 years ago, as many scientists think, or even earlier, there is plenty of evidence to prove the existence of the dry land which provided the route and a relative abundance of game—the woolly mammoth, the mastodon, and other large animals—which could have provided the motive for the Indians' passage from Asia eastward into North America.

From the Bering Strait groups of Indian hunters followed herds of wild animals, moving slowly but inexorably—as climatic changes dictated and new pastures beckoned—eastwards and southwards, eventually to populate both North America and South America. The period encompassed by these prehistoric "folk wanderings" must be measured in thousands rather than hundreds of years. And, as climatic conditions changed and ecological opportunities were heightened for some groups and lessened for others, specific group responses resulted in most tribes becoming specialized hunters, fishermen, or seed gatherers. The evidence for these prolonged migrations is widely dispersed across two continents and is often enigmatic and fragmentary. Understandably, in many instances it is less than conclusive, and consequently no detailed or precise chronology of the peopling of the Americas has yet been agreed upon.

The Indian groups that arrived in the Pacific Northwest, and particularly in Washington, appear to have used three main routes on their journey from the north:

The Coastal Route. This most westerly and possibly earliest of the three routes skirted the ice sheets and glaciers which adjoined the present-day North Pacific coastline along a coastal plain that today forms part of the continental shelf. Sea mammals, fish, shellfish, and a variety of berries were the Indians' main items of food on this route.

The Cordilleran Route. This was chronologically the last of the three routes to be used. Lying between the Rockies and the Coast Ranges and following the interior valleys of modern-day British Columbia, this route opened up some eight thousand years ago as the continental ice sheets began to shrink and valley glaciers retreated into the higher reaches of the adjacent mountains. As the ice melted, grasses and other vegetation appeared to lure the game animals south, and with these herds came the Indians who depended on them for their food supply. Probably it was along this route

that a significant percentage of the groups who populated Washington in the prehistoric period made their way south.

The Main Route. This route ultimately went along eastern foothills of the Rockies. It started in northwest Alaska within sight of the Brooks Range and north of the Yukon River, where the virtually unglaciated lowland provided a habitat for an abundant wildlife for thousands of years during the Pleistocene epoch. The opening of the corridor southwards along the foothills of the Rockies provided an extension of that habitat. This corridor—between the western ice sheets of today's British Columbia and the much larger continental ice sheets that covered all of eastern Canada from the islands of the Arctic to the Great Lakes—opened much earlier than that through the cordilleran region on the west. Along it moved the herds and the attendant Indian groups who were eventually led to the nonglaciated plains of what is today the United States. Of the three routes this is the one that scientists believe was taken by the largest number of Indian groups, although how many of them moved west across the Rockies into Washington in the latitude of the state is as yet unknown.

Shown on the main map are the three routes and their approximate locations and divergences. The inset map, which covers an area from eastern Siberia to southern Oregon, shows the probable shoreline at the time of maximum glaciation, as well as the extent of the continental ice sheets.

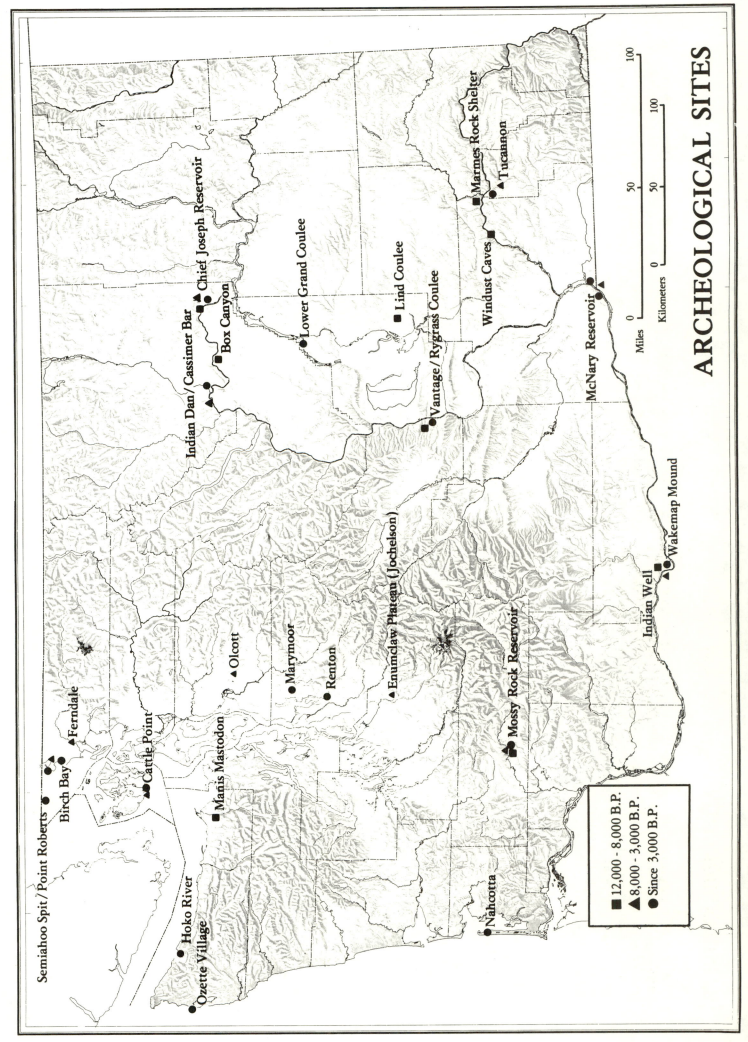

ARCHEOLOGICAL SITES

Semiahoo Spit/Point Roberts
Birch Bay
Ferndale
Cattle Point
Hoko River
Ozette Village
Nahcotta
Manis Mastodon
Olcott
Marymoor
Renton
Enumclaw Plateau (Jochelson)
Mossy Rock Reservoir
Indian Well
Wakemap Mound
McNary Reservoir
Windust Caves
Tucannon
Marmes Rock Shelter
Lind Coulee
Vantage/Rygrass Coulee
Lower Grand Coulee
Chief Joseph Reservoir
Indian Dan/Cassimer Bar
Box Canyon

■ 12,000 - 8,000 B.P.
▲ 8,000 - 3,000 B.P.
● Since 3,000 B.P.

100
100
50
50
0
Kilometers
0
Miles

10. ARCHEOLOGICAL SITES

Although the arrival of Indian groups in the Pacific Northwest cannot be dated with any great precision, evidence of the presence of man in Washington as early as 12,000 years ago was revealed in 1977 at the Manis mastodon site near Sequim on the Olympic Peninsula. There the remnant of a spearpoint found in the mastodon's rib attested to the presence of human hunters in the region when Vashon-Fraser glaciation was still present in the area. The carbon-14 dating technique, which was used on the mastodon remains and spearpoint, has been used on artifacts and other remains recovered at hundreds of sites across the state, and although none of them has yet proved as venerable as the Manis mastodon remains, dates of 9,000 to 10,000 B.P. (before the present) are not uncommon, as at Marmes Rock Shelter and in Lind Coulee.

With more than 5,000 Indian sites on record, and only a relatively few of these professionally worked as yet, there seems little doubt that further significant archeological finds will be made in Washington. Chance discoveries, often coming in the wake of public or private work projects (road building, dam construction, excavation for large buildings) or the preparation of something as mundane as digging a ditch or a duck pond (as was the occasion with the Manis mastodon find),

have kept professional archeologists continuously occupied during the past three or four decades. Systematic digs at all known sites—where these have not already been lost, as many have been because of rising waters behind federal dams—would take hundreds of man-years and more trained archeologists than are presently available, not to mention the millions of support dollars such digs would require. Consequently, our knowledge of events in the distant past and their detailed chronology is at best very imperfect.

Only a very few, twenty-two in all, of the more than 5,000 archeological sites scattered across the state are shown on this map. Generally, such sites are in the river valleys and along the coast. For example, there are hundreds of known sites on the lower Snake River and the lower and middle Columbia. There are also numerous sites in the Yakima valley, around Puget Sound, along the Pacific Coast, and in the Okanogan, upper Columbia, Sanpoil, and Nespelem river valleys.

The sites shown have been selected for three principal reasons. First is the temporal spread—from 12,000 B.P. to the recent past just prior to the arrival of the first white explorers. The sites have been grouped into three rather broad time periods: early sites (12,000 to 8,000 B.P.), middle-period sites (8,000 to 3,000 B.P.),

and late-period sites (3,000 B.P. to the immediate prehistoric past). Secondly, the map shows the broad distribution of sites in various environments and habitats, east and west of the Cascades, during all three time periods. And third, all the sites shown have been the subject of publications, unlike most of the remaining 5,000 sites, on which little or nothing has been recorded beyond their existence.

In general, the items recovered at most of the sites have been relatively imperishable—stone axes, adzes, and hammers, obsidian knives, bone needles, hooks, and similar items. Also encountered are the bones of human beings, domestic animals, and animals hunted and trapped for food—mastodon, bison, deer, and smaller mammals, as well as the all-important salmon and shellfish. At sites such as the Ozette Village on the Olympic Peninsula, however, the continuously humid ground has helped preserve organic artifacts of wood and vegetable fibers. Elsewhere the remains of fishing nets and weirs have been found, and with these, as well as careful investigation of the sites, the professional archeologist has been able to reconstruct and provide abundant detail on the cultural and economic life of these first settlers of the present state of Washington.

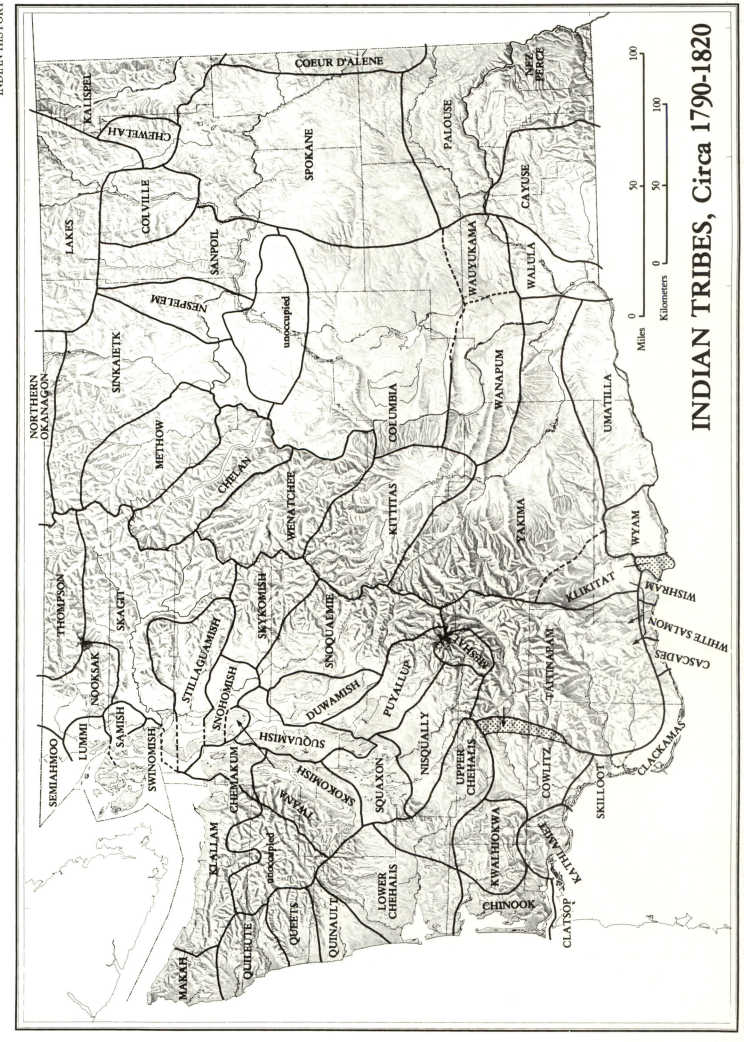

INDIAN TRIBES, Circa 1790–1820

NEZ PERCE
COEUR D'ALENE
PALOUSE
KALISPEL
CHEWELAH
SPOKANE
CAYUSE
COLVILLE
LAKES
SANPOIL
NESPELEM
WAUYUKAMA
WALULA
NORTHERN OKANAGON
SINKAIETK
unoccupied
WANAPUM
UMATILLA
METHOW
COLUMBIA
CHELAN
WENATCHEE
KITTITAS
YAKIMA
THOMPSON
SKAGIT
SKYKOMISH
SNOQUALMIE
MESHAL
WYAM
STILLAGUAMISH
KLIKITAT
WISHRAM
NOOKSAK
SNOHOMISH
DUWAMISH
PUYALLUP
TAITINAPAM
WHITE SALMON
CASCADES
SEMIAHMOO
LUMMI
SAMISH
SWINOMISH
CHEMAKUM
SUQUAMISH
SKOKOMISH
NISQUALLY
UPPER CHEHALIS
COWLITZ
CLACKAMAS
SKILLOOT
KLALLAM
TWANA
SQUAXON
MAKAH
QUILEUTE
unoccupied
QUEETS
LOWER CHEHALIS
KWALHIOKWA
CHINOOK
KATHLAMET
CLATSOP
QUINAULT

100
100
50
50
Miles
Kilometers
0
0

During the early years of white-Indian culture contact the explorers and fur traders soon discovered that a large number of different tribes and bands inhabited the Pacific Northwest region. These Indian groups enjoyed varied life-styles, spoke diffrent languages, and displayed marked differences in dress, ceremonies, and adornments. Elaborate social rituals were developed in some tribes. Successful trading became a major economic activity among the Chinook, for example; while artistic talents were widely displayed by most of the tribes.

Systematic study of Pacific Northwest Indian tribes did not begin until long after the first European landfall. Fortunately, a good deal of valuable information can be gleaned from the journals and logbooks of European and American sailors and traders, and from the finely executed drawings and paintings of contemporary artists such as John Webber. Recent ethnohistorical research has greatly expanded our knowledge of the economic, social, and artistic achievements of the region's tribes around 1800.

A basic division is usually made between the coastal tribes of western Washington and those of the interior. In general, the coastal tribes were heavily dependent on the rivers and tidal waters for their staple foods of fish and shellfish, whereas the interior tribes relied more heavily on plants and berries, as well as game and other animals.

Coastal tribes. Over hundreds of years the Northwest Coast Indians developed elaborate and highly successful cultures in a narrow zone between Alaska and Oregon, cultures that have been broadly divided into three groups—Northern, Wakashan, and Coast Salish—Chinook. It was the third of these that occupied most of the Washington coast and its adjacent valleys and lowlands. The sole exception was the Wakashan-speaking Makah tribe of the Olympic Peninsula. Salmon, steelhead, and shellfish provided the basic diet of the coastal Indians. A portion of their catch was smoked

and dried, some for local consumption, but much of it for trading with interior tribes. Supplementing their diet were berries, fruit, and nuts, as well as various roots and tubers, notably camas and wild carrot. Land mammals and birds provided part of the diet of some tribes, and among the Makah, sea mammals were an important food item.

Settlements tended to be large, occasionally with as many as 400 residents, and for the most part they were permanent. Some groups, like the Lummi, travelled during the summer months to offshore islands where they usually erected temporary shelters. All of the coastal tribes made permanent houses of wood, but the large cedar-plank houses in the north, with high gabled ends, were considerably modified in shape and appearance farther south. Adornment of houses, including carved totem poles at entrances, was common. Personal and group possessions were far more numerous than in most North American tribes: carved masks for dances and ceremonies, clothing made of bark cloth and furs, utensils for cooking and eating, as well as many domestic tools, fishing gear, and weapons of many kinds.

Social organization varied from group to group, but throughout the coastal region the potlatch ceremony was common. In general, the northern tribes of southeast Alaska and British Columbia were more powerful and aggressive, and raids by the Haida and Kwakiutl on the tribes of Puget Sound and the Strait of Georgia were common. Around the mouth of the Columbia the Chinook-speaking tribes were more economically motivated, and over many centuries they developed important trade links along the coast and into the interior. A Chinook jargon became the principal lingua franca of the Pacific Northwest.

Interior Tribes. The intermontane region between the Cascades and the Rockies provided diverse physical environments for more than a score of Indian groups. From the beginning of the eighteenth century most of

the Columbia Plateau Indians were in possession of the horse, which had greatly modified their way of life by the time of the arrival of the first whites.

Salmon and other fish provided a major portion of the diet of many of the interior tribes—according to Angelo Anastasio (see References, Map 11) between one-third and one-half—and at sites along the Columbia, particularly Kettle Falls, spear fishing was a major activity of the men. Dried salmon pemmican was a valuable item of trade. Plant foods included camas and wild carrot, as well as various berries, nuts, and miscellaneous roots. Game animals were plentiful in many areas, but although elk, deer, bison, and smaller animals were hunted regularly, they seldom were a reliable source of food.

Most of the plateau Indians settled in small villages along the rivers. Usually comprising three to five families, the villages were semipermanent settlements. The houses varied in type and structure. Most important and most widespread were semisubterranean dwellings, circular in shape, which were entered by ladder from the pole and mat-covered roofs. Seasonal dwellings erected during the hunting/collecting season were usually of poles overlaid by mats.

Social organization was somewhat simpler on the plateau than among the coastal groups. Villages had their headman, and groups of adjacent villages joined from time to time in larger social units, but these were seldom long-lasting. The arrival of the whites, and the subsequent threats to the Indians' survival posed by outbreaks of smallpox and other epidemics, and the imminent takeover of their territory, led to military operations that forged new links between village groups and alliances of formerly unfriendly tribes. This availed little. With the eventual defeat of the plateau Indians (see Map 28) and their removal to reservations (see Map 14) traditional tribal territories became meaningless, and Indian cultures were destroyed or transformed beyond recognition.

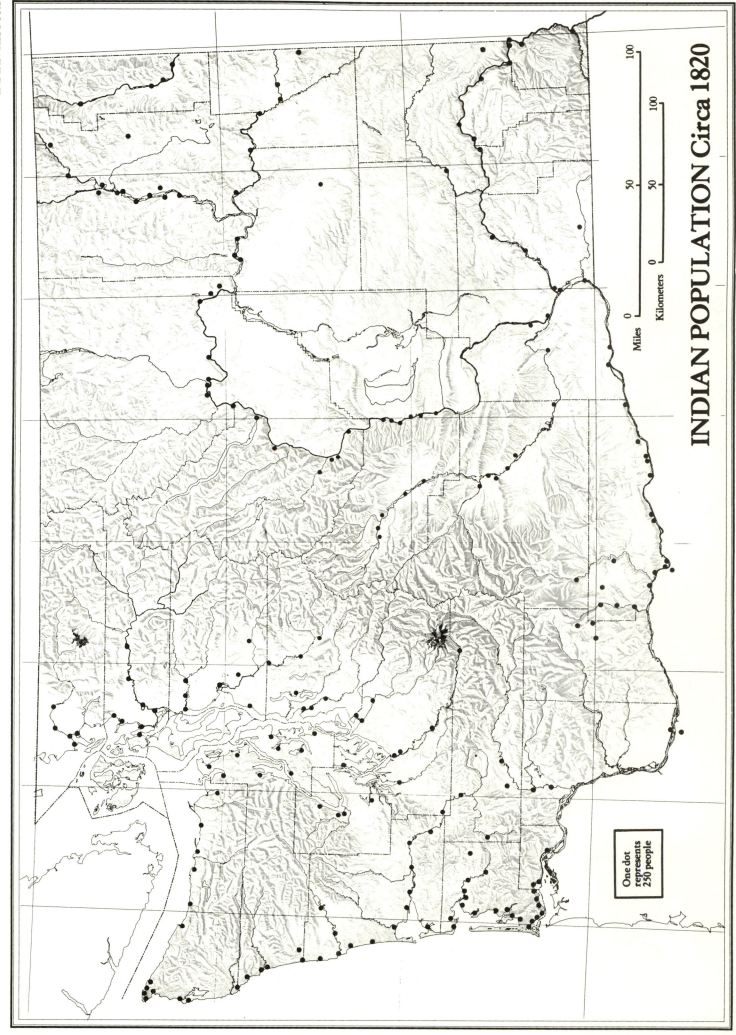

INDIAN POPULATION Circa 1820

One dot represents 250 people

100

100   50   0   Miles
100   50   0   Kilometers

The problems of determining the size of Indian populations in the first years of Indian-white culture are many. No accurate information is available because no official census was taken until the seventh census of 1850. Furthermore, records of other sorts are sparse and seldom reliable. Many of these, such as personal diaries and ships' logs, have little or nothing to report on the size of Indian groups, and even when reliable, they tend to deal only with specific groups and limited areas.

Not until the Hudson's Bay Company began to make population estimates in the years after 1825 do we begin to get some notion of the size and demographic structure of the various Indian tribes and bands. Later contemporary information can be gleaned from such sources as the reports of the Wilkes expedition and the writings of Samuel Parker, George Gibbs, and James G. Swan. Of course, by the time these estimates were made the Indians throughout the Pacific Northwest had been greatly affected by such newly introduced diseases as measles, smallpox, syphilis, and cholera, the ravages of which had caused the decimation of virtually every tribe of the region.

The best-known estimates of Indian population are those of James Mooney, whose "Aboriginal Population of America North of Mexico" has been used by virtually all later writers, and A. L. Kroeber, whose *Cultural and Natural Areas of Native North America* has become one of the classics of American anthropology. Although the two scholars are not always in accord, the figures proposed by Kroeber are usually very similar to those of Mooney. More recently a Washington anthropologist, Herbert C. Taylor, Jr., has analyzed these estimates for the coastal tribes of Northwest America, and compared both scholars' statistics with those recorded by officials of the Hudson's Bay Company, notably Chief Factor James Douglas. Although Mooney's estimates are for the year 1780, and those of the Hudson's Bay Company are for the actual years when the estimates were made between 1825 and 1846, there appear to be unusually large discrepancies for some groups of Indians, even taking into account the ravages of diseases that reduced most Indian populations.

Using both archeological and ethnohistorical evidence, Taylor has produced his own estimates for the year 1780, which suggest that in most cases Mooney's were underestimates. A few examples will suffice. Mooney's estimate for the Puget Sound Salish population in 1780 is 6,000, while Taylor's is 10,300 and that of the Hudson's Bay Company for a half century later is 5,175. And while the total figure given by Mooney for the Makah, Quileute, and Quinault tribes of the Olympic Peninsula is 4,000, Taylor suggests a figure of 5,000. In one notable exception, the population of the Chinook tribe, Mooney's estimate is grossly out of line with that of Taylor—5,000 as against 22,000. The figure reported for the later period by the Hudson's Bay Company is 2,585. For the southern part of the Northwest Coast, Mooney's estimate is 57,000, compared with Taylor's of 72,300. By the end of the fur-trade era the total must have been not much more than half the figure for the region as a whole, and in the coastal regions of Washington, especially around the Columbia River, the reduction of population during the period must have been considerably more than half. There were similar reductions east of the Cascades, although the total population there was much smaller than the population west of the mountains.

In the distribution and density of Indian population around 1820, the period for which the present map has been drawn, there remained marked differences between the coastal and the interior tribes. The coast tribes, depending heavily on a diet of salmon, shellfish, and wild roots and berries, tended to live in larger communities of one hundred or more, and in permanent lodges close to tidewater or rivers. Groups ventured away from the water only occasionally to collect seasonal items of food. Although salmon was an important item of diet for most of the plateau Indians, their heavier dependence on gathering and collecting inevitably resulted in a more nomadic type of settlement. Nevertheless, the importance of river sites for their permanent settlements is amply supported by the evidence of the hundreds of known sites along the Columbia, Snake, and other rivers of the plateau. In his map of North American Indian population density, Harold E. Driver shows the region west of the Cascades as having a density of from four to ten per square mile, whereas population on the east drops to less than two per the square mile.

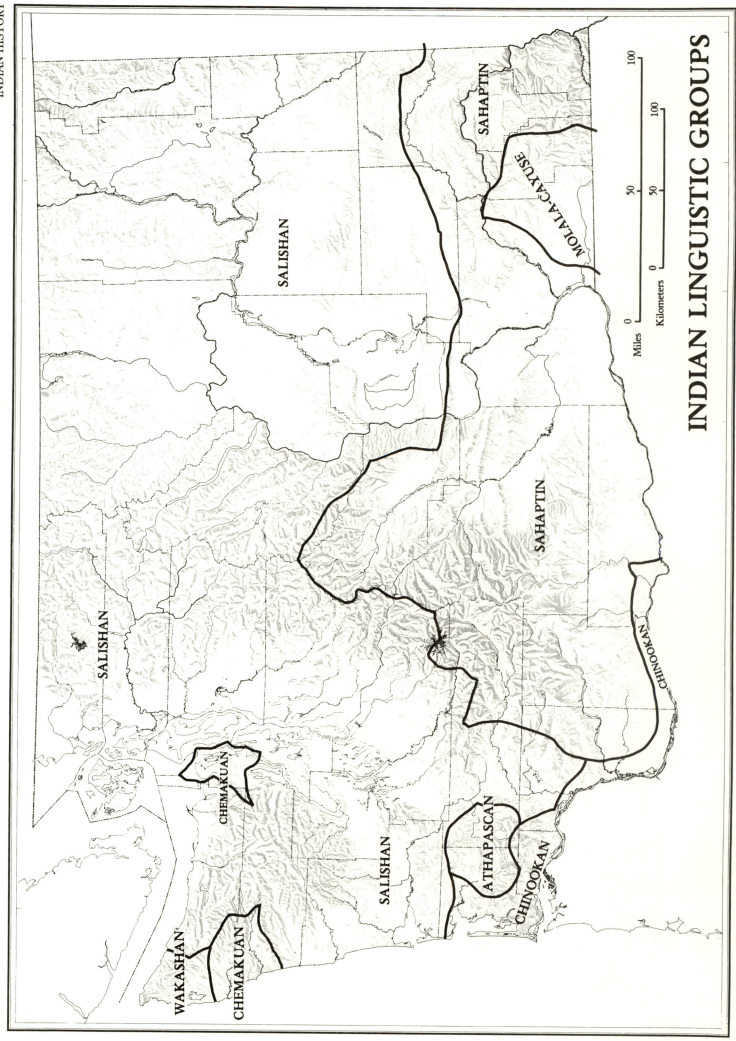

INDIAN LINGUISTIC GROUPS

13. INDIAN LINGUISTIC GROUPS

There neither is, nor ever has been—at least for many thousands of years—a single, ubiquitous Indian language. Perhaps as many as two thousand languages were spoken by the Indians of the Americas at the time of initial Indian-white culture contact, two-thirds of the number in South America alone. In their grammar, vocabulary, and intellectual sophistication, these languages—despite the absence of any written form—have long been considered the equivalent of languages spoken in other parts of the world. Indian languages at the time of European contact and conquest were in no way primitive. Unfortunately, their complexity—size of vocabulary or grammatical construction—provided no keys to levels of material or spiritual culture, technological achievement, or political organization.

But with such a variety of languages spoken—more than two hundred of them in North America north of Mexico—intertribal relationships must inevitably have suffered, or at least been constrained, despite the evolution of widespread sign languages and, eventually, the adoption of notably effective lingua francas such as Chinook.

The classification of Indian languages has been underway since John Wesley Powell's pioneering efforts of the 1880s and 1890s, but there remain numerous problems to be unravelled. In the end, it is thought, settlement of these thorny problems might uncover a host of facts regarding Indian migrations, dispersals, and inter-minglings. That time, however, is still far off. Powell's basic arrangement and organization remain essentially unchanged, although the regrouping of Indian languages into families and still larger phyla has taken place. Notable contributions to Indian linguistic research in recent years have included the emergence of *lexicostatistics*, the statistical study of words and language relationships, and *glottochronology*, an associated study that determines the rate at which language changes over time. While offering many promising and fascinating possibilities, these controversial approaches require further research before the riddles of Indian language relationships can be precisely determined.

In Washington, Indian linguistic groups are reasonably well authenticated and accepted, although the precise details are far from settled. The languages appear to fall into three distinct phyla, each divided into a number of families or isolates. In the northern part of the state the Indian languages are for the most part included in the Vogelins' eighth phyllum of "language isolates and families with undetermined phyllum affiliations." The largest of these families is the *Salishan*, individual languages of which were spoken by tribes or clans from the Pacific east to the Rockies, and from north of the U.S.–Canadian border almost to the Columbia River. Salishan-language subfamilies include (1) the Okanogan–Sanpoil–Colville–Lakes, (2) the Flathead–Pend d'Oreille–Kalispel–Spokane, (3) the Upper Chehalis–Cowlitz–Lower Chehalis–Quinault, (4) the Snoqualmie-Duwamish-Nisqually, and (5) the Lummi-Songish-Klallam.

Two other families of languages in the same phyllum, but spoken by much smaller numbers of Indians, were the *Wakashan*, represented in the state by the Makah language, and the *Chemakuan*, which included the Quileute and Chemakum languages.

Much of the southern portion of the state from Willapa Bay to the Blue Mountains, and stretching northwards along both sides of the Cascades to about the latitude of Mount Rainier, was occupied by tribes and clans speaking languages classified as families or isolates of the Penutian phyllum. The most widely spread were the languages of the *Sahaptin* family, which included Nez Perce and Sahaptin. Along the lower Columbia River valley as far as the eastern end of the Columbia Gorge, speakers of the *Chinookan* family of languages—Lower Chinook and Upper Chinook—were settled. Two isolates of the Penutian phyllum—*Molala* and *Cayuse*—were intermingled in the western portion of the Blue Mountains south of the Snake River.

There remains but one language family to be noted. This is the *Athapascan*, the language spoken by groups of Indians in the Willapa Hills north of the Columbia and east of Willapa Bay. Part of the Na-dene phyllum, this language family is related to the Tlingit language isolate and the Haida language isolate, languages spoken far north of Washington in British Columbia and Alaska.

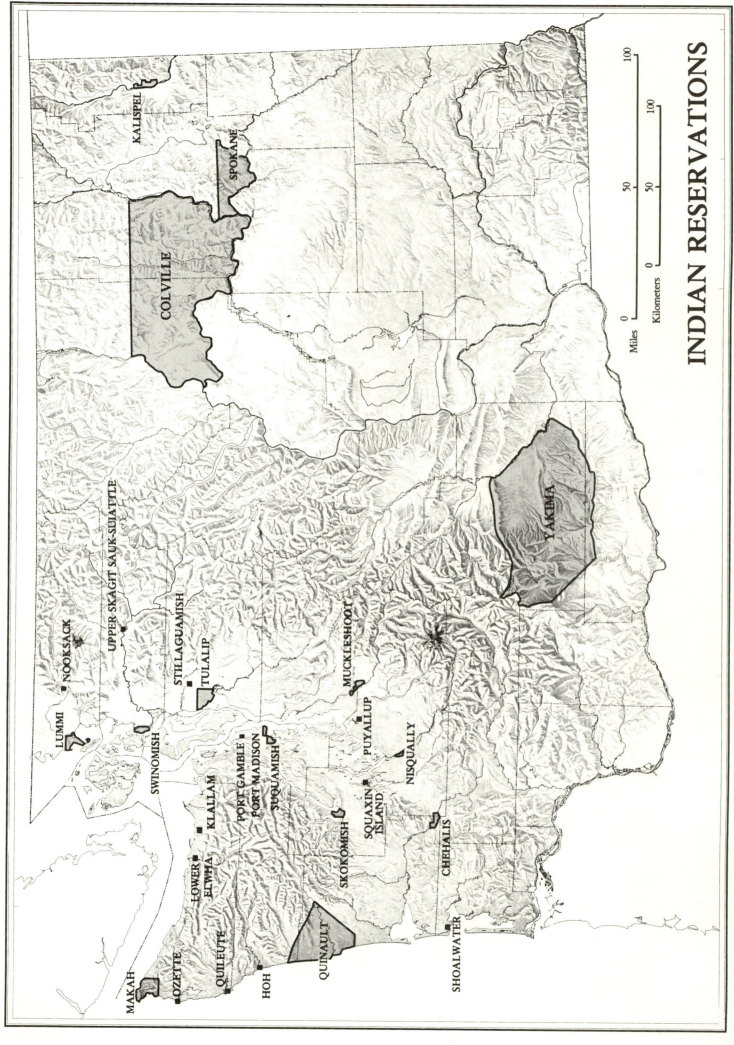

INDIAN RESERVATIONS

MAKAH
OZETTE
QUILEUTE
HOH
QUINAULT
SHOALWATER

LOWER ELWHA
KLALLAM
PORT GAMBLE
PORT MADISON
SUQUAMISH
SKOKOMISH
SQUAXIN ISLAND
CHEHALIS

SWINOMISH
LUMMI
NOOKSACK

UPPER SKAGIT SAUK-SUIATTLE
STILLAGUAMISH
TULALIP

MUCKLESHOOT
PUYALLUP
NISQUALLY

COLVILLE
KALISPEL
SPOKANE

YAKIMA

Miles
Kilometers
0   50   100
0   50   100

Barely one hundred years after the Northwest Territory Ordinance of 1787 had declared, "The utmost good faith shall always be observed toward the Indians," the Indian tribes of the continental United States had been deprived of all but a tiny fraction of their original patrimony. Of the 1.9 billion acres they had roamed over and occupied in the late sixteenth century, a mere 53 million acres remained in their hands at the beginning of the twentieth.

Before 1850 it was the practice of the United States government to delay conveyance of title to any public lands until, among other things, all Indian titles were extinguished by treaties signed between the individual tribes and representatives of the United States government. Ratification of such a treaty by the Senate was the final procedure in appropriating Indian land. Removal of Indian tribes to locations west of the Mississippi was carried out prior to white settlement wherever possible, and always in advance of the conveyance of title to any lands granted to settlers.

Problems of an altogether different and unique sort came with the conclusion of the dispute over the Oregon Territory in 1846. Before then settlement had already taken place throughout the Willamette valley, along the shores of the Lower Columbia, and around southern Puget Sound. The granting of such lands by the Provisional Government of Oregon had created problems that took more than a decade to settle.

The Organic Act of 1848, which established the Oregon Territory, guaranteed the rights of Indians prior to extinguishment of title by treaty, and, at the same time, it annulled the land grants that had been made by the Provisional Government. No provision was made for the negotiation of treaties until the Indian Treaty Act was signed in 1850. The act authorized negotiations only with tribes west of the Cascades, as well as arrangements for their removal to the east. Four months later the survey of public lands was initiated by the Oregon Donation Act. By the end of 1851 nineteen treaties had been negotiated, but although their lands were ceded, these Indians were not moved eastward over the mountains. Instead reservations west of the mountains were designated. The Senate refused to ratify these treaties, and it was not until 1854 that the Senate acted and ratified the treaties earlier negotiated. Immediately thereafter Isaac Stevens, territorial governor of Washington, and Joel Palmer, superintendent of Indian affairs in Oregon Territory, were instructed to negotiate treaties with other Indian tribes in the vicinity of white settlement, and to proceed "to concentrate all tribes in a few reservations of limited extent."

In western Washington, Stevens quickly concluded four treaties with various groups of Indians: those of Medicine Creek (Nisqually, Puyallup, Steilacoom), Point Elliott (Duwamish, Suquamish, and allied tribes as far north as Bellingham Bay), Point No Point (Klallam, Chemakum, Skokomish) and Neah Bay (Makah). Attempts to conclude treaties with the remaining tribes of southwest Washington were unsuccessful, although shortly after the breakdown of negotiations a treaty was concluded with the coast tribes living north of Grays Harbor (Quinault, Quileute, and Hoh).

Turning his attention to the eastern part of the territory, Stevens called the tribes of the south and southeast—Yakima, Nez Perce, Walula, and Cayuse—to a meeting at Walla Walla, where after tortuous negotiations a treaty was signed by all four tribes, plus the Umatilla band. Before similar arrangements could be worked out with the tribes of north-central and northeast Washington, the Yakima War erupted in September 1855.

Just as hostilities were about to end in 1858 (see Map 28), Congress determined that eastern Washington was not to remain Indian Country; and in the following year all the treaties negotiated in 1854 and 1855 were ratified by the Senate, although no appropriations were approved to deal with these until 1860. No further trea-

ties were signed, and in 1871, Congress formally abolished the treaty system, after which reservations of various sizes were organized east and west of the Cascades.

The map of Indian reservations shows only their modern-day locations and extent. Some important changes during the second half of the nineteenth century should be noted, including (1) the reduction by approximately one-half of the Colville Reservation, which from 1871 to 1892 extended northwards from the Columbia River to the Canadian border and occupied all the land from the Columbia on the east to the Okanogan River in the west; and (2) the elimination of the Columbia or Moses, Reservation, which was established in 1879–80 as a reward for Chief Moses and his Nez Perce band, who had remained neutral during the Bannock War. In 1883 this reservation, which had stretched from the Okanogan River to the Cascades, was greatly reduced in size by moving its northern border from the forty-ninth parallel fifteen miles to the south. In 1886 the reservation was dissolved, and Indians living on it were offered the choice of 640-acre allotments in the vicinity or removal to the Colville Reservation.

Since the reduction of the Colville Reservation in 1892, only minor adjustments have been made in the size of reservations in Washington. Encroachments on these and on other Indian lands continued after that date, however, despite the Dawes Severalty Act of 1887. The latter was aimed at making Indian allotments inalienable for a period of twenty-five years. Nevertheless, during the operation of the Dawes Act between 1887 and 1934, the total acreage of reservation land in Washington declined from 4,680,000 acres to 2,755,000 acres. In addition to the loss of acreage, extensive mineral rights and leases of timberlands and grazing lands were acquired by non-Indians. As historian Frederick Yonce has noted, "the story of white land settlement is the story of the dispossession of the Indians."

PART III

EXPLORATION OF THE PACIFIC NORTHWEST

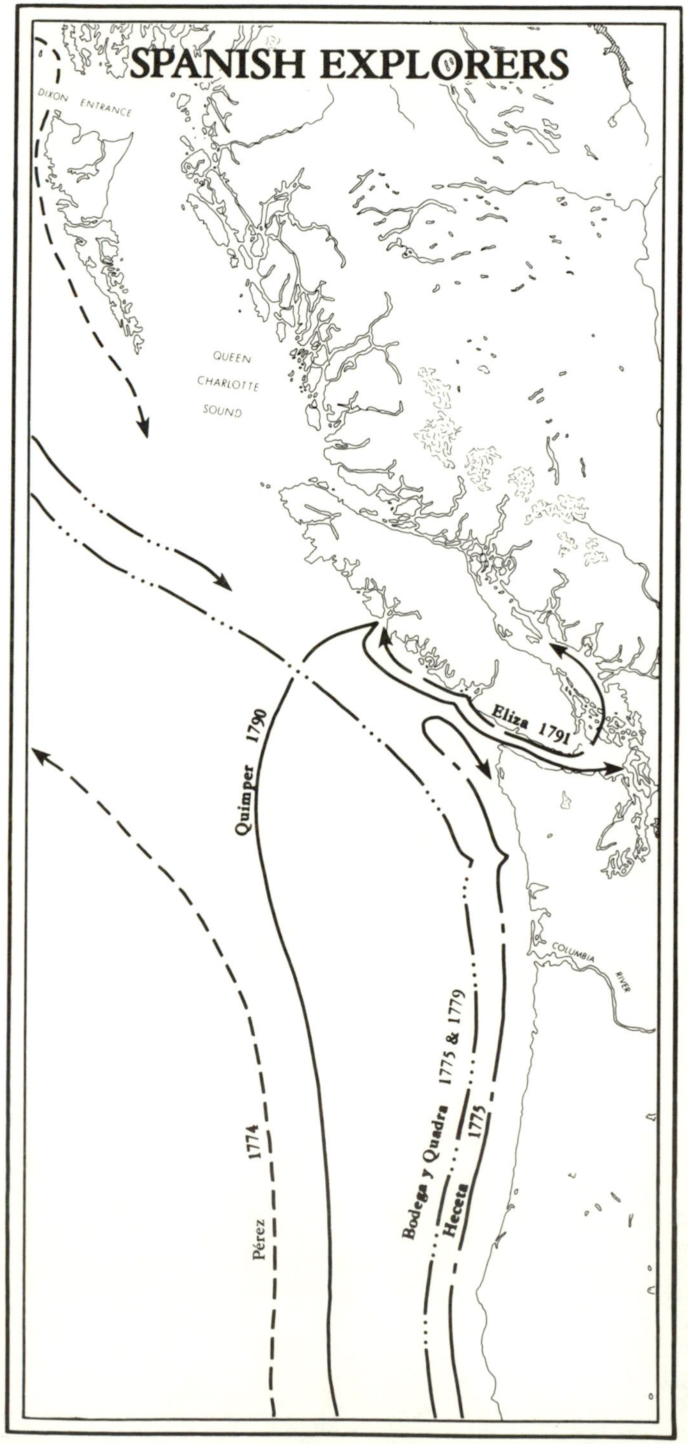

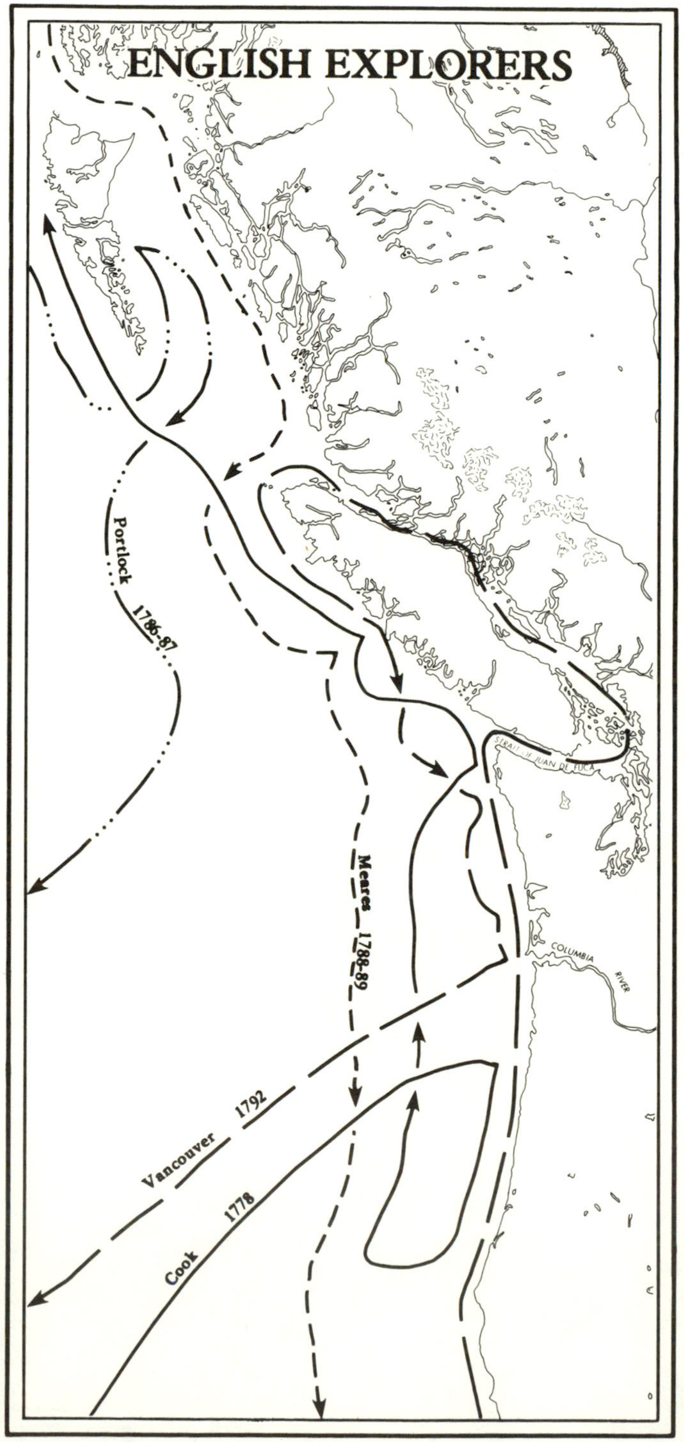

FRENCH & AMERICAN EXPLORERS

Lapérouse 1786

Gray 1791-92

Gray 1791-92

Wilkes 1841

COLUMBIA RIVER

QUEEN CHARLOTTE SOUND

DIXON ENTRANCE

ENGLISH EXPLORERS

Meares 1788-89

Portlock 1786-87

Vancouver 1792

Cook 1778

COLUMBIA RIVER

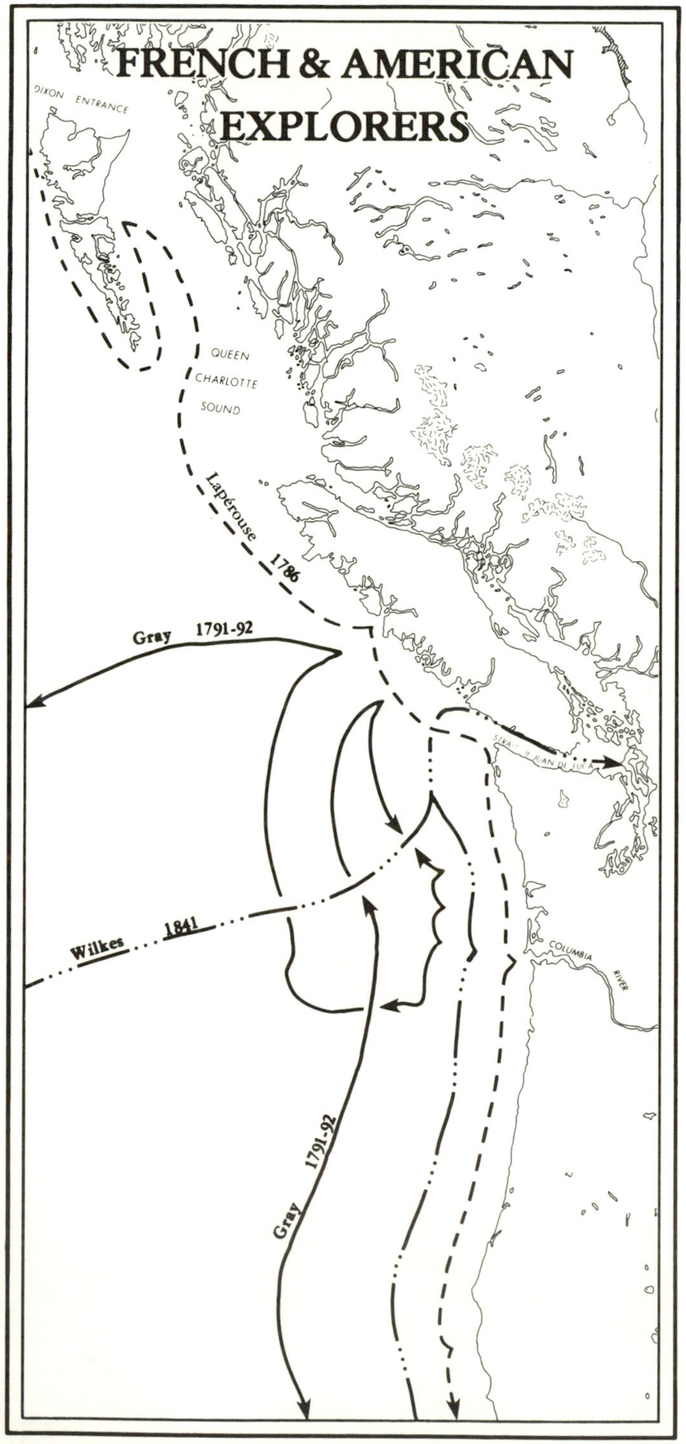

SPANISH EXPLORERS

Eliza 1791

Quimper 1790

Hecate 1775

Bodega y Quadra 1775 & 1779

Pérez 1774

COLUMBIA RIVER

QUEEN CHARLOTTE SOUND

DIXON ENTRANCE

EXPLORATION OF THE NORTHWEST COAST OF AMERICA

© 1988 by the University of Oklahoma Press

15. EXPLORATION OF THE NORTHWEST COAST OF AMERICA

Those eighteenth-century explorers who, after Francis Drake's 1577–80 voyage, piloted their ships and crews into the mist-enshrouded waters north of 46° north latitude on the Pacific coast of North America were not the first to glimpse the shores of what became Washington state. Oral traditions combine with artifacts to suggest many earlier visitors, and of course, for thousands of years fishermen and warriors from Indian settlements had plied coastal, sound, and river waters, gathering a mass of details about the region's waterways and landforms. But the Europeans who arrived in the eighteenth century were different. They were driven by novel motives, besides the desire to survive and natural curiosity: religious zeal, scientific curiosity, and nationalism urged them forward and shaped their plans. They were beneficiaries of new science and technology; they travelled aboard ships designed for long-range expeditions on the high seas, and they possessed new navigational instruments that provided surer passage and a better measure of position. They were aided by, and assisted in turn, skilled cartographers. They recorded their findings in carefully kept journals, logs, and artists' renderings and used the recently invented printing press to broadcast news of their explorations.

First to reach the southern coast of the hemisphere, Spain pressed her advantage by exploring northward. In 1774, Juan Pérez was sent to take possession of the whole west coast of North America as far north as latitude 60°, but he reached only 54 N before turning back. Shortly thereafter Bruno de Heceta and Juan Francisco de Bodega y Quadra commanded the first recorded European landings on Washington's Pacific coast on July 14, 1775, near Point Grenville and within sight of the Olympic Mountains; and Heceta probably was the first European explorer to sight the entrance to the Columbia River, although he mistook it for the Strait of Juan

de Fuca. Neither the voyage of James Cook nor that of Jean François de Galaup, comte de la Lapérouse, added anything substantive to what was already known about the coast of Washington, although both made important contributions to knowledge elsewhere in the north Pacific Ocean. Early in the summer of 1790 an exploring party led by Manuel Quimper made the first verifiable visit to the Strait of Juan de Fuca, examining initially the northern shoreline, then Bahia de Quimper (now Dungeness Bay) and Puerta de Bodega y Quadra (Port Discovery). Quimper's men saw Puget Sound, but thought it a shallow bay; they also discovered Haro's Strait and Núñez Gaona (Neah Bay) and took extensive soundings. Anxious at least to limit British incursions in the northwest, sending Francisco de Eliza in 1791 to reconnoiter again Haro Strait and examine Nuestra Señora de los Angeles (Port Angeles) on the southern coast of the Strait of Juan de Fuca). They established the first European settlement in what became Washington at Neah Bay in May 1792—planned as a major naval base to guard Spain's interest in the region—and dispatched two officers formerly with the famed Malaspina scientific expedition, Dionicio Alcalá Galiano and Cayetano Valdés, to explore methodically the shore and waterways within the Strait of Juan de Fuca.

Alcalá Galiano and Valdés reached Neah Bay early in June 1792 and with the help of a cooperative native chief, Te-ta-koos, explored Puget Sound, including Bellingham Bay, from which they could hear erupting Mount Baker. The expedition sailed northward through the San Juan Islands. On June 21, near the present site of Vancouver, British Columbia, the Spaniards were surprised to encounter an expedition flying British colors and commanded by Captain George Vancouver.

Vancouver's ships, *Discovery* and *Chatham,* had departed England in April 1791, travelling to the Pacific via the Cape of Good Hope with stops for surveying work and provisioning in Australia, New Zealand, Chatham, Tahiti, and Hawaii. The vessels had made landfall at 39° 20′ north altitude, then sailed up the coast, missing the mouth of the Columbia River but anchoring inside the Strait of Juan de Fuca at the close of April 1792. Vancouver's men explored and mapped much of Puget Sound, its islands and channels (see Map 16), working cooperatively with the Spanish explorers for a time. The cooperation was born of mutual respect and a shared interest in advancing knowledge of the region, but did not erase conflicting national aims. Going ashore near present-day Everett, Washington, Captain Vancouver lay official claim to the area for Great Britain. Alcalá Galiano and Valdés, for their part, were in a desperate race to reinforce Spain's claim in the Pacific Northwest—an effort historian Warren Cook has likened to "locking the barn door after the proverbial theft."

Vancouver wintered in Hawaii and returned in the summer of 1793 to survey Washington's Pacific coastline. A Spanish expedition, commanded by Juan Martinez y Zayas, also charted the coastline, visiting Grays Harbor and crossing the Columbia River bar to penetrate some fourteen miles, before running aground, then withdrawing. Lacking the will and power for a protracted struggle, Spain retreated in 1797 from the waters north of 42°. The British, meanwhile, had learned of other rivals: Vancouver had encountered the American trader, Robert Gray, who had made an earlier visit to the area and on his second voyage, in May 1792, had found and entered the Columbia River. That discovery, as well as Gray's entry into Grays Harbor, provided an opening wedge for later United States claims to the Oregon Country.

The Wilkes expedition is depicted in Map 18.

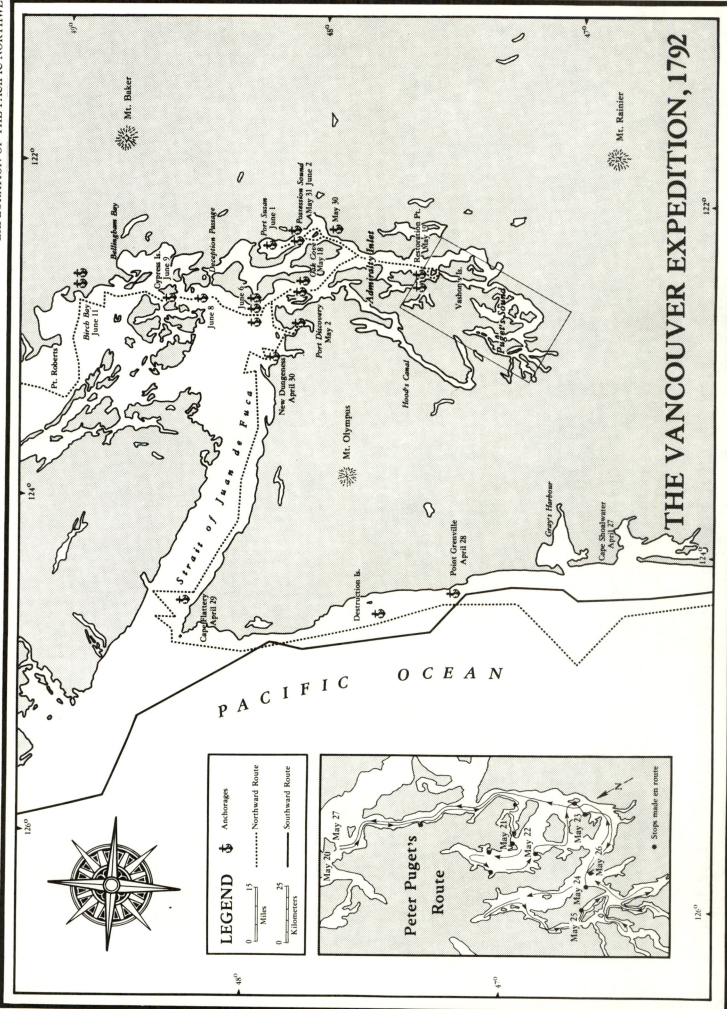

THE VANCOUVER EXPEDITION, 1792

The two British ships that sighted California's shore at 39° 27' north latitude late in the afternoon of April 17, 1792, were engaged in a momentous enterprise. Under the command of Captain George Vancouver, the *Discovery* and the *Chatham* were engaged in one of history's longest oceanic exploring expeditions. Their officers and crews had orders to examine and record the principal features of the North Pacific coastline of North America to further document and support British claims in the region. They were bound for Nootka, where Vancouver was to seek a solution to the dangerous impasse with Spain. He would ultimately succeed in this mission and would preside over the beginning of the Spanish retreat from the waters north of 42°. And with equally impressive amounts of skill and tenacity, he would lead his expedition in investigating and charting much of the coast and inland waters of Washington.

Vancouver's ships had weighed anchor on April 1, 1791, and sailed by way of the Cape of Good Hope to South Africa's Simon's Bay, where the vessels were repaired and newly provisioned and four crew members replaced. The expedition sailed east for New Holland, New Zealand, and Tahiti in mid-August 1791 and arrived off the western coast of Australia on September 26. After some coastal exploration the two ships moved on to South Island, New Zealand, dropping anchor at Dusky Bay at the beginning of November. They were almost destroyed by heavy winds while moored there, and were separated during the subsequent passage to Tahiti. *Discovery* and *Chatham* departed Matavia Bay for the North American coast via Hawaii on January 24, 1792.

Passing Cape Disappointment and the mouth of the Columbia River, Vancouver's ships encountered Robert Gray's *Columbia* on April 29, 1792. After consultation with Gray, the British exploring party continued northward, arriving off Cape Flattery at midday of April 29 (and leaving the Boston trader to his imminent discovery of the Columbia River). *Discovery* and *Chatham* entered the Strait of Juan de Fuca, proceeded along the southern shore, and stopped April 30 at New Dun-

geness. As they approached that harbor, a third lieutenant aboard the *Discovery*, Joseph Baker, scanned the eastern horizon and was the first to spy the volcanic peak that henceforth bore his name.

Vancouver next ordered the methodical survey of the coast, using small, open boats. The two ships were moved to Port Discovery, which was found by the survey crews on May 2. The survey continued while other crewmen made repairs to ships, sails, and rigging; collected fresh water supplies; and set to work brewing a vile concoction known as spruce beer, useful in warding off scurvy. Between May 7 and 15 several survey parties—led by Vancouver; James Johnston, master of *Chatham*; Lieutenant Peter Puget of *Discovery*; and the expedition botanist, Archibald Menzies—discovered and explored Port Townsend and Hood Canal and sighted and named Mount Rainier. *Chatham* sailed north on May 18 to explore the area's islands. Puget and Master Joseph Whidbey meanwhile were placed in charge of a launch and cutter and directed to examine Puget Sound. Their surveying party arrived at the inlet where Olympia now is located on May 25. Vancouver and Baker explored the western portion of that inlet and returned to *Discovery*, after circling Vashon Island, on May 29.

Chatham sailed north on May 28 and was joined at Port Susan by *Discovery* on May 30. The onset of poor weather slowed both ships' progress. *Chatham* found herself stranded in shallow water on June 1, but was freed by high tide. The two ships turned back to Port Susan, where they were rejoined on June 2 by a party of explorers, commanded by Whidbey and Lieutenant James Hanson, who had examined Whidbey Island's east coast, including Penn Cove. Whidbey and Puget next were dispatched on June 7 to complete surveys of the Whidbey Island vicinity. Meanwhile, the main body of the expedition, after conducting an official ceremony on June 4 laying claim to the region examined to date, made its way northward and paused just to the west of Cypress Island. From there the British ships progressed slowly to Birch Bay (so named because of Menzies's

discovery of a stand of birch there), where during a brief pause, repairs to the vessels and planning for further exploration were initiated. The following day, Vancouver and Puget set out northbound in two small boats. Whidbey took a survey party to examine the area to the southeast and found and explored a bay which was named in honor of the British Navy's controller of storekeeper's accounts, Sir William Bellingham. Returning to the anchorage at Birch Bay, Whidbey sighted two Spanish vessels near the north entrance of Bellingham Bay, the *Sutil* and the *Mexicana*, commanded by Alcalá Galiano and Cayetano Valdés.

Vancouver encountered these two ships later near Burrard's Inlet, which is today part of the city of Vancouver, British Columbia. Temporarily, national rivalries were submerged in a common search for information, and for a time the two expeditions conducted joint surveys of the coast north of the forty-ninth parallel. The onset of foul weather forced a cessation in the explorations, but when Vancouver led his ships into Nootka on August 28, 1792, he and his men had completed an impressive reconnaissance of much of the coastal area of Washington. Protracted negotiations with the Spanish would follow, and Vancouver's ships, wintering in Hawaii, would later retrace Robert Gray's entry into the shoal-bound mouth of the Columbia River, but the Vancouver expedition's major contributions to knowledge of Washington's coastal areas were already virtually complete. Hundreds of miles of coastline had been examined and charted with painstaking care. Important geographical features such as Mount Rainier and Mount Baker had been discovered, and the peoples, vegetation, and game of the region were described in detail. The Vancouver expedition's work, moreover, had been carried out with a degree of accuracy that would surprise and impress explorers and cartographers of later generations. In Vancouver's wake, the ambiguities and fables left intact or even invented by earlier explorers ceased to clutter charts and maps. The coastal outline of Washington stood revealed and documented.

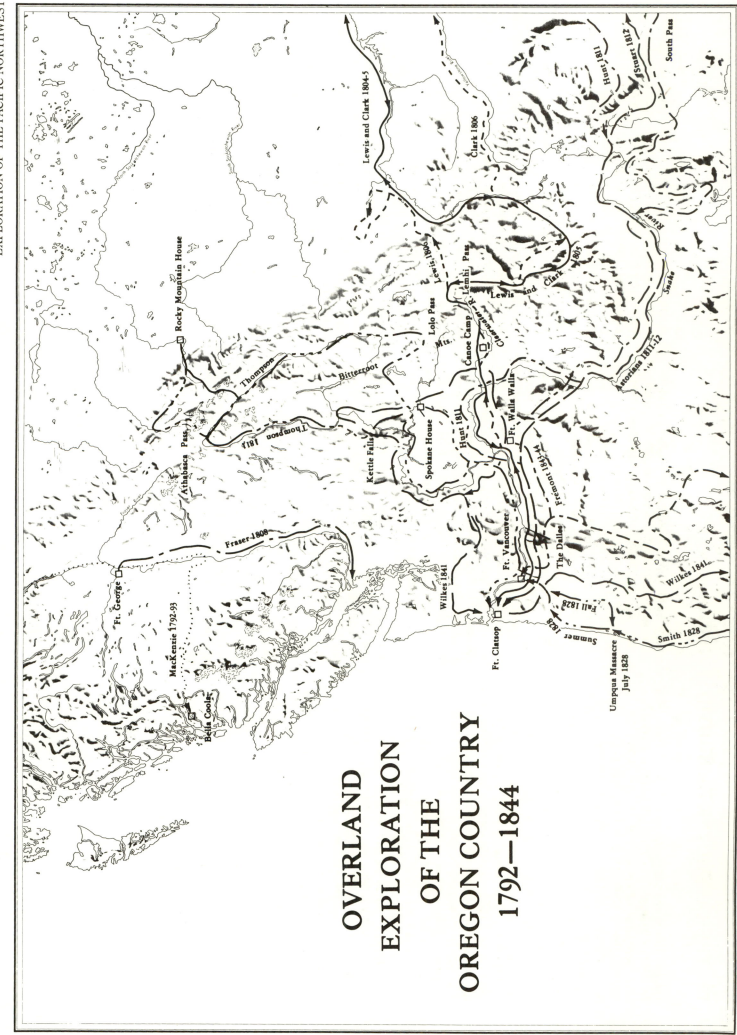

OVERLAND
EXPLORATION
OF THE
OREGON COUNTRY
1792—1844

17. OVERLAND EXPLORATION OF THE OREGON COUNTRY, 1792–1844

The four-nation race to chart and claim coastal areas of the Pacific Northwest was not replicated by land-based explorers. The Oregon Country, a half million square miles in area (see Map 19), possessed a daunting variety of natural obstacles. Exploration and survey progressed slowly, being advanced primarily by official American expeditions and by the fur companies.

It was, in fact, a fur trader, Alexander Mackenzie of the North West Company, who first penetrated the interior of the Pacific Northwest. In 1787, Mackenzie was sent to replace Peter Pond at the North West Company's Fort Athabasca in what is now central Canada. A winter spent in Pond's company helped fire Mackenzie's imagination with dreams of finding a passage to the Pacific, and on June 3, 1789, he made his first attempt to reach the "western ocean." The attempt was a failure of sorts: the ocean discovered was not the Pacific but the Arctic; the river, the Mackenzie—named by him the Disappointment River—was not the "great river of the West." Three years later, in October 1792, Mackenzie's second expedition got underway. Following the Peace River and struggling through terrifying rapids and across rugged mountain terrain, the group, reached salt water near Bella Coola on July 20, 1793.

Although Mackenzie's march to the Pacific did not ensure immediate success for the North West Company in the Oregon Country, it did give the company—and also Great Britain—a substantial claim to the region. It also inspired further British exploration. Simon Fraser, another Nor'Wester, conducted a trading and exploratory expedition through the Rockies in 1806, and in the process he bestowed on the area the name New Caledonia. Late in May 1808, Fraser descended the Fraser River to the site of present-day New Westminster on the British Columbia coast, adding much new information to the map of northwest North America.

Still another North West Company officer, David Thompson—geographer, astronomer, and the company's chief surveyor—made contributions second only to those of Mackenzie. In 1798, Thompson conducted the first systematic survey of the upper Mississippi river basin, and during the next few years he explored and mapped extensive areas of the Rockies. In 1807 he decided to seek out the headwaters of the Columbia River, and in the course of the next few years the complex hydrography of the upper Columbia region was skillfully unravelled by him. Early in 1811, Thompson discovered Athabasca Pass, and from near there he followed the Columbia downstream to Kettle Falls. He explored parts of the Colville, Spokane, and Snake rivers before journeying downriver to the ocean. Not only was Thompson the first explorer to trace the Columbia from source to mouth, but also he discovered Athabasca Pass, which was to serve as the major route across the Rockies for decades to come. He pieced together a map of the West that was to serve travellers and government officials for more than a generation.

Meanwhile, the Americans had not been idle. Thomas Jefferson's dream of dispatching an American-sponsored expedition to the Oregon Country finally was realized when Meriwether Lewis and William Clark set out from Saint Louis on May 14, 1804. The expedition travelled up the Missouri River and wintered with the Mandan Indians. Crossing Lemhi Pass, they reached the Clearwater River, which led them first to the Snake and then to the Columbia. On November 7, 1805, they were camped within sight of the Pacific. After spending the winter at Fort Clatsop, the expedition started back late in March 1806. The Lewis and Clark expedition had achieved a number of significant scientific successes, and most important of all, it firmly established the claims of the United States to Oregon. It also kindled American interest in the fur trade of the West.

After gaining a share of the existing fur trade through his American Fur Company, John Jacob Astor in 1810 formed the Pacific Fur Company and launched a two-pronged expansion plan in the Pacific Northwest. The *Tonquin* was dispatched to establish a trading post near the mouth of the Columbia and commence trade with nearby Indian tribes, while Wilson Price Hunt was appointed to lead an overland expedition and establish a usable trade route between Saint Louis and the Pacific Coast. Hunt left the Missouri Territory late in April 1811 in command of a party of sixty including David Stuart. By mid-October they were moving down the south branch of the Snake River. It took them close to three months more, however, to traverse the rugged terrain of the Rockies, and it was not until early January 1811 that they arrived on the banks of the Columbia. Ten days later Astoria was reached. In the ensuing year the Astorians mounted expeditions to different parts of the Oregon Country, establishing forts and exploring the surrounding country, but following the outbreak of the War of 1812, the Pacific Fur Company withdrew from the region, leaving the field to the North West Company. The sale of Astoria and subsequent British dominance in the fur trade of the Pacific Northwest, first by the North West Company, then after 1821 by the Hudson's Bay Company, discouraged American exploration for a time, although much detailed geographical knowledge was added by the British fur traders.

Later American expeditions added only slightly to the general knowledge of the Oregon Country. Jedidiah Smith in 1824 explored the headwaters of the Snake River, and in the following year led a larger group of trappers west and then south into California, before turning north again. When ambushed by Indians near the mouth of the Umpqua River in 1828, Smith and three of his companions escaped to make their way to Fort Vancouver. Then in the 1840s the Wilkes expedition (Map 18), though mainly concerned with coastal exploration, was able to achieve a small amount of overland exploration in the Cascades and the Columbia Basin. Finally, in the summer of 1843, John C. Frémont headed an exploring party through parts of the Pacific Northwest, as a result of which a few additional details were added to the map of Oregon.

THE WILKES EXPEDITION

18. THE WILKES EXPEDITION

A generation would intervene between completion of the highly successful Lewis and Clark expedition of 1804–5 and another official United States effort to explore the Oregon in Country in 1841. Captain Edmund Fanning had proposed to President James Madison an expedition to the Pacific Northwest and the ocean beyond, but the War of 1812 had upset the scheme. A similar plan was advanced by President John Quincy Adams in 1825. Congress responded tardily and inadequately, voting approval in 1828 but neglecting to fund the project. Secretary of the Navy Samuel Southard made available a sloop, commissioned an inquiry of experienced seafarers to ascertain what kinds of data an expedition should gather, and sent Lieutenant Charles Wilkes to England to purchase navigational instruments. Nothing came of these efforts, and an attempt by Captain Fanning to combine a search for new sealing grounds with the collection of scientific information in the Pacific in 1829 and 1830 had disappointing results.

Pressure from commercial and whaling interests, as well as the scientific community, for an expedition that would make possible more accurate and detailed charts and information for the Pacific Ocean finally compelled action. The command went first to Captain Thomas ap Catesby Jones, but he resigned in a dispute with the Navy secretary at the close of 1837 and was replaced by Charles Wilkes. Wilkes was ambitious and strongwilled, and his appointment and leadership stirred controversy among his contemporaries. He has been called energetic, decisive, and competent, and a martinet who displayed "puerile petulance." Perhaps his most serious flaw was his lack of experience as a naval explorer. His second and third officers, Lieutenants William L. Hudson and Cadwalader Ringgold, also lacked survey experience.

The United States Exploring Expedition, as it was called, departed Hampton Roads, Virginia, on August 18, 1838. It consisted of two sloops of war, *Vincennes*

and *Peacock*, a survey brig, *Porpoise*, and storeship, *Relief*, and two former New York Harbor pilot tenders, renamed *Sea Gull* and *Flying Fish*. Aboard, in addition to the officers and men, were nine scientists and artists. Wilkes's instructions stipulated extensive explorations of the Pacific Ocean, especially the Samoan and Fiji islands, and the Antarctic, as well as the northwest coast of North America north of the Golden Gate. It was April 1841 before Wilkes was ready to sail for the Oregon Country with *Vincennes* and *Porpoise*, leaving Hudson to complete the exploration of some smaller Pacific Islands. The expedition was to be reunited later.

In the meantime Wilkes, having tried and failed to cross the bar into the Columbia River, sailed north for the Strait of Juan de Fuca and anchored in Port Discovery on May 2. He sent off a letter to Fort Nisqually requesting a pilot, but on May 6, after having examined the harbor and adjacent shore, he moved his ships to Port Townsend. On May 8 the exploring party traveled eight miles to the entrance to Hood Canal (called Port Lawrence by Wilkes). Wilkes's English pilot from Nisqually met the Americans on the west side of Admiralty Inlet across from the southern tip of Whidbey Island in a cove henceforth called Pilot Cove. He led them up the inlet to an anchorage near Port Madison. They next passed to the west of Vashon Island, pausing for the night immediately below the narrows leading into Puget Sound. They reached Fort Nisqually on May 11.

Hudson had been delayed by unexpectedly protracted survey work and then had wrecked his ship, *Peacock*, in attempting to enter the Columbia. His continued absence forced Wilkes to curtail his planned explorations. He sent Lieutenant Augustus L. Case to survey Hood Canal and Lieutenant Ringgold to explore Admiralty Inlet. Lieutenant Robert E. Johnson was given command of an overland exploring party bound for Fort Colvile, the Lapwai Mission, and Fort Walla Walla, which was scheduled to return in two months via the Yakima River. Crossing the Puyallup River, Johnson

led his men east through Naches Pass, then travelled north, reaching the Yakima River on June 2. They continued north, arriving at Fort Okanogan six days later. Moving east to Fort Colvile, then south to Lapwai and Walla Walla, they left the philologist Horatio Hale to complete a survey of the region and then returned to Nisqually. Wilkes and four companions went by horse to Cowlitz Farm and on to Astoria by canoe. Returning from a visit to the Willamette Valley settlement, Wilkes met Peter Skene Ogden at Fort Vancouver, and he and artist Joseph Drayton accepted an invitation to travel with him, Wilkes as far as Cowlitz Farm, Drayton all the way to Walla Walla.

Meanwhile, Wilkes had ordered a small party under Midshipman Henry Eld to conduct a thorough survey of Grays Harbor, which was completed with dispatch. Another group, aboard *Porpoise*, weighed anchor at Nisqually on May 15 and initiated an examination of the region at the mouth of the Puyallup River (Commencement Bay), then moved north. The passage between Port Orchard and Port Madison was explored, as was Penn Cove on Whidbey Island. Some of the expedition took Deception Passage to the northern outlet of Possession Sound. After spending July 4 near Point Roberts and reconnoitering at the mouth of the Fraser River the following day, this party, under Lieutenant Maury, joined the *Vincennes* and the main body of the expedition at New Dungeness on July 20.

News of Hudson's loss of the *Peacock* ended further exploration, including a projected overland journey to the Yellowstone River. Wilkes's ships gathered off the mouth of the Columbia on August 6. The expedition's surveys of portions of the Pacific would stand the test of time. Surveys of the Pacific Northwest, although hurried by circumstances, nonetheless inspired a growing public awareness of the region and supported a firm United States position in the approaching negotiations with Britain of the Oregon Question.

PART IV

THE OREGON COUNTRY AND WASHINGTON TERRITORY

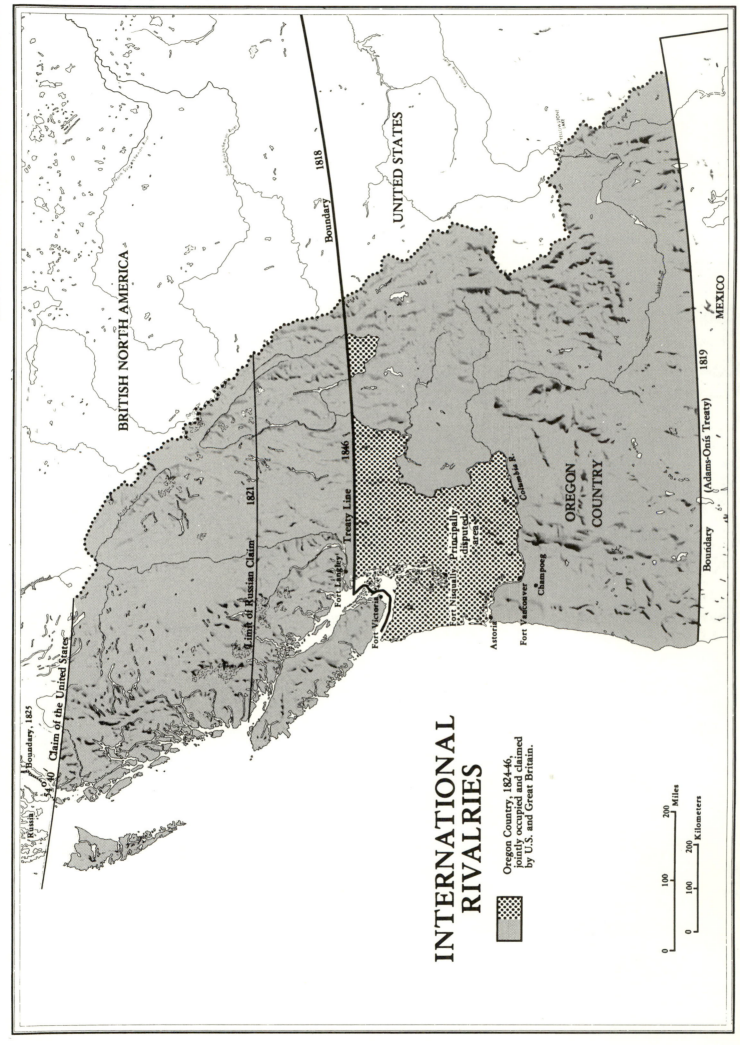

BRITISH NORTH AMERICA

1818 Boundary

UNITED STATES

Boundary, 1825

Claim of the United States

54° 40'

Russia

Limit of Russian Claim 1821

1846 Treaty Line

Fort Langley

Fort Victoria

Fort Nisqually — Principally disputed area

Astoria

Fort Vancouver

Champoeg

Columbia R.

OREGON COUNTRY

MEXICO

Boundary (Adams-Onis Treaty) 1819

YELLOWSTONE LAKE

INTERNATIONAL RIVALRIES

Oregon Country, 1824-46, jointly occupied and claimed by U.S. and Great Britain.

200 Miles

100   200

0   100   200 Kilometers

19. INTERNATIONAL RIVALRIES

From the moment on July 14, 1775, when Spanish explorers stepped ashore near Point Grenville, future European control over the Pacific Northwest was a certainty. But which nation would succeed in exercising that control? The once-preeminent empire builders of New Spain, who had explored much of the coastline of the region, projected a naval base at Neah Bay and attempted to interdict overland access to the Oregon Country by Lewis and Clark. However, they retreated from a major confrontation after the Nootka Convention of 1790 with Great Britain and sold all claim to the area north of 42° to the Americans in 1819. The Russians had explored Alaska's coastline and begun a long-lasting trade there by the 1780s. Despite commissioning raids on California's otter population by Aleut hunters under Yankee command and establishing an agricultural and trading station well within Spanish territory, they made no sustained, serious efforts to examine or settle the region between 42° and 54° 40'. An imperial ukase was issued in 1821 that appeared to extend Russian claims south to 51°, but it was nullified when, in treaties with the United States in 1824 and Great Britain in 1825, the czar surrendered title to the area south of 54° 40'.

This left the British and Americans the sole contenders. Their dispute, alternately dormant and tense, would continue for over two decades. Since the British navy was at least temporarily in control off the coast, and British traders monopolized the fur trade after 1812, once Astor's men were gone, the British had

every reason to press for an early settlement of the Oregon Question. The Americans resisted, adopting what one secretary of state would characterize as a "policy of wise and masterly inactivity." The best the English diplomats could get following the War of 1812 was a ten-year agreement to leave Oregon open to both countries' nationals. This arrangement was renewed in 1827 for an indefinite period, subject to a mutual right of abrogation upon one-year's notice. By April 1846, when the United States Congress voted to give notification of termination, subsequent British offers to compromise had reduced the area of disputed ownership to essentially the land lying between the Columbia River and the forty-ninth parallel, which already was the international boundary from the Lake of the Woods to the Rockies.

By the early 1840s American settlers had followed the earlier missionaries, and the question of sovereignty over Oregon had become a powerful political issue. To a claim resting on the explorations of Gray, Lewis and Clark, the Astorians, and others, and the acquisition of Spanish claims in the Adams-Onís Treaty, the Americans added an emphasis on what they regarded as the logic of an ever-expanding march westward: Oregon would be theirs, as all that aly to the east had become so. Congressmen proposed the building of forts along the Oregon Trail, and press and politicians took up the cause of manifest destiny.

Elected on that plank in 1844, President James K. Polk pressed the issue. He cleverly played upon his

countrymen's nationalistic feelings, but there is evidence that he was prepared to accept less than all of Oregon, that his chief objective was the establishment of American ports on the North Pacific coast. The British, too, were willing to make sacrifices. Troubles in Ireland and continued unrest because of the Corn Laws, as well as the realization that war with the United States would disrupt a major portion of the empire's commerce, encouraged moderation. At a time when British leaders harbored doubts about the profitability of Britain's far-flung possessions, the notion of a war largely in defense of the unpopular Hudson's Bay Company's waning interest in distant Oregon was very unattractive.

Initial differences over the fate of Vancouver Island and the Columbia River gave way to a compromise. The international boundary that was decided in 1846 followed the forty-ninth parallel to a channel between the mainland and Vancouver Island, all of which remained in British hands. The Americans gave the Hudson's Bay Company navigational privileges on the Columbia River—an empty gesture, since the company already had shifted most of its activities north to Fort Victoria and the interior of British Columbia. As it turned out, the agreement did not wholly settle questions of title in the Pacific Northwest, and confusion about exactly where the dividing line ran between the mainland and Vancouver Island nearly precipitated military action later. The ultimate question of title was resolved only in the Treaty of Washington of 1871.

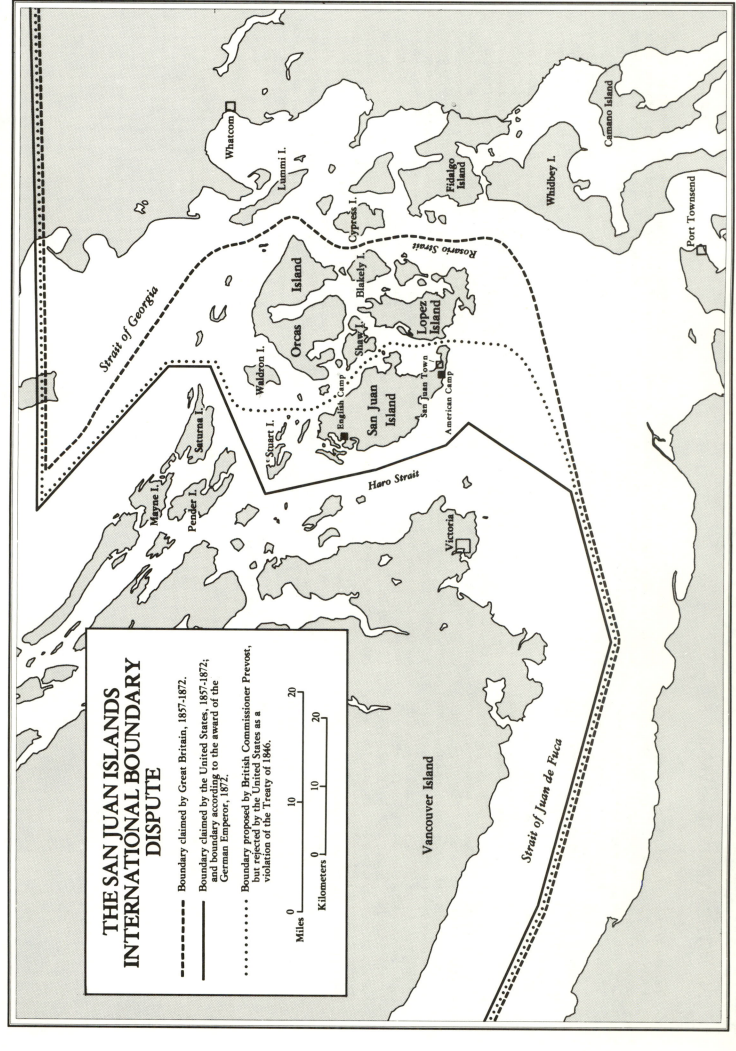

THE SAN JUAN ISLANDS
INTERNATIONAL BOUNDARY
DISPUTE

- - - Boundary claimed by Great Britain, 1857-1872.

——— Boundary claimed by the United States, 1857-1872;
and boundary according to the award of the
German Emperor, 1872.

········· Boundary proposed by British Commissioner Prevost,
but rejected by the United States as a
violation of the Treaty of 1846.

Miles   0   10   20

Kilometers 0   10   20

Strait of Georgia

Whatcom

Lummi I.

Cypress I.

Orcas Island

Waldron I.

Blakely I.

Rosario Strait

Fidalgo Island

Camano Island

Whidbey I.

Port Townsend

Shaw I.

Lopez Island

English Camp

San Juan Island

San Juan Town

American Camp

Stuart I.

Saturna I.

Mayne I.

Pender I.

Haro Strait

Victoria

Vancouver Island

Strait of Juan de Fuca

20. THE SAN JUAN ISLANDS INTERNATIONAL BOUNDARY DISPUTE

The signing of the original Treaty of Washington on June 15, 1846, left one Oregon boundary issue outstanding. Ignorance of the precise geography of the region, on the part of both the English and American commissioners, resulted in a vague reference to "the middle of the channel which separates the continent from Vancouver's Island." In fact, two such channels existed, and specifying one, the Canal de Haro (Haro Strait), as the international line would give the United States possession of the San Juan Islands, while choosing the other, Rosario Strait, would place those islands under British control. Compared to the amount of territory already divided, the San Juan Islands might appear insignificant. Yet land hunger, misguided patriotism, and overzealous officials on both sides almost managed to precipitate war over the matter.

For several years there was no trouble over the commissioners' oversight. When the Oregon Territorial Legislature created a county government for the islands of upper Puget Sound, including Whidbey and the islands of the Haro Archipelago, the British did not protest; and there was no American reaction when, between 1843 and 1846, the Hudson's Bay Company began depositing small numbers of sheep on San Juan Island. Tension developed in 1846 when George Bancroft, United States ambassador to Great Britain, reported that the Hudson's Bay Company, desirous of having San Juan Island for a permanent sheep-raising station, was pressing for an official government espousal of the Rosario Strait boundary. Tension rose further in December 1853 when the Hudson's Bay Company steamer *Beaver* transported thirteen hundred sheep and a sheepherder, Charles Griffin, to San Juan Island. The American customs collector, Isaac Ebey, attempted to claim customs duties, the British refused to pay, but after an unpleasant exchange between James Douglas, governor of Vancouver Island, and the Washington territorial governor, Isaac Stevens, tempers cooled, and the issue again was postponed.

When the question was transformed into a dangerous controversy in the summer of 1859, the occasion itself was ludicrous. The Hudson's Bay Company employee, Charles Griffin, remained on the island, watching over a growing number of sheep and other livestock, which were permitted to roam freely. In the meantime, however, American settlement had grown appreciably, largely because of the influx of people drawn northwestward by the Fraser River gold discoveries. One of the settlers, Lyman Cutler, had taken up a claim adjacent to Hudson's Bay Company land. He had watched in growing exasperation while company pigs broke through his fences and rooted in his garden, and after receiving no satisfaction from Griffin, he shot a pig on June 15, 1859.

Cutler offered to pay for the dead animal, but in the inept hands of area officials the incident grew quickly into an international crisis. Governor Douglas dispatched his son-in-law and two other men to threaten Cutler. General William S. Harney, commander of United States Army units in the northwest, talked the Americans on the island into drawing up a petition requesting protection, then sent to their aid a small detachment of troops from nearby Fort Bellingham, under the leadership of Captain George E. Pickett. The British responded, and soon over a thousand men faced one another on the island. Left to their own devices, Harney and Douglas doubtless would have embroiled their countries in war at this juncture, but on the British side, Captain Geoffrey Hornby and Rear Admiral R. Lambert Baynes pressed for caution, and United States Army Major Grenville O. Haller managed to inject some calm into American councils.

Officials in Washington, D.C., learned of the crisis in September, 1859. The venerable General Winfield Scott hurried west, arriving at the scene of the confrontation just in time to prevent hostilities. He reached a temporary agreement with the British: all but one infantry company would be withdrawn by the Americans, and the British would remove their menacing naval forces from the island's environs. Citizens of both nations would have equal rights on the island. Although Harney attempted to reverse Scott's orders soon after he departed, Harney was reprimanded and removed from his command in October. The truce held.

The Civil War distracted both sides, although Douglas did briefly contemplate an invasion of Washington Territory early in the sectional struggle. Following the war, negotiations were begun in 1868 to settle a number of unresolved differences between Great Britain and the United States, including the San Juan boundary dispute. It was agreed in a new Treaty of Washington, approved May 8, 1871, to submit the matter to arbitration by the German emperor. After consulting a distinguished group of jurists and geographers, Kaiser Wilhelm announced on October 21, 1872, his decision in favor of the American claim, rejecting the boundary that had been proposed by British Commissioner James Charles Prevost.

EVOLUTION OF TERRITORIAL BOUNDARIES

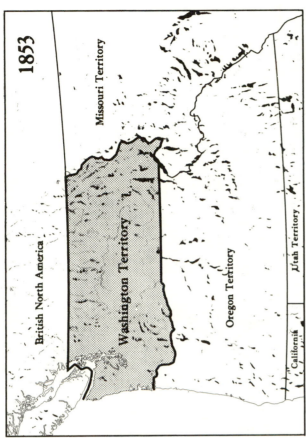

1853

British North America

Missouri Territory

Washington Territory

Oregon Territory

California

Utah Territory

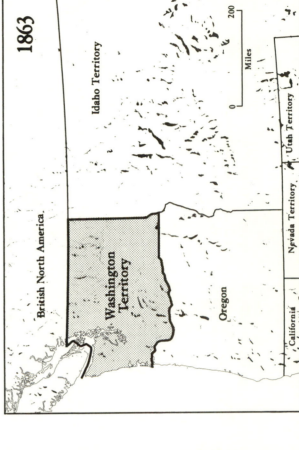

1863

British North America.

Idaho Territory

Washington Territory

Oregon

California

Nevada Territory

Utah Territory

0 200

Miles

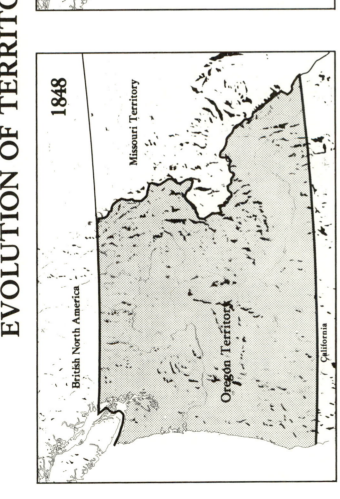

1848

British North America

Missouri Territory

Oregon Territory

California

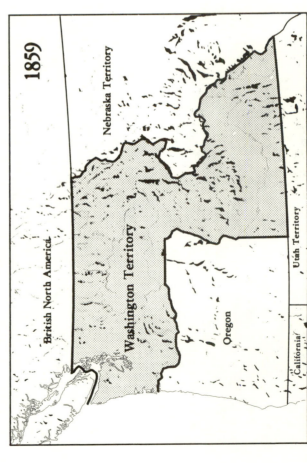

1859

British North America

Nebraska Territory

Washington Territory

Oregon

California

Utah Territory

When Congress established the Territory of Oregon in August 1848, the future Washington Territory was, of course, within the Oregon Territory borders defined in the 1846 agreement between the United States and Great Britain. Forty-two degrees north latitude divided Oregon from California. The use of the forty-ninth parallel as the line between British and American territory had been extended from the Rockies to the Pacific Ocean. The summit of the Rockies marked the eastern boundary of the Oregon and Washington territories; the Pacific Ocean, the western boundary. Although settlers were few in number—the federal census of 1850 reported but 1,049 whites north of the Columbia River—nonetheless, the Americans in the northern portion of the new territory began immediately to lobby for separation. At successive Fourth of July celebrations Olympia orators called for division. Olympia and the area's earliest newspaper, *The Columbian*, vigorously campaigned for carving up Oregon, and citizens gathered at Cowlitz Landing in late August 1851 to memorialize Congress on the issue. The Oregon Assembly, it was argued, was too far away for adequate communication, and its legislators neglected the needs of those living north of the Columbia.

Heeding the pressure, Congressional Delegate Joseph Lane, on the opening day of the 1852–53 session of Congress, introduced a resolution urging an inquiry into the potential utility of dividing the territory. His request gained support from resolutions forwarded by citizens who had met the preceding November at Monticello (located where Longview is today) and from the Oregon Assembly, which recorded its agreement with the idea in January 1853. Congress approved division and established Washington Territory on March 2, placing within its borders all of the original Oregon Territory north of the Columbia and the forty-sixth parallel. Included in the territory were all of present-day Washington, plus northern Idaho, and Montana west of the Rockies.

That configuration survived until Oregon became a state, with its present boundaries, in 1859. Then Washington Territory was redefined to include what was left of the original Territory of Oregon, so that Idaho and northwest Wyoming were added. This clumsy change was shortlived. Gold discoveries in Idaho drew a rush of new population to the diggings—a population, Olympia-based Republicans noted, that included a dangerous preponderance of Democrats. Soon a movement for territorial status for Idaho was under way, supported less by the apathetic Idaho miners than concerned Republicans west of the Cascades. The resulting division, in March 1863, which sheared off the Idaho mining districts but reserved the agriculturally developed area surrounding Walla Walla, gave Washington its current boundaries.

PART V
THE FUR TRADE ERA

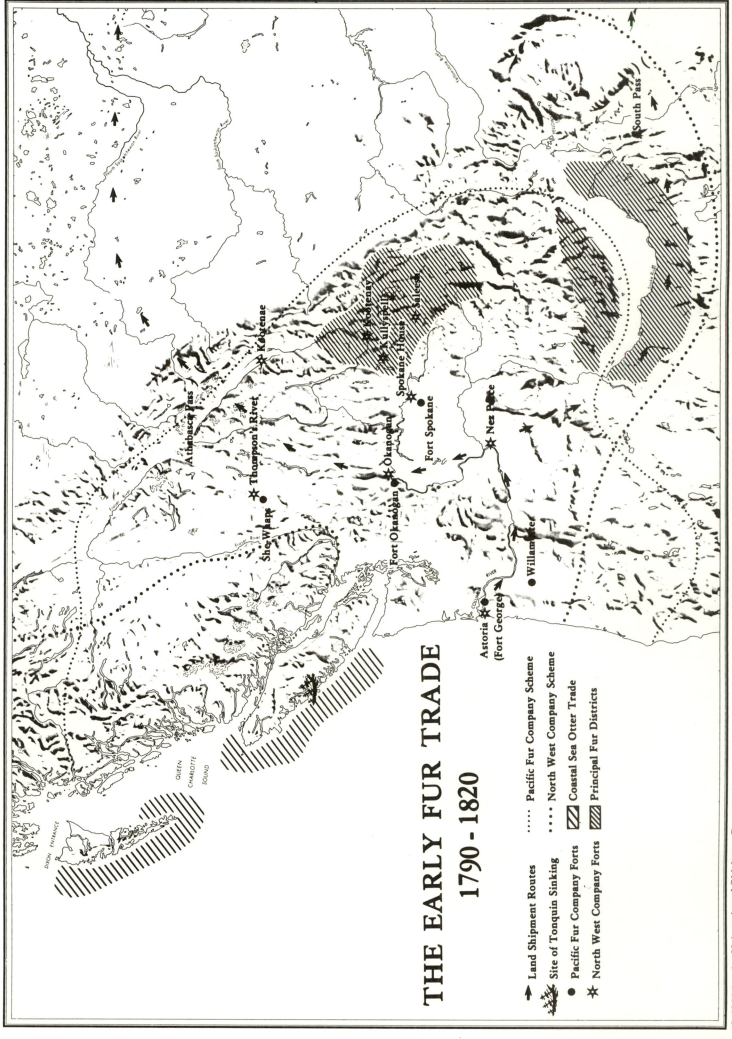

THE EARLY FUR TRADE
1790 - 1820

↑ Land Shipment Routes	⋯⋯ Pacific Fur Company Scheme
⚡ Site of Tonquin Sinking	⋯⋯ North West Company Scheme
● Pacific Fur Company Forts	▨ Coastal Sea Otter Trade
★ North West Company Forts	▨ Principal Fur Districts

South Pass

Kootenae

Athabasca Pass

Thompson's River

She Whaps

Okanogan
Fort Okanogan

Kootenay
Kullyspell
Saleesh
Spokane House
Fort Spokane

Nez Perce

Willamette

Astoria
(Fort George)

COLUMBIA RIVER

Fraser River

North Saskatchewan River
South Saskatchewan River

QUEEN CHARLOTTE SOUND

DIXON ENTRANCE

The fur trade is a major component of the early history of the Pacific Northwest. Not only did the fur trade result in thorough exploration of most of the region, the furs collected and sold constituted the earliest of the region's natural resources to be exploited. Initially it was the magnificent sea otter pelts that were sought, but after 1810 beaver skins replaced these as the principal object of the trade.

Although sea otter pelts acquired by members of Captain James Cook's last expedition were sold in Canton in 1779, organized commercial operations did not begin until 1784, when British traders started systematically to exploit what was to become in a mere twenty-five years a virtually extinct species. The pioneer trader was Captain James Hanna, whose 1785 visit to the northwest coast was followed in the next few years by a score of British, as well as American and European, vessels. Notable among the British captains were Nathaniel Portlock, George Dixon, Charles Barkley, and John Meares (Portlock and Meares's routes are shown in Map 15).

Concentrated along the west coast of Vancouver Island and the Queen Charlottes, the resounding success of the sea otter trade alarmed the Spanish, whose early claims to the region had been reaffirmed by the expeditions of Juan Pérez and Heceta in the mid-1770s (see Map 15). The arrival of Don Esteban José Martínez at Nootka in 1789 and his seizure of Meares's ships *Iphigenia* and *North West America* precipitated a crisis that led to the eventual signing by Britain and Spain of the Convention of October 1790. The latter, which ended the dispute, gave the British the right to fish, trade, and establish settlements wherever in the South Seas the Spanish were not already established, and it effectively removed Spain from further participation in Pacific Northwest affairs. The British were not left in sole possession of the northwest fur trade, however. Even at the time of the arrangement, American traders, including Robert Gray and John Kendrick, had begun operations in the fur trade there, which within ten years they were to dominate. In the decade between 1785 and 1794 more than thirty British vessels were engaged in the coastal fur trade, compared with scarcely a dozen American ships. In the ensuing decade between 1795 and 1804, American vessels outnumbered British seven to one. Thereafter the numbers of both American and British vessels dropped dramatically as fur resources were depleted and harvests plummeted.

Accurate statistics for the sea otter trade are not possible, as few lists were ever compiled and fewer still survive. On occasion seasonal sales are estimated to have reached 15,000 pelts in Canton alone. It seems probable that between 1785 and 1810 not fewer than a half million sea otter pelts were harvested by coastal Indians for trade with the Americans and British.

Meanwhile, the exploitation of the region's land mammals was already under way, and once again the contention for control was between the British and Americans. The Lewis and Clark expedition (1804–1806) had sparked the interest of New York entrepreneur John Jacob Astor in a Pacific Northwest fur trade, and led to the establishment in 1810 of the Pacific Fur Company based in Saint Louis. Earlier the 1793 transcontinental expedition of Alexander Mackenzie had led to further explorations by Simon Fraser and David Thompson and the establishment of a handful of British posts in the upper Columbia region by the Montreal-based North West Company. A two-pronged land-sea effort sponsored by Astor led to the establishment of Fort Astoria at the mouth of the Columbia in 1811 and other forts further inland soon thereafter. Rival British posts were constructed near present-day Kamloops (Thompson's River and She-Whaps), at the confluence of the Okanogan and Columbia rivers, and on the Spokane River. Ultimately, however, the Pacific Fur Company was sold to the North West Company in 1813, after Astor lost a trading vessel, the *Tonquin*, to unfriendly Indians off Vancouver Island in 1811, and the outbreak of the War of 1812 and the refusal of Canadians—who constituted the majority of the traders of both companies—to fight one another.

Following the War of 1812, the Northwest Company began its exploitation of the Snake River country and continued operations in the Kootenay and upper Columbia regions. In all of these ventures business proceeded in a less than systematic way. Desultory operations of little commercial value continued until 1821, when the North West Company was forced by the British government into an amalgamation with its principal rival, the Hudson's Bay Company.

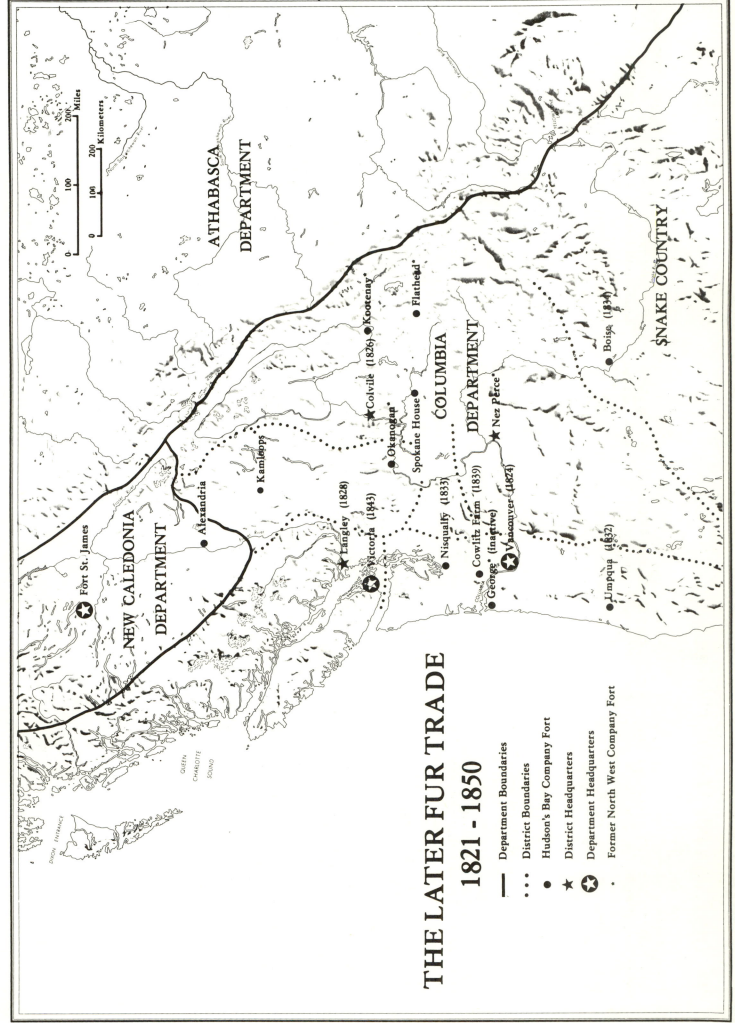

ATHABASCA
DEPARTMENT

NEW CALEDONIA
DEPARTMENT

Fort St. James

Alexandria

Kamloops

Langley (1828)

Victoria (1843)

Kootenay
Colvile (1826)
Okanogan
Spokane House
Flathead

COLUMBIA
DEPARTMENT

Nez Percé

Nisqually (1833)
Cowlitz Farm (1839)
George (inactive)
Vancouver (1824)

Umpqua (1832)

Boise (1834)

SNAKE COUNTRY

QUEEN
CHARLOTTE
SOUND

DIXON ENTRANCE

Miles
200
Kilometers
200
100   200
100
0

THE LATER FUR TRADE
1821 - 1850

——— Department Boundaries
····· District Boundaries
• Hudson's Bay Company Fort
★ District Headquarters
✪ Department Headquarters
· Former North West Company Fort

The arrival of the Hudson's Bay Company in the Pacific Northwest in 1821 initiated numerous and far-reaching changes, and between 1821 and 1846 the company proved itself the dominant force in the region. All parts of the Oregon Country were systematically exploited for their furs, occasionally, as in the Snake Country, to the point of extinction of a few preferred species.

Permanent posts were established at Fort Vancouver and Kettle Falls (Fort Colvile) on the Columbia, and at points on the Fraser River (Fort Langley), the Snake (Fort Boise), and Puget Sound (Fort Nisqually), posts which were to become in many cases major centers for American settlement and economic activity in later years. Other posts, such as Spokane House and Fort George (Astoria), were either closed or relegated to inactive status. And while the collecting of furs remained the main concern of the "Honourable Company," important commercial ventures in farming, dairying, lumbering, and fishing also were successfully initiated in the Pacific Northwest.

Lying wholly west of the Rockies, the Oregon Country was never legally part of the huge territory of Rupert's Land granted to the Hudson's Bay Company by the royal charter of 1670. Nevertheless, it was administered as part of the company's Northern Department. The region was divided initially into two regions, New Caledonia and Columbia, and the latter was loosely subdivided into rather ill-defined districts. In charge of all British North American operations was the gover-nor, Sir George Simpson; and directing operations west of the Rockies was the superintendent, Dr. John Mc-Loughlin, a chief factor of the Hudson's Bay Company and a former employee of the North West Company. Posts, variously called forts or houses, were manned by officers and men of the company, supported by large numbers of French-Canadian *engagés* (company traders) and smaller numbers of workmen from the Sandwich (Hawaiian) Islands, usually known as Kanakas. Depending on the size of the post, the officer in charge might be a chief factor or chief trader or, in the smaller posts, a clerk. Other categories of employees, in addition to workmen and skilled craftsmen, were postmasters and interpreters.

Unlike the independent fur-trading mountain men on the upper Missouri River and in the Rockies, who most often did their own trapping of beaver, the Hudson's Bay Company relied solely on the Indians for skins and pelts. An elaborate trade which went beyond simple bartering was organized, with the value of the various furs determined in terms of the most highly prized animal, the beaver, for which trade tokens were issued. In turn, the tokens were redeemed for a wide range of goods such as four- and six-point woolen blankets, pots and pans, buttons and cloth, axes and knives, and muskets and other arms.

Pacification of the Indians and good relationships with individual tribes were a sine qua non of company policy, and so long as the Hudson's Bay Company remained in control of the Oregon Country, interracial problems were relatively minor. The fur brigades who journeyed out each spring to the fur-rich districts—the Snake, the Willamette and Umpqua, the Kootenay, the Okanogan, and so on—made contact with the tribes, purchased their pelts, and provided them with desired trade goods. The furs were ultimately assembled at Fort Vancouver and sent in annual shipments by sea to London.

The greatest challenge to the company's monopoly came not from the American fur traders but rather from the settlers who followed in the wake of the Methodist and American Board missionaries who had travelled west in the mid-1830s to set up missions in the Willamette valley and Columbia Basin.

By the time of the 1844 presidential election the company had already made preparations for withdrawal and for reorganization of the department. Fort Victoria on Vancouver Island, built in 1843, became in 1845 the new headquarters.

Although settlement of the Oregon Question left the Hudson's Bay Company's property south of the new boundary intact, during the next decade fur trade activities, which had been declining for some years, dwindled to negligible proportions. When the company closed its Fort Vancouver operations in 1860, it was little more than a trader in miscellaneous merchandise, and with the company's withdrawal the fur trade era may be said to have come to an end.

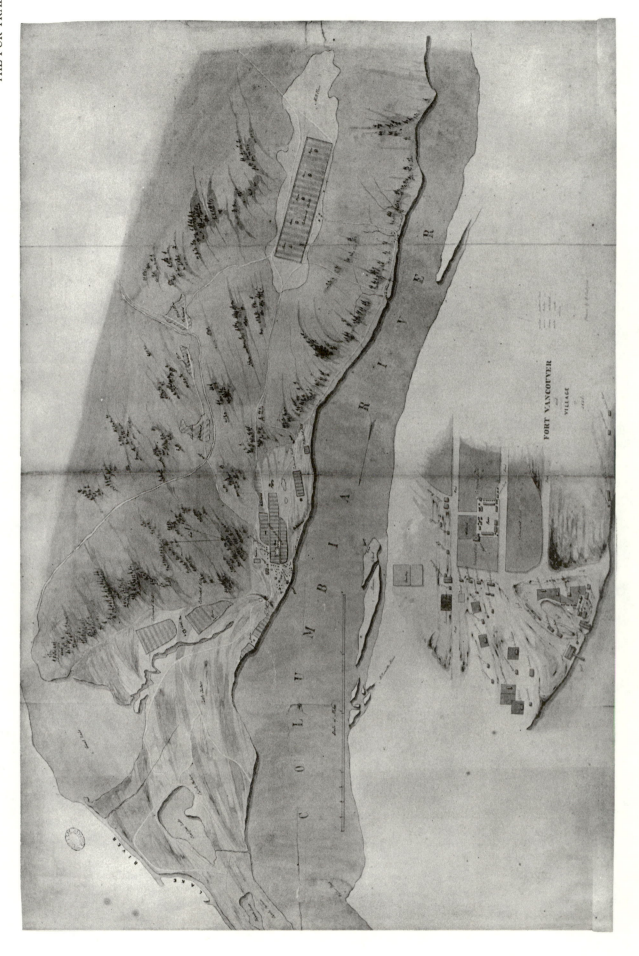

FORT VANCOUVER
and
VILLAGE

Fort Vancouver, called by one authority the "heart and nerve center" of the Oregon Country, was not only the headquarters of the Hudson's Bay Company's Columbia Department for more than twenty years but also the principal outpost of the British Empire on the northwest coast and the social and cultural center of the region.

Built in 1824 to replace Fort George as the control center of company operations, for reasons that were as much political as economic, the new fort was placed close to Belle Vue Point (today's Scenic Point) on the north shore of the Columbia River, some six miles upstream from the mouth of the Willamette. The site was on a benchland prairie overlooking the river, but it was more than a mile inland. The new fort occupied about three-fourths of an acre and comprised a dwelling house, two stores, an Indian hall, and some smaller buildings. Although it seemed comfortable enough at first, it was soon found to be overcrowded and increasingly inconvenient. It was too far away from the river for trading purposes, and more irritating to the residents, there was no suitable supply of fresh water from either a stream or a well. Consequently, a new and much larger fort was constructed in 1829 closer to the water.

Richard Covington's sketch of the fort reproduced here—one of several that he prepared for the Hudson's Bay Company during the 1840s and 1850s—shows the second Fort Vancouver and its environs with great clarity and detail. The stockade enclosing the fort was constructed of Douglas fir pickets eight to ten inches in diameter and eighteen to twenty feet in length. In 1846 the stockade extended 226 yards from east to west and 106 yards from north to south, enclosing an area of approximately five acres. Inside were buildings of many

shapes and sizes. Lieutenant George Foster Emmons of the Wilkes expedition, who visited the fort in 1841, made a sketch and appended a list of nineteen buildings within the palisade. These included the chief factor's residence, quarters for the officers and their families, the central stores and clerical office, a residence for the chaplain, a bakery, a blacksmith's forge, and carpenters' shop. All except a brick-built powder magazine were wood buildings.

In the immediate vicinity of the fort were scores of farm buildings, including barns and stables, an "ox byre" (cow shed), a piggery, and various root houses. North of the fort were two schoolhouses, a stable, a gristmill, the Roman Catholic church, and houses for the workmen. Directly south of the fort was a hospital, a boat shed, the salmon smokehouse, and a distillery; and in the village west and southwest of the fort were most of the workmen's houses and adjacent sheds and outhouses. Downstream from the fort on the lower plain were three more houses, a diary, a barn, and a pigpen; and on Sauvie Island were more houses, four dairies, and a granary.

The total area of land occupied by the Company in the vicinity of Vancouver was 8,960 acres (about fourteen square miles), of which about 1,400 acres were cultivated. On adjacent pastureland and open forest land some thousands of sheep, horses, and cattle were raised, as well as pigs and poultry. Also under control of the company were other nearby structures, including a sawmill seven miles east of the fort (near the present town of Camas) and a water-powered gristmill, capable of milling more than 20,000 bushels of grain a year, which was on Mill Creek close to the north bank of the Columbia and about five miles east of the fort.

Encroachments by American settlers on company land, following the 1846 partition of the Oregon Country, were only one of the problems that led to the final decision to abandon the fort in 1860, and although the Company claimed more than $1.2 million in compensation for its lands and properties, it was offered only $450,000 in 1869, a sum it promptly accepted.

Throughout its more than twenty years of service as the headquarters of the Company on the West Coast, Fort Vancouver remained a magnet for a wide variety of visitors, American and European as well as British. Among them were explorers Jedediah Smith and Charles Wilkes; missionaries Jason Lee, Marcus Whitman, and Pierre Jean De Smet; artists Paul Kane and John Mix Stanley; botanists David Douglas, Thomas Nuttall, and John Kirk Townsend; American trader Nathaniel Wyeth; and Boston propagandist Hall J. Kelley. While not all the visitors were enamored of the commercial activities of the Honourable Company, or in favor of British occupance of the Columbia River, few left unappreciative of the warm hospitality accorded by the company superintendent, Dr. John McLoughlin, and his officers. With its schools and hospital, its chapels and churches, and its social life, Fort Vancouver was widely regarded as a cultural oasis in a savage wilderness.

In 1954 the site of Fort Vancouver was named a National Historic Site. Since then the stockade and bastion have been rebuilt on their original sites, the Chief Factor's Residence has been replicated according to original plans and descriptions, and various other buildings, such as the bakery, have been erected on their original sites.

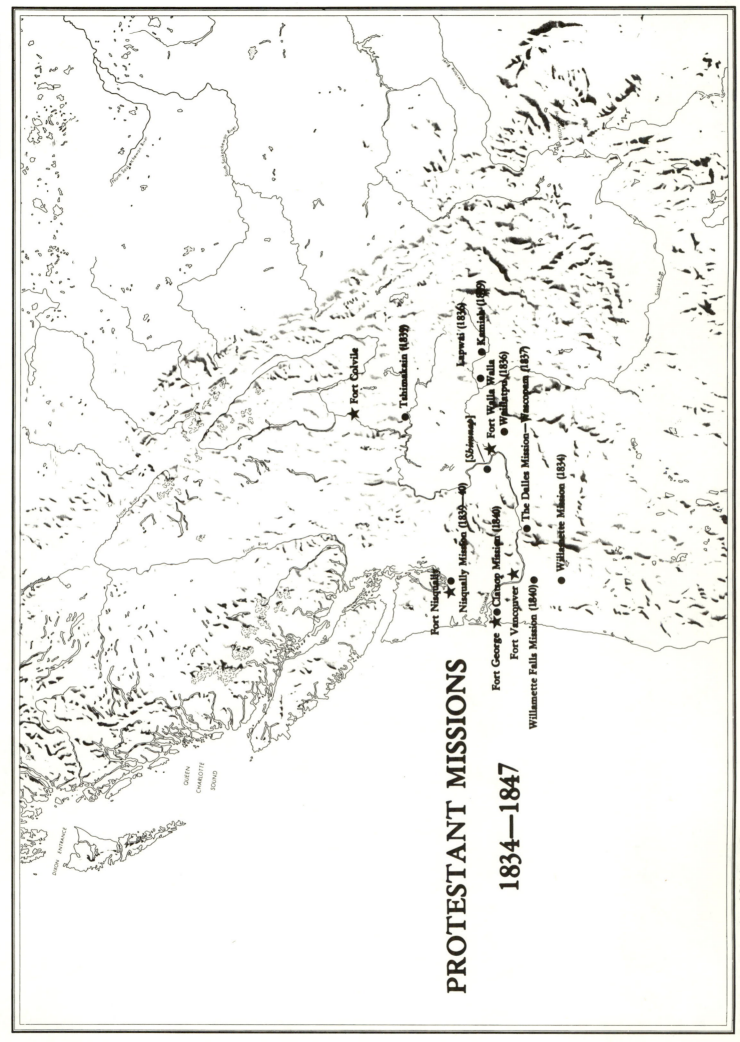

PROTESTANT MISSIONS

1834—1847

Fort Nisqually
Nisqually Mission (1839—40)
Fort George
Clatsop Mission (1840)
Fort Vancouver
Willamette Falls Mission (1840)

[Skimoonaq]

The Dalles Mission — Wascopam (1837)

Willamette Mission (1834)

Fort Colville

Tshimakain (1839)

Lapwai (1836)

Kamiah (1839)

Fort Walla Walla
Waiilatpu (1836)

Columbia

25. PROTESTANT MISSIONS, 1834–1847

Perhaps no period in the history of the Pacific Northwest has elicited such widespread and continued interest as the short-lived missionary era that began so modestly in the spring of 1834 and ended so disastrously with the Whitman Massacre of November 1847.

The possibility of establishing protestant missions in the region was under consideration at least as early as 1821, but it was not until 1829 that the Reverend J. S. Green of the American Board of Commissioners for Foreign Missions arrived to assess the possibilities. Reporting unfavorably, Green returned to his duties in Hawaii. The establishment of the first mission by the Methodist Church—not the American Board—was not until five years later.

METHODIST MISSIONS

Traditionally the inception of missionary activity in the Northwest has been tied to the visit of a delegation by Nez Perce and Flathead Indians to Saint Louis in 1831 and their subsequent meeting with Governor William Clark. Yet it was not until the publication of William Walker's letter in the *Christian Advocate and Journal* some eighteen months later that attention was paid to the Indians' request that a mission be established among them. Action followed quickly as public attention was riveted on the opportunity that beckoned. By May 1833 the Reverend Jason Lee of Stanstead, Quebec, had accepted the call and been approved by the Methodist mission board. His task was to journey across the country to settle among the Flatheads and establish a mission. His nephew, the Reverend Daniel Lee, was chosen as his assistant, and Cyrus Shephard was appointed as schoolteacher. After travelling in the company of Nathaniel Wyeth and his fur traders as far as Fort Hall in present-day Idaho, the missionary party continued northwestward with traders of the Hudson's Bay Company, reaching Fort Vancouver on September 15. Doubts regarding the wisdom of establishing a mission among the Flatheads, which had been sown by Wyeth, were fanned by the comments of Dr. John McLoughlin. As a result, the decision was made to establish the first mission west of the Cascades in the Willamette valley.

For some years valiant but ineffective efforts were made to Christianize and "civilize" the Indians. Reinforcements of thirteen men and women arrived in 1836, including Dr. Elijah White, a medical missionary. Soon afterward, Daniel Lee and H. W. K. Perkins were able to establish the Wascopam mission at The Dalles on the south bank of the Columbia. More reinforcements of almost 100 persons arrived in 1840. New missions were established near Fort George (the Clatsop Mission), at Nisqually, and at the Falls of the Willamette, but such little success attended them that eventually the missionaries turned their attention to their own farming activities, and to the American settlers who were arriving yearly in increasing numbers. The Wascopam Mission was sold to the American Board in 1845, and soon thereafter regular Methodist churches replaced the missions. More significant than their missionary activities were the successes of the Methodists in bringing into being a Provisional Government of Oregon in 1843, and the establishment of Willamette University, the first institution of higher learning in the Pacific Northwest.

AMERICAN BOARD MISSIONS

American Board missionaries began their activities in the Pacific Northwest in 1835 and established their first mission a year later. In 1835 the Reverend Samuel Parker and Dr. Marcus Whitman, a medical missionary, were chosen by the board to journey to the Flathead country and establish a mission there. When they reached the Rockies, Parker sent Whitman back east for reinforcements, while he continued on to Fort Vancouver.

Whitman was able to recruit the services of the Reverend Henry Harmon Spalding and a layman, William H. Gray, an experienced carpenter. Together with the ministers' new wives, Eliza Hart Spalding and Narcissa Prentiss Whitman, the party of five travelled across the country and reached Fort Vancouver on September 12, 1836. Two months later the Whitmans had established their mission at Waiilatpu in the Walla Walla valley, and the Spaldings began their mission at Lapwai in the Clearwater valley. The support of the Hudson's Bay Company's personnel at Forts Vancouver, Nez Perce, and Colvile was invaluable in providing necessary supplies, animals, and mail services.

Reinforcements for the missions arrived in 1838 when three other missionaries, all with new brides, travelled across the continent in the company of Gray, who had been sent back for this purpose some months earlier. In turn, two new missions were established, and a third was contemplated but never, so far as is known, begun. Elkanah Walker and Cushing Eells were sent to establish a mission, called Tshimakain, among the Spokane Indians, while Asa Bowen Smith was sent to the upper Clearwater River to establish a second mission, Kamiah, among the Nez Perces. The proposed mission among the Yakima Indians, Shimnap, to which Gray was assigned, was never begun.

Internal strife among the missionaries, the threat of closure of the most successful of the missions—Waiilatpu—by the American Board, its reprieve following Whitman's breakneck ride east in 1842, and the arrival of increasing numbers of settlers, accompanied by frequent and occasionally devastating outbreaks of diseases such as smallpox and cholera, were only a few of the problems encountered. Then in November 1847 occurred the massacre of Marcus and Narcissa Whitman and a dozen others by leaders of the Cayuse Indians. With their deaths the end of the missionary era came quickly. Today the site of the Whitman mission at Waiilatpu is a National Historic Site, while the Lapwai and Kamiah missions are included in the Nez Perce National Historic Park.

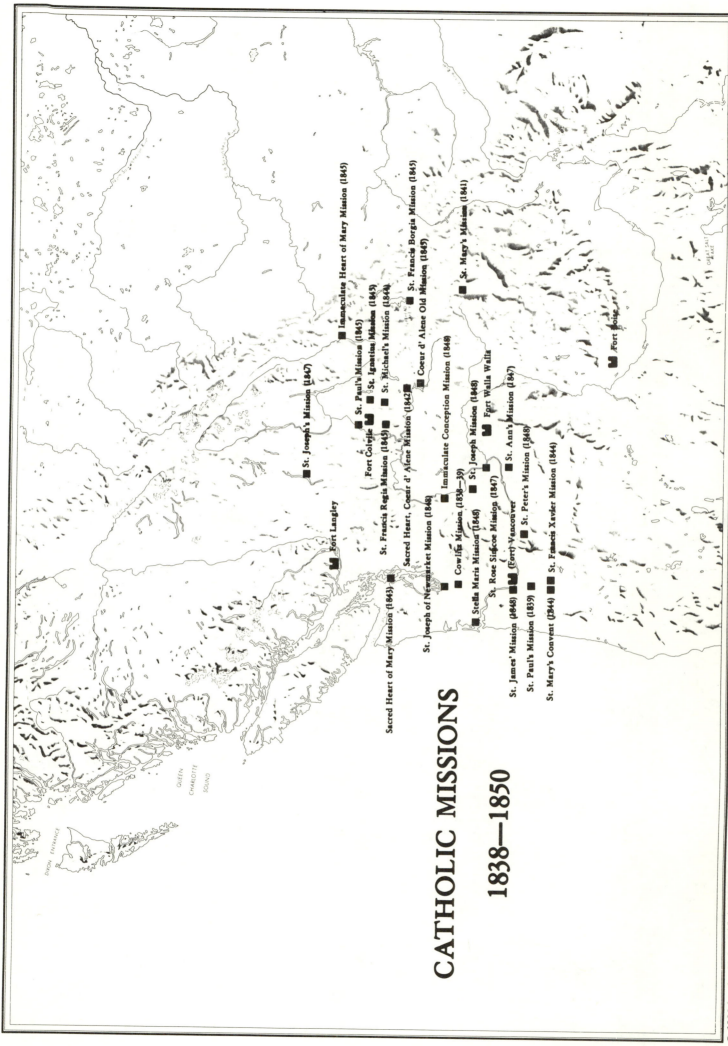

Immaculate Heart of Mary Mission (1845)

St. Paul's Mission (1845)

St. Ignatius Mission (1845)

St. Michael's Mission (1844)

St. Francis Borgia Mission (1845)

Coeur d' Alene Old Mission (1845)

St. Mary's Mission (1841)

Fort Boise

GREAT SALT LAKE

St. Joseph's Mission (1847)

Fort Colvile

St. Francis Regis Mission (1845)

Sacred Heart, Coeur d' Alene Mission (1842)

Immaculate Conception Mission (1848)

St. Joseph Mission (1848)

Fort Walla Walla

St. Ann's Mission (1847)

Fort Langley

Sacred Heart of Mary Mission (1849)

Cowlitz Mission (1838—39)

St. Peter's Mission (1848)

St. Joseph of Newmarket Mission (1848)

Stella Maris Mission (1848)

St. Rose Siscoe Mission (1847)

(Fort) Vancouver

St. Francis Xavier Mission (1844)

Sacred Heart of Mary Mission (1843)

St. James' Mission (1848)

St. Paul's Mission (1839)

St. Mary's Convent (1844)

QUEEN CHARLOTTE SOUND

DIXON ENTRANCE

CATHOLIC MISSIONS
1838—1850

Although the first mass in the Pacific Northwest, so far as is known, was celebrated in July 1774 by priests accompanying the Pérez expedition, it was another nineteen years before the first Spanish priest took up residence at Nootka Sound on Vancouver Island, and more than sixty years before the first Catholic mission was established in the Pacific Northwest.

Knowledge of the work of the Black Robes, as the priests were called by the Indians, had filtered through to the region, in particular to the territories of the Flatheads and the Nez Perces, from the Red River Colony in Canada and from Saint Louis. It was brought west by tribal members who had journeyed east, or by French-Canadian and Métis voyageurs of the fur companies, most of whom were nominally Catholic.

The decision of a number of former *engagés* of the Hudson's Bay Company to settle in the Willamette valley in spite of official objections led to petitions being sent in 1834 and 1835 to the bishop of Red River for a priest to serve them, and in 1836 to the building of the first Catholic church in Oregon, some four miles from Champoeg. In the same year the Northwest was "annexed" to the Vicariate Apostolic of Red River, Canada, and despite considerable resistance on the part of the Company governor, George Simpson, and the Committee of the Company, permission was granted for two priests to journey to the Oregon Country with the transcontinental party of 1838. The expectation of the officials was that the priests would help persuade their French-speaking congregations to move north of the Columbia and settle around Fort Nisqually or near Cowlitz Farm. In late November 1838, Father (later Archbishop) François Norbert Blanchet and Father Modeste Demers arrived at Fort Vancouver, and within less than a month they had chosen a section of land near Cowlitz Farm for their mission, the first in the present state of Washington. In the next few years numerous other sites were selected east and west of the Cascades for similar ventures.

Meanwhile, in midsummer 1839, a Flathead–Nez Perce delegation arrived in Saint Louis, the fourth such delegation to have been sent since 1831, to request the services of the Black Robes in setting up missions among them. There the delegation met with Father Pierre Jean De Smet, who was destined to become one of the major figures in not only the spread of Christianity throughout the Pacific Northwest but also the exploration of many of the interior valleys of the region. Less than a year later De Smet reached the Flathead Country and, after a quick reconnaissance, made the decision to return to Saint Louis for reinforcements. With the arrival the following year of five additional priests, including Father Nicholas Point, the opportunity for rapid diffusion of Catholic missions throughout the Columbia Basin and northwards into present-day British Columbia became a reality.

A historic meeting between Blanchet, Demers, and De Smet took place at Fort Vancouver in 1842, and shortly thereafter an orderly arrangement of church control and governance was set in motion. During the next few years the priest and Jesuit fathers visited and established friendly relations with a large number of tribes, and as the map shows, more than a score of missions were constructed.

The Whitman Massacre of 1847 brought into the open the growing antagonism between Protestant missionaries and Catholic priests. Blanchet's cool reception of attempts by Willamette settlers to form a provisional government added to the vituperations and accusations regarding the priests' role during the massacre of the Whitmans, and it did much to increase the resentment of Catholics among the predominantly Protestant American settlers. Yet the Catholic priests continued to have greater impact among the Indians. While the Indian wars of the 1850s and later years greatly added to the dangers facing the Catholic missionaries, these dangers did little to deter their continued advance into Indian territory, including that of the much-feared Blackfoot tribe.

By the end of the Indian troubles the number of Catholic missions had tripled, and instead of simple log structures, magnificent, richly decorated, and painstakingly constructed edifices were beginning to appear. Some of the mission churches built after 1850 remain to this day as witnesses to the intrepid determination and faith of countless Black Robe pioneers.

PART VII

EARLY TERRITORIAL HISTORY

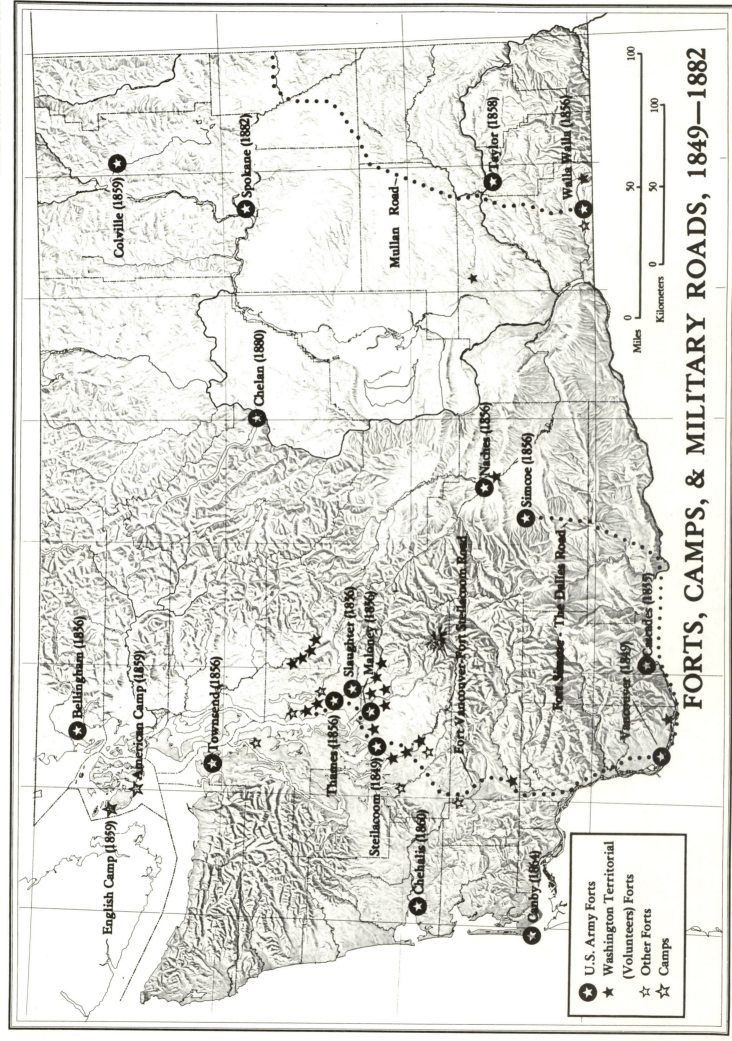

English Camp (1859)

Bellingham (1856)

American Camp (1859)

Colville (1859)

Spokane (1882)

Chelan (1880)

Townsend (1856)

Slaughter (1856)
Maloney (1856)

Thinner (1856)

Steilacoom (1849)

Chehalis (1860)

Canby (1864)

Naches (1856)

Simcoe (1856)

Taylor (1858)

Walla Walla (1856)

Mullan Road

Fort Vancouver–Fort Steilacoom Road

Fort Simcoe–The Dalles Road

Vancouver (1849)

Cascades (1855)

FORTS, CAMPS, & MILITARY ROADS, 1849–1882

Miles
Kilometers

100
50

100
50

0
0

U.S. Army Forts
Washington Territorial (Volunteers) Forts
Other Forts
Camps

© 1988 by the University of Oklahoma Press

American settlement in the Pacific Northwest preceded by some years the arrival of the United States Army. It was the resistance of the native peoples to steadily increasing immigration that forced President James Knox Polk to order the dispatch of troops to this new frontier.

The most serious outbreak of violence in the 1840s was the Whitman Massacre of November 1847, during which the Whitmans and a dozen other whites lost their lives at the hands of a group of Cayuse Indians. Reaction came swiftly: volunteers assembled in the Willamette valley were dispatched to fight the indecisive Cayuse War of 1848.

In 1849 units of the United States Army arrived to take charge of military matters in the newly created Oregon Territory and to relieve settlers of the task of organizing volunteer units for action against the Indians. Vancouver was chosen as the army headquarters, and the Columbia Barracks were constructed close by the Hudson's Bay Company's Fort Vancouver. Fort Steilacoom was established at the same time on Puget Sound near to the Company's Fort Nisqually.

Following the capture and execution of the Cayuse leaders responsible for the Whitman massacre, the presence of United States troops helped create a semblance of tranquility and ensured the conditions for further white settlement and economic growth. In 1853, however, a series of events provoked further actions by Indians east and west of the Cascades. Subsequently, a half-dozen years of intermittent white-Indian hostilities resulted in the construction of more than thirty forts and the building, or at least planning, of several military roads.

The need for roads, as much as any political goal, prompted the successful petition of settlers north of the Columbia for separate territorial status in 1853, and it was anticipated that it would be the army that would provide these. The selection of Major Isaac I. Stevens as territorial governor and Indian superintendent came at the same time he was appointed to undertake the railroad survey between the forty-seventh and forty-ninth parallels. His arrival in the territory and his completion of the railroad survey were to have far-reaching results for the future of Indian-white relations.

One of Stevens's first acts was his appointment of Captain George B. McClellan as leader for the western end of the survey. McClellans's orders were to find the best route across the Cascades between Walla Walla and Fort Steilacoom and to begin construction of a military road along this route for the use of new settlers travelling the Oregon Trail. For this purpose the Congress had already appropriated $20,000. McClellan explored the Cascades, but ignored Snoqualmie Pass—a costly mistake—and eventually he undertook some survey work along Naches Pass, which was chosen as the route. The citizens of Washington Territory bore the brunt of the cost, in both labor and materials, of making usable the difficult route over Naches Pass. The Emigrant Road, as it was named, was never a success, nor did it ever become a military road.

Meanwhile Governor Stevens had completed his railroad survey and commenced his treaty-signing activities with Indian tribes. Initial successes were followed by adverse Indian reactions and the outbreak of the Yakima War of 1855–56. Dispatch of troops from The Dalles, Oregon, northward into Yakima tribal lands emphasized the need for new army forts in eastern Washington and the construction of reliable military roads. At the same time Indian attacks—or fears of such—on communities around Puget Sound led to frequent and urgent requests for army protection and the building of more forts.

Army forts were established east of the mountains at the Cascades in 1855, and at Simcoe, Naches, and Walla Walla in 1856, together with the construction of a mili-

tary road connecting The Dalles and Fort Simcoe. West of the Cascades, Forts Slaughter, Maloney, Thames, Townsend, and Bellingham were built in 1856, and the old Hudson's Bay Company trail between Fort Vancouver and Puget Sound was upgraded to become a military road capable of carrying wagons. In addition, more than a score of other forts, most of them built and manned by Washington Territorial Volunteers, were erected at points along the Puget Sound–Cowlitz corridor and in the Cascades adjacent to important settlements in King, Pierce, and Thurston counties.

Proposals for the construction of additional military roads were considered periodically by the U.S. Congress during the 1850s, and in a few instances appropriations were approved. Only one of these, the Mullan Road connecting Walla Walla and Fort Benton, was surveyed and eventually completed. Others were never completed, including the projected military road from Fort Steilacoom to Fort Bellingham and another from the mouth of the Columbia to Fort Townsend. Work on the Mullan Road was halted due to the outbreak of the Spokane War in 1858, during which additional forts were required, including Fort Taylor (1858) on the Snake River and Fort Colville (1859) east of Kettle Falls.

With the cessation of hostilities in 1859, an uneasy truce was eventually transformed into a lasting peace. This was interrupted only by the outbreak of violence among the Nez Perces in 1877, which culminated in the now famous march of Chief Joseph that ended in his surrender at Bear Paw, Montana, in the same year. By this time settlement of eastern Washington was far advanced, and its agricultural and mineral resources were being rapidly developed. The need for a military presence receded as the Indians were confined to reservations, though not before two additional army forts were established: Fort Chelan in 1880 and Fort Spokane in 1882.

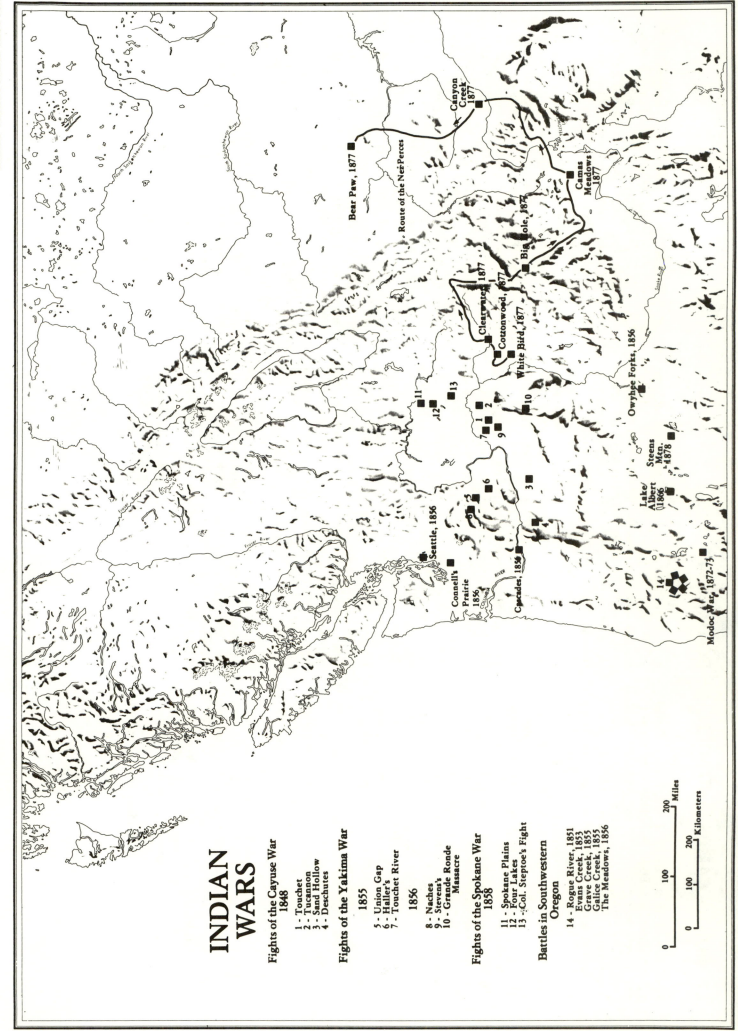

INDIAN WARS

**Fights of the Cayuse War
1848**

1 - Touchet
2 - Tucannon
3 - Sand Hollow
4 - Deschutes

Fights of the Yakima War

1855

5 - Union Gap
6 - Haller's
7 - Touchet River

1856

8 - Naches
9 - Stevens's
10 - Grande Ronde
 Massacre

**Fights of the Spokane War
1858**

11 - Spokane Plains
12 - Four Lakes
13 - Col. Steptoe's Fight

**Battles in Southwestern
Oregon**

14 - Rogue River, 1851
 Evans Creek, 1853
 Grave Creek, 1855
 Galice Creek, 1855
 The Meadows, 1856

Bear Paw, 1877

Canyon Creek, 1877

Route of the Nez Perces

Camas Meadows, 1877

Big Hole, 1877

Clearwater, 1877

Cottonwood, 1877

White Bird, 1877

Owyhee Forks, 1856

Steens Mtn. 1878

Lake Albert 1865

Seattle, 1856

Connell's Prairie 1856

Cascades, 1856

Modoc War, 1872-73

Miles
Kilometers
0   100   200
0   100   200

28. INDIAN WARS

A series of bloody wars between whites and Indians erupted shortly after the division in 1846 of the Oregon Country from British North America (see Map 21), and continued, with occasional intermissions, for more than three decades. In the long run the wars availed the Indians nothing. White mistrust and hatred of Indians mounted as battle followed skirmish, and truces were arranged, or peace treaties signed, only to be broken soon thereafter. In seeking to maintain their way of life and to secure their traditional hunting grounds from white encroachment, the Indians of the Pacific Northwest were forced to meet the white settlers head on. Their defeat, if not total extermination, was foredoomed from the day of the first white arrival, although it took longer than a generation for the seemingly inevitable series of encounters to begin.

Despite the incidents that had led up to the sinking of the *Tonquin* in 1811, troubles with the Indians were kept to a minimum throughout the fur trade era. In fact, relations then were generally friendly. The role played by Dr. John McLoughlin, whom the Indians called the "White-Headed Eagle," has likely been overstated, for other officials of the Hudson's Bay Company were no less solicitous in their efforts to maintain good relations with the native population. If for no other reason, it made sound economic sense to do so: trading for furs and salmon depended on willing cooperation, not suspicion and antagonism.

The arrival of permanent white settlers threatened the good relationships established during the fur trade era. In the mid-1840s, after several years of successful overland crossings and outbreaks of smallpox and other "white man's diseases," tensions rose to danger point. In November 1847 they reached a climax in the bloody massacre of the Whitmans at the Waiilatpu Mission. Within weeks the Cayuse War had broken out.

With the Provisional Government still in control in Oregon, and with no United States troops within many

hundreds of miles, the settlers' only recourse was to raise a volunteer militia. By mid-December, 1847, a 500-man force had formed, and a month later, under the command of Colonel Cornelius Gilliam, it headed east to the Walla Walla valley in search of the Cayuse murderers. During the ensuing three months a series of minor skirmishes and indecisive battles were fought at Deschutes, Sand Hollow, Touchet, and Tucannon. The war ended with little achieved apart from driving the Cayuses from their traditional hunting grounds. The next two years were difficult ones for the tribe. In February 1850 five Cayuse leaders surrendered and stood trial for the murder of the Whitmans. On June 3, 1850, all five were hanged in Oregon City.

Hardly had the Cayuse War been settled before encroachments of white settlers on the territory of tribes in southwest Oregon led to troubles that were to erupt spasmodically over the next few years and result in loss of life and property on both sides. And just as these troubles were ending, new white encroachments led to skirmishes and battles with the Snakes of southeast Oregon.

Meanwhile in Washington Territory, Governor Isaac Stevens was signing treaties with the tribes of western Washington before proceeding east to arrange similar treaties with the tribes of the Columbia Basin. The first Walla Walla Council in May and June 1855, despite the resistance of the Cayuses and the Yakimas, ended with the signing of treaties by all the southern tribes. They were not to remain intact for long, for while Stevens was arranging treaties with the Coeur d'Alenes and Flatheads, and later with the Blackfeet, the Yakima War of 1856 broke out.

As in the earlier Cayuse War, the campaign began well for the Indians, with the early defeat of Major Granville O. Haller and his troops from The Dalles. His successor did little better, but with the arrival of troops from Oregon, the United States Army registered suc-

cesses in the Walla Walla country and Blue Mountains, while cleanup operations were carried out in the Cascades and western Washington. A second Walla Walla Council was called by Stevens in September 1856, but it failed to pull in the Yakimas, and when negotiations broke down and skirmishes ensued, Stevens and the accompanying U.S. troops decided to withdraw to The Dalles. For the moment hostilities were terminated, and with the interior officially closed to settlers, this standoff rather than truce between settlers and Indians was allowed to pass without incident for eighteen months.

With the discovery of gold on the upper Columbia near Colville, however, and the arrival of thousands of miners, the interior was again forced open, Indian lands were encroached upon once more, and hostilities resumed in the Spokane War of 1858. Once again it was the Indians who registered the initial successes with the defeat of Lieutenant Colonel Edward J. Steptoe at Rosalia and the hasty retreat of U.S. forces to the Snake River. Major Robert Garnett's successful raid on the Yakimas and the decisive battles of Four Lakes and Spokane Plains, in which Colonel George Wright's forces inflicted heavy losses on the Indians, quickly brought hostilities to a close with the surrender of the Indians.

The final phase of the Indian Wars in the Pacific Northwest was the Nez Perce War, which broke out in 1877 following incidents in Oregon's Wallowa valley and elsewhere. After the heroic march of the Nez Perces through parts of Idaho, Wyoming, and Montana, which culminated in the battle of Bear Paw, their leader, Chief Joseph, lay down his arms and surrendered, announcing in words that have been enshrined in American History: "From where the sun now stands, I will fight no more forever." After Joseph's followers were removed to the Colville Reservation, Washington's Indian wars were over.

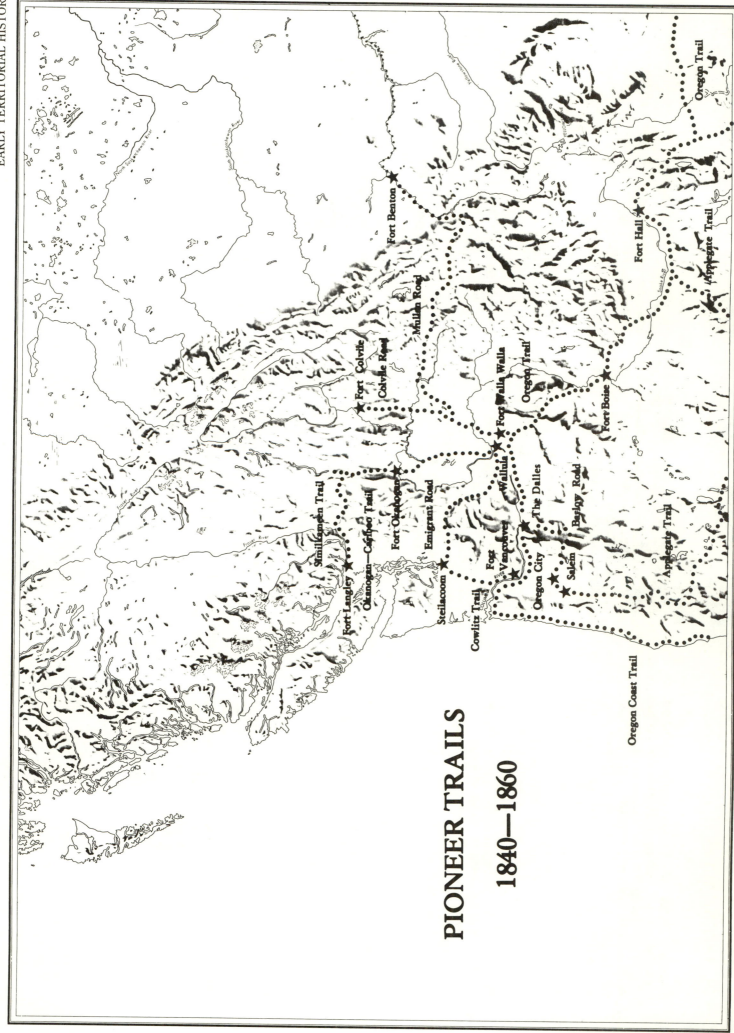

PIONEER TRAILS
1840—1860

Throughout the pioneer era water routes rather than land routes carried most of the freight and passenger traffic. For this reason virtually all pioneer settlements were located on or very close to tidewater or navigable waterways.

Nonetheless, land travel became increasingly necessary in all parts of the Pacific Northwest in the 1850s and 1860s. Many already-existing trails, the work of Indians or fur traders, were pressed into service, and new ones were laid out and developed as settlements were connected with other settlements, both east and west of the Cascades. The condition of these trails, which tended to vary markedly from winter to summer, was a subject frequently remarked upon in letters, diaries, and journals. Sometimes they were quagmires, at other times dusty, deeply rutted paths. Robert Greenhow, in his *History of Oregon and California* (1845), noted, "Below the Walla Walla, the obstacles to the passage of wheel carriages are, at present, such as to preclude the use of them almost entirely." And it must be admitted that, despite the building of an occasional wagon road, things did not change much until the 1870s. The trails were much more suited to men on foot or horseback.

The most important and most famous of all the immigrant trails—used almost exclusively to bring pioneers into the region and of little or no use for later trade purposes—was the Oregon Trail. The date of its initiation may be disputed, depending on one's interpretation of its early use by fur traders and trappers, missionaries, and explorers; but in fact, it was not until May 15, 1842, when 112 Americans and their 18 wagons left Independence, Missouri, that the route can be said to have become a major overland route with a well-marked, if not always easily negotiated, trail. One year later 1,000 pioneers and 120 wagons began the overland passage, and in succeeding years increasing numbers joined the trek to the Willamette and lower Columbia rivers and Puget Sound. The Oregon Trail continued in use for the next

half-century, by which time more than 300,000 persons had moved along it, nine-tenths of them completing the journey.

Crossing the Rockies at South Pass, the Oregon Trail led southwest towards Fort Bridger, from which point it turned northwest to Fort Hall on the Snake River. From there the trail followed the riverbanks as far as Fort Boise, near which it moved off in a northwesterly direction towards the Blue Mountains. This crossing proved a major obstacle to the earliest pioneers, who were always greatly relieved to reach the Whitman Mission on the far side of the Snake River. The trail followed the Columbia River west from Wallula Gap and eventually reached its end at The Dalles. After a perilous trip by raft or boat down the Columbia the emigrants reached Fort Vancouver or Oregon City to begin their new lives as settlers in the Oregon Territory.

Various shortcuts were found and used in later years, and some of the early stopping points such as Fort Bridger and the Whitman Mission were bypassed. Not all of these shortcuts were much of an improvement, and some in fact presented new dangers of their own. The one that became the most renowned was the Barlow Road, which was really an extension of the Oregon Trail from The Dalles to the Willamette valley. The road owed its origin to the determination of settlers already established in the valley to find an alternative to the dangerous and often costly river route from The Dalles westward. Authorized by the Provisional Government, Samuel K. Barlow eventually explored the route and built the road that was to bear his name. Completed in time to be used by 152 wagons of the large 1846 party, the road was indeed more than a trail, and in fact was the first real wagon road in Oregon. It continued until 1912 to act as a toll road skirting the southern flanks of Mount Hood and connecting The Dalles with the Willamette valley.

Hardly less famous was the Applegate Trail, a route pioneered by Jesse Applegate and his brothers, which

led from the Snake River and the Oregon Trail across southern Idaho, northern Nevada, and southern Oregon to the Ashland Basin and thence northwards to the Willamette valley. Its dangers were equal to those of the Oregon Trail, and despite its vaunted advantages, it was no rival to the latter in numbers of immigrants using it.

North of the Columbia River, many of the trails pioneered centuries before by Indians and used more recently by traders of the Hudson's Bay Company were pressed into service, notably the Cowlitz Trail between the Columbia River and Puget Sound. Of more limited use were the eastern Washington trails. These included the Colvile Road from Walla Walla to Fort Colvile, and the Okanogan-Caribou and Similkameen trails, which were used heavily by miners in the later 1850s.

The problems of transportation on the lower Columbia west of The Dalles for settlers en route to Puget Sound helped push the proposal for an alternate route across the Cascades, and in October 1853 the Emigrant (Cascades) Road from Walla Walla to Fort Steilacoom was declared finished. This road was 234 1/2 miles in length, reached an elevation of approximately 5,000 feet on Naches Pass, and crossed the Naches River many times.

The remaining road of significance shown on the map is the Mullan Military Road, which connected Walla Walla with Fort Benton on the upper Missouri River in Montana. Completed much later than the other roads, and crossing as it did much more difficult terrain, the road never attained the importance of the Oregon Trail as an alternate route for settlers.

Other trails were opened during the 1850s in the Puget Sound region, on the Lower Columbia, in the Willamette valley, and along the Oregon coast; and many of them became in later years the routes of various state highways or county roads (see Map 49).

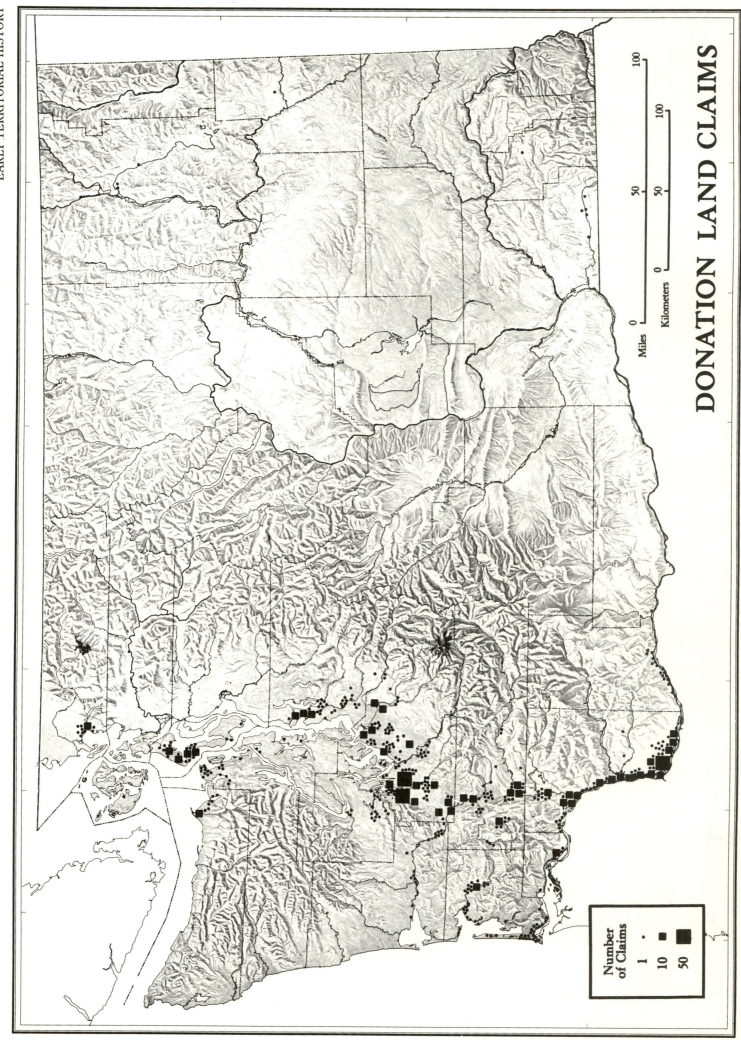

DONATION LAND CLAIMS

Miles
Kilometers

0   50   100
0   50   100

Number
of Claims
1   ·
10   ■
50   ■

The Donation Land Law was enacted by Congress on September 27, 1850, shortly after the creation of the Oregon Territory. Its purpose was twofold: first, to provide for the survey and the distribution of public lands in the territory; and second, to authorize the outright donation of public lands to settlers. The latter provisions helped greatly to regularize the occupance of the more accessible lands in the Willamette, lower Columbia, and southern Puget Sound regions by settlers who had arrived before that date. It also made possible the acquisition of free land by later comers, thus providing an important inducement to emigrants from other parts of the country.

The first three sections of the act deal with the appointment of a surveyor-general and details of the survey. Section four goes on to stipulate:

There shall be, and hereby is, granted to every settler or occupant of the public lands, American half-breed included, above the age 18 years, being a citizen of the United States, or having made a declaration on or before the first day of December, 1850, and who shall have resided upon or cultivated the same land for four consecutive years, and shall otherwise conform to the provisions of this act, the quantity of one half section . . . if a single man, and if a married man, or if he shall become married within one year from the first day of December 1850, the quantity of one section . . . one half to himself and the other half to his wife to be held by her, in her own right.

For those arriving in the territory after December 1, 1850, and before December 1, 1853, the act authorized the granting of one-quarter section to a single man and one-half section to a married couple. Later amend-

ments to the act extended the date of qualification to December 1, 1855, and permitted settlers to patent their claims after only two years occupancy on payment of $1.25 an acre. Furthermore, widows were allowed to receive full title even when the full period of occupancy had not been completed.

As a result, 1,018 claims were registered in the state of Washington for which patents were eventually prepared by the surveyor-general of the territory. The claims comprised a total of more than 300,000 acres of some of the state's most accessible and fertile land, particularly in western Washington. Donation claims were registered in twenty-two of Washington's present thirty-nine counties. Only thirteen claims were established in five of eastern Washington's twenty counties, including five in Walla Walla County and three in Stevens County, all of them close to the Whitman Mission and the Hudson's Bay Company's Fort Colvile,* respectively. The 1,005 claims in western Washington were more widely distributed, with all nineteen existing counties except Skagit and Snohomish having one or more. Nevertheless, as the map indicates, the claims were heavily concentrated in a few counties of southern Puget Sound and the lower Columbia. Thurston County with 234 claims had close to one-fourth of the total, followed by Clark with 161 and Pierce with 108. The claims varied a good deal in size; not always were they recorded as 160, 320, or 640 acres. The smallest on record was

John Lovelace's 38-acre claim in Vancouver; the largest, the David Sturgess claim of 652 acres, also in the vicinity of Vancouver. Four mission claims—three Roman Catholic, one protestant—were awarded—two west and two east of the mountains. The most interesting grant made was the one to George Bush and his wife, Lacey—mulatto by birth and normally not eligible—by special act of Congress.

Important though the act was in encouraging settlement, there were various concomitant problems and drawbacks. Among these should be noted the occupance of lands not already surveyed or of lands not yet ceded by Indian tribes or else claimed by the Hudson's Bay Company. Certainly, some of the Indian troubles of the 1850s and later stemmed from such encroachments, and although the Hudson's Bay Company was eventually compensated for its losses, the seizure of the company lands did little at the time to promote Anglo-American goodwill.

So far as the occupance of unsurveyed land was concerned, as George W. Fuller points out, "a curious result of locating claims previous to surveys was that the shape of many claims was very irregular, following the whims of the settlers, and it became the duty of the Surveyor-General to make the boundaries as claimed" (A History of the Pacific Northwest, p. 211). More serious than the awkward shapes of many of the claims was the scattered, dispersed pattern of settlement that ensued as a result of claims that were as much as a square mile in size. In the words of Johansen and Gates, the size "isolated the settlers" and "impeded the growth of the towns and the diversification of occupations, industry, and crops" (Johansen and Gates, p. 291).

---

*Fort Colvile, named for Andrew Wedderburn Colvile, deputy-governor of the Hudson's Bay Company, was at Kettle Falls, some miles from the present city of Colville.

Location of Townships

Township 20 North,
Range 43 East, W.M.

Township 32 North,
Range 1 East, W.M.

Township 2 North,
Range 2 East, W.M.

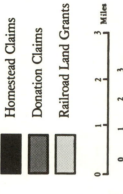

HOMESTEAD CLAIMS

■ Homestead Claims
▨ Donation Claims
□ Railroad Land Grants

0   1   2   3   Miles

0   1   2   3   Kilometers

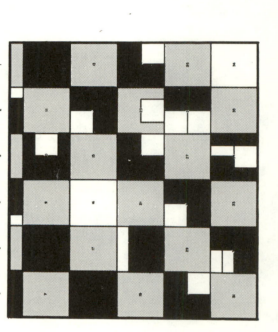

Township 20 North, Range 43 East, W.M.,
Rosalia, Whitman County

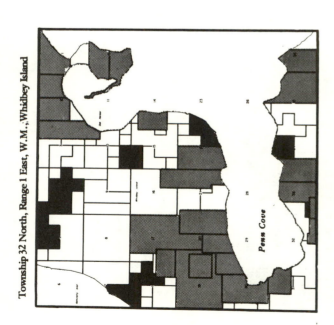

Township 32 North, Range 1 East, W.M., Whidbey Island

Penn Cove

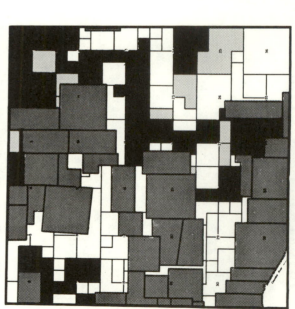

Township 2 North, Range 2 East, W.M.,
Vancouver, Clark County

31. HOMESTEAD CLAIMS

Although the 1862 Homestead Act, which came into effect on January 1, 1863, greatly extended the settlers' ability to acquire land in Washington Territory, it was not the only means available nor, as convincingly shown, the preferred one. The Donation Act, which operated until 1855, transferred more than 300,000 acres to more than one thousand claimants, while the preemption laws of 1841 and later, which were extended to Washington in 1854, enabled others to acquire up to 160 acres of land on payment of $1.25 an acre. And as such land might be obtained within one year of a declaratory statement of intent being registered, many settlers opted for this means of land acquisition in preference to the free homestead with its always burdensome restrictions and requirements.

Under the Homestead Act any head of household or any individual over twenty-one, including single, independent women, was allowed to file on a quarter section of 160 acres. The homesteader had then to cultivate and reside on the land for five consecutive years, at the end of which a final certificate and title would be granted to him or her. In western Washington, however, at the time of passage of the act the most accessible land was already taken in donation claims or preempted by other settlers, and in eastern Washington much of the best land was to be included in the eighty-mile-wide strip of the Northern Pacific Railroad's land grant. The odd-numbered sections of each township within this strip were allocated to the railroad, and homesteads of only eighty acres could be entered in the even-numbered sections open to settlers.

Between 1863 and 1880 fewer than 10,000 homesteads were entered in Washington, compared with more than 63,000 in Minnesota and close to 57,000 in Nebraska during the same period. The preemption laws were repealed in 1891, and a commutation provision was introduced in the Homestead Act that allowed homesteaders to purchase their land for $1.25 an acre. These changes helped improve matters in Washington. East of the Cascades help was provided by a number of other federal acts that did much to increase the number of homesteads. The 1877 Desert Law Act, which allowed acquisition of 640-acre tracts on condition that part of the area was irrigated, led eventually to 6,085 original entries totalling 998,708 acres, though only 1,121 of these, for a total area of 138,090 acres, were ever completed. In 1909 the Enlarged Homestead Act permitted entries of 320 acres on specified nonirrigable dry lands, and the 1916 Grazing Homestead Act allowed 640-acre entries on dry lands suitable for grazing only. As a result more than one million acres of additional homestead land were entered under the two acts.

In the century following passage of the Homestead Act, more than 15 million acres were entered, although only about two-thirds of the acreage was carried to final certification and the issuance of titles. Before 1961, 65,007 entries were made in the state of Washington on 9,442,387 acres. Of the total, 34,981 entries were made after 1900 with a total of 5,139,698 acres. Roughly one-fourth the entries made since 1900 have been enlarged, grazing, or reclamation homesteads.

The distributional patterns of homesteads in the state's more than 1,500 townships vary so greatly that no generalizations will be attempted, and as it has not been possible to obtain, or to compute, totals for all townships, three sample townships have been selected to show representative patterns of homestead and other land grants.*The Whidbey Island Township shows the absolute dominance of donation claims in that region. The Vancouver Township, which also had many donation claims, shows concentration of homestead claims on less accessible land away from the river. The Rosalia Township shows a regular alternation of homesteads and railroad land grants. Only in the Rosalia map, however, are the two sections (16 and 36) allocated for the upkeep of schools left unclaimed. In the other two, prior entries predating the Homestead Act had already acquired some of these lands.

*Maps like these are available for all surveyed townships of the state. They are obtainable for a fee from the Bureau of Land Management, successor to the General Land Office which prepared them.

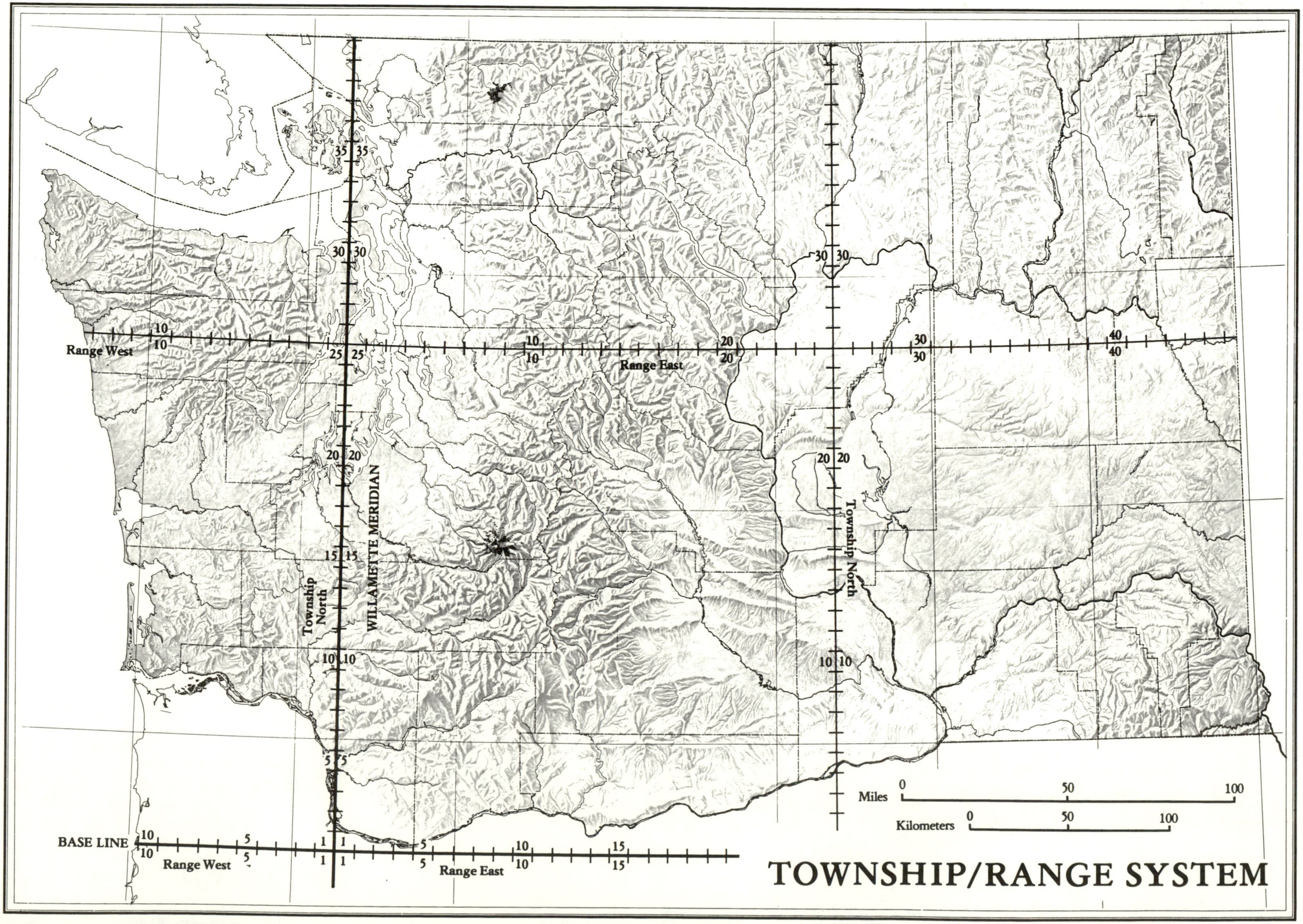

TOWNSHIP/RANGE SYSTEM

Township North

Range East

WILLAMETTE MERIDIAN

Township North

Range West

Range East

BASE LINE

Range West

Miles

Kilometers

The Land Ordinance of 1785, which initiated the rectangular cadastral survey in the first seven ranges of Ohio that same year, provided the method by which virtually all the public lands of the United States surveyed after that date were brought into legal ownership. Although the Donation Land Act of September 27, 1850, offered the option of utilizing a geodetic method dependent on triangulation, the secretary of the interior never saw fit to recommend its adoption, despite the urging of various surveyors general of Oregon and Washington and of Washington Territorial Governor Isaac I. Stevens, himself an expert surveyor. Consequently, the surveyors of Washington were plagued well into the twentieth century by inordinate problems encountered in attempting to apply rigidly the principles of rectangular survey in terrain as rugged as that of the Cascades or the Olympics and over country as heavily forested as western Washington. Even today close to six million acres of the state's almost forty-five million acres remain unsurveyed.

The rectangular survey necessitated choice of a north-south *principal meridian*, along which east-west township lines six miles apart would be extended at right angles, and an east-west *base line*, along which north-south range lines would be similarly extended. The Willamette Meridian chosen for the survey of Oregon Territory was already in use when Washington Territory was created in 1853, so that Washington's principal meridian remained unchanged. The base line, which intersected the principal meridian near the confluence of the Columbia and the Willamette, was also already adopted.

The more than 1,500 townships of Washington are numbered from 1 North to 40 North, while the ranges extend from 16 West to 46 East.

During the years of active survey ten *standard parallels*, north of the base line and twenty-four miles (or four townships) apart, were surveyed, in some cases in their entirety, in others with interruptions. Additional township lines between the standard parallels were surveyed as demanded, as were the section lines within these. Range lines six miles apart were surveyed east and west of the Willamette Meridian as required. However, east of the Cascades two additional *guide meridians* were also required. Chosen were the Columbia Guide Meridian, from Wallula Gap to north of the Columbia, and the Colville Guide Meridian, from the fifth standard parallel to the Columbia River immediately

south of the Canadian border. In the more difficult terrain of the Okanogan Highlands and west of the Okanogan River short subsidiary meridians that stretched from four to seven townships—twenty to forty-two miles—were also required. These were, from west to east, the Ruby, Moses, Sanpoil, Joseph, and Kettle River guide meridians. Local accommodation was needed also in the much-indented and island-studded Puget Sound region, where the Willamette Meridian passed only through small islands of the sound so that many of the required markers could not be located.

Inaccuracies in the surveying of many parts of the state, when added to the physical impossibility of imposing an exact grid of six-mile-square townships, each of thirty-six one-mile square sections, have resulted in a myriad of irregularities in the boundary lines and total acreage of perhaps a thousand sections and a hundred townships within the state. Yet, considering the immense difficulties inherent in the application of such a system—particularly the long-continued practice of employing private individuals, some with little experience of survey work and with inadequate contracts to do the job—what is perhaps surprising is that the system worked so well and was administered so efficiently.

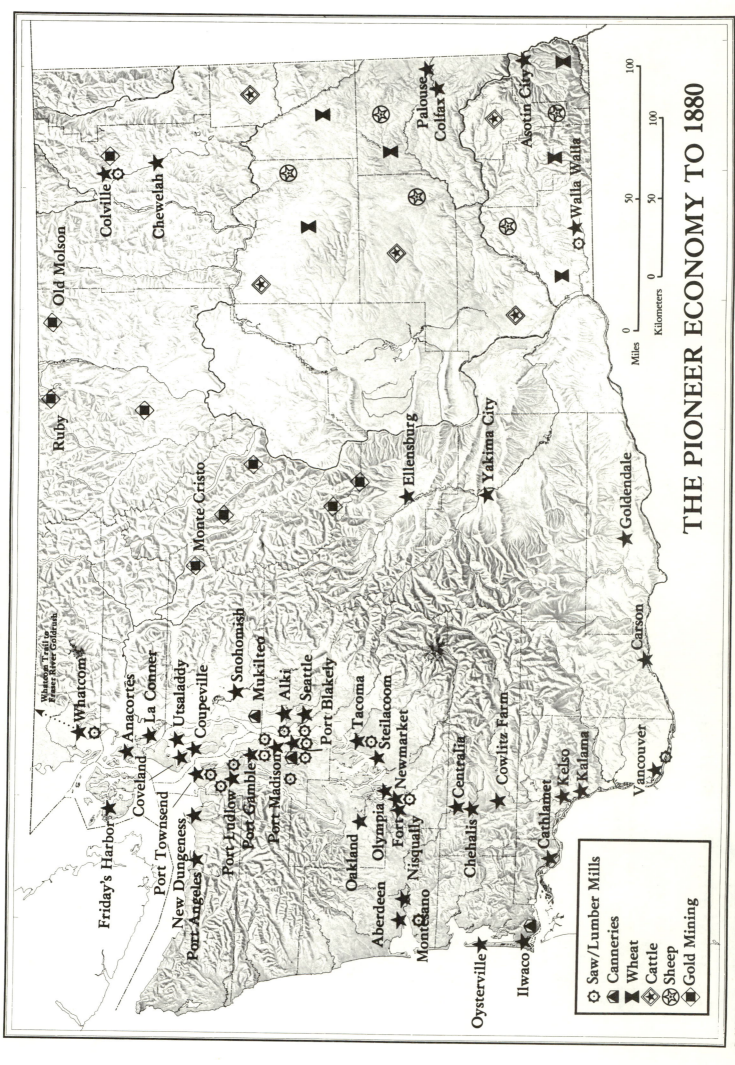

THE PIONEER ECONOMY TO 1880

Legend:
- ✪ Saw/Lumber Mills
- ▲ Canneries
- ◼ Wheat
- ⋈ Cattle
- ✪ Sheep
- ◆ Gold Mining

33. THE PIONEER ECONOMY TO 1880

Between the arrival of the first permanent settlers and the beginning of the railroad era in the last two decades of the nineteenth century, Washington's pioneer economy underwent transformation from a subsistence economy to one based on intensive commercial exploitation of its abundant natural resources. By the 1880s the agriculture, fishing, lumbering, and mining industries were each making significant contributions to the territory's economy, although none of them by that date had reached its full potential.

The exploitation of the region's natural resources had begun, in fact, long before the arrival of the first American settlers in the 1840s. Furs were the first resource to be developed. The sea-otter trade begun in the 1780s lasted about twenty years and had all but disappeared by the time Lewis and Clark reached the Columbia in 1805. The trade in beaver and other pelts began soon afterwards and lasted, although with greatly diminished returns, until the division of the Oregon Country in 1846. Thereafter furs became a relatively unimportant part of the region's economy. Meanwhile, however, the Hudson's Bay Company was laying the foundations of three industries that were to play an increasingly important role in later decades: agriculture, lumbering, and fishing.

The region's first commercial agriculture was initiated by the Hudson's Bay Company in 1824 when Fort Vancouver was built and the first of its eventual 6,000 acres of cultivated land were brought into production. Agriculture was developed on a more restricted scale at Fort Colville and other Company posts in the interior and eventually, with the establishment of the Puget Sound Agricultural Company, at Fort Nisqually and Cowlitz Farm. Field crops, fruits and berries, garden produce, and livestock products were produced in amounts sufficient to ensure self-sufficiency among the company's personnel, as well as to provide food for local Indians and a surplus for sale in Alaska and Hawaii. Three years later, in 1827, with the help of Kanakas from the Hawaiian Islands, the first sawmill in the Pacific Northwest was begun at Camas and sawn lumber made available for both local use and overseas sale. Commercial fishing, the last

of the three resource industries to be developed, was based on the purchase of salmon from the Indians. At Fort Langley on the Fraser and at Fort Vancouver, salmon were dried and salted, or packed in brine, and exported in large 500-pound barrels. Despite the obviously commercial intent of these activities, all were practiced on a relatively small and geographically restricted scale, but it was not until years later that the American settlers were able to match the company's activities in wider international markets.

In the first few years of American settlement economic activities also were on a small scale and restricted, as land was cleared, mills established, mines sought and sunk, and markets found. Then the California gold rush of 1849 had a marked effect on the Pacific Northwest. Not only did it draw many settlers south, it also appeared to offer promising markets for sawn timber, coal, and agricultural products.

Lumber mills were set up hurriedly at tidewater on the lower Columbia, the Olympic Peninsula, and around Puget Sound. Few of the mills developed as large a trade as owners and operators anticipated. Consequently, the next twenty to thirty years were to prove precarious ones for the lumber trade. Among the well-known mills were Yesler's mill in Seattle, the Pope and Talbot mill at Port Gamble, and mills at Seabeck, Port Ludlow, Port Blakely, and Whatcom.

The discovery of gold near Colville in the 1850s set off a new gold rush as prospectors from many parts of North America flocked to the area. Other gold rushes affecting the territory were those on the Fraser (1858) and the later ones in the Okanogan Highlands, the Cascades, and the Rockies during the 1860s, 1870s, and 1880s. Seldom did the mineral strikes result in anything of permanent significance—many of them, in fact, were very short-lived—but wherever they were made settlement tended to follow, and in many instances, as the mineral deposits were exhausted, agriculture and ranching helped provide new and more permanent inducements to settlement. Many of the mine settlements today are no more than ghost towns, among them Ruby,

Monte Cristo, and Old Molson, but out of those early mining activities came benefits that greatly enhanced the significance of two settlements that were to become two of the state's major cities. Spokane, which rose to prominence as railroad and supply center for the mining settlements of the inland empire of the Hudson's Bay Company (eastern Washington, Idaho, and southeast British Columbia), never lost its early lead as a regional center, and Tacoma, which had been chosen as the terminus of the Northern Pacific Railroad in the 1870s, became in the next decade the site of the state's major nonferrous smelting operations—an industry that closed only recently in 1984.

The opening of mines and the exploitation of the region's timber resources drew thousands of workers, as did the promise of free land under the Homestead Act. And with the increase of population came increased demand for food supplies. Centered initially on the lowlands of western Washington, agriculture by the 1870s was shifting its focus increasingly to the more extensive grassland regions of eastern Washington. The range cattle and sheep industries that heralded the change there had been joined by the late 1870s by wheat farming in the Palouse Hills. By the end of the territorial period these new wheatlands were being eyed as a potential breadbasket of more than regional significance.

Finally, the introduction of canning in the California fisheries in 1860s sparked the interest of northwesterners in this hitherto-neglected resource, although it was not until 1876 that the first cannery on Puget Sound was constructed at Mukilteo. It was to be joined by scores of others in the next quarter century, as this basic Indian food resource, particularly the salmon, became a favorite food of millions of customers in Western Europe and elsewhere. By that time, however, the pioneer economy of subsistence farming, sawmilling, and metal mining had entered a new phase. The development of national and international markets, made possible by a transportation revolution involving both ships and railroads, was rapidly transforming the economic scene.

PART VIII

POPULATION GROWTH AND CHARACTERISTICS

POPULATION DISTRIBUTION AND DENSITY

1860

INHABITANTS PER SQUARE MILE

• Each Dot Represents 100 Inhabitants

1920

0 - 9   10 - 24   25 - 74   75 Plus

1940

0 - 9   10 - 24   25 - 74   75 Plus

1980

0 - 9   10 - 24   25 - 74   75 Plus

Where people live and why, and in what concentrations and numbers, have been matters of interest and concern to legislators, government officials, planners, and businessmen since the earliest days of the republic. Written into the federal constitution, in fact, is the requirement that the nation's population be counted once every ten years in order to reapportion state congressional representations for the ensuing decade. At the state level population statistics are required for a great many purposes, including the appropriation and apportionment of funds and the regional provisioning of such state services as transportation, health facilities, and schools. And in the private sector the development and success of economic and social activities are closely geared to population distributions and densities: in general, a high density of population encourages, and a low density (or sparsity) of population discourages, these activities.

Various geographical features, all of them reviewed in earlier maps in this atlas, are the principal reasons for the very uneven distribution of population across the state of Washington. Generally, more fertile soils, better water supplies, and ease of access have tended to encourage settlement in the lowland regions; conversely, the rugged upland areas have repelled settlement. Apart from sporadic mining ventures, the Cascades, the Olympics, the Okanogan Highlands, and the Blue Mountains have never supported sizeable populations, whereas the lowlands of Puget Sound and the Strait of Georgia, the lower Columbia valley, and many parts of the Columbia Basin have provided a variety of opportunities for successful settlement and economic development. Climatic, edaphic, and hydrographic factors have likewise influenced in varying degrees the peopling of the state. To these geographical features must also be added a number of historical, cultural, and economic factors, including fortuitous choices of town sites, dramatic early development of major resource industries, and the growth of regional and national trade links and markets. Economic inertia, which helps

maintain an activity in a location no longer ideally suited for it, also plays a part in the continuation of communities, and therefore of established settlement patterns.

The maps shown on the opposite page have been drafted using the census information for the years 1860, 1920, 1940, and 1980. The years have been chosen to highlight some of the changes that have occurred in the distribution and density of population in the state during the past century and a quarter.

The map for 1860 shows the distribution of the white population only. With a total of only 11,594 persons it has been possible to show the approximate location of these by means of dots that each represent 100 inhabitants. The importance of such major centers as Vancouver, Walla Walla, Olympia/Tumwater, and Fort Steilacoom is readily apparent. Northern Puget Sound remained sparsely settled, as did the Olympic Peninsula north of Aberdeen. Whites in eastern Washington were domiciled largely in the Walla Walla valley, with much smaller clusters in the Colville and Spokane valleys. The Big Bend of the Columbia and the eastern foothills of the Cascades had virtually no white population at all.

By 1920 the distribution of population was very much closer to present-day patterns. King, Pierce, and Spokane counties had emerged as the most densely peopled areas in the state, and their largest cities—Seattle, Tacoma, and Spokane—had established their claims to be the leading cities. Clark County, including Vancouver, remained well settled, while three counties on northern Puget Sound—Snohomish, Skagit, and Whatcom—as well as most of the counties south and west of Seattle and Tacoma, showed markedly increased population densities, largely as a result of the widespread and intensive exploitation of the natural resources of land and sea. Population densities remained uniformly lower east of the mountains except in a few successful farming counties, notably Walla Walla, Whitman, and Yakima. Irrigation was still largely confined to the Spokane and Yakima valleys.

The 1940 map shows some changes, but none of them very pronounced. Population densities west of the mountains continued to rise more steeply than elsewhere in the state, with King County reaching 237 per square mile and Pierce County 109. Only Jefferson County and Skamania County, both of them mountainous and thickly forested, had densities below ten per square mile. The decentralization of population into suburban areas around the major cities cannot be indicated on maps that show only county averages, but by 1940 the spillover of King County's population was helping to increase the densities of adjacent counties, notably Snohomish and Kitsap. With major irrigation projects still in their early stages of construction in the Columbia Basin, and agriculture still in a somewhat depressed state due to the Great Depression, fewer changes occurred in eastern Washington, although Spokane County's density had risen from 80 per square mile to almost 100.

Between 1940 and 1980 the changes initiated by the automobile revolution of the 1920s and 1930s continued at a rapid pace, with suburban populations booming and inner-city populations starting to sag. This latter phenomenon is displayed and discussed in Maps 36 and 64 and the texts for those maps. Perhaps more notable than the suburban shift of population were some regional shifts that affected south-central and central Washington. The initiation of nuclear power development in Benton County and the growth of the Tri-Cities region increased Benton County's population from 7 per square mile in 1940 to 63 in 1980, and the population of neighboring Franklin County from 5 to 28 per square mile. Somewhat less dramatic, but still of considerable significance, were the increases in central Washington due to the initiation there of large-scale irrigation farming and the growth of the necessary service sector. Grant and Adams counties were the main beneficiaries of these developments.

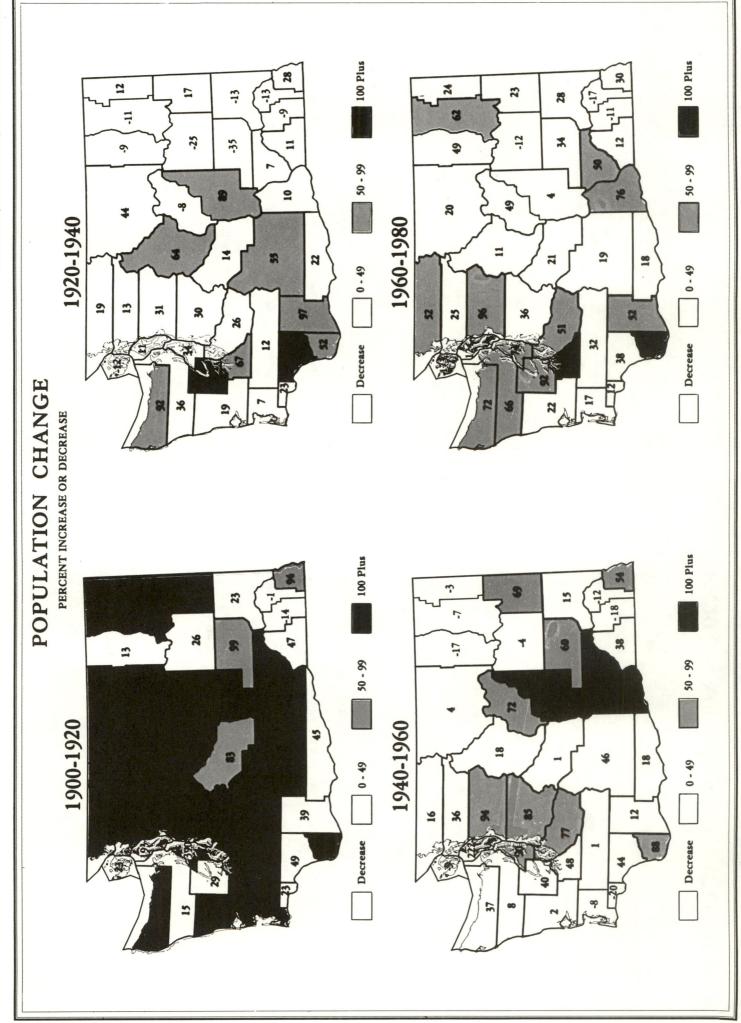

POPULATION CHANGE
PERCENT INCREASE OR DECREASE

35. POPULATION CHANGE

Although Washington's population increased dramatically during some decades in the recent past, the changes were far from uniform across the state. In some counties growth has been considerable in each decade since the beginning of white settlement; in others early growth has been followed by contraction as conditions of life deteriorated or economic opportunities failed to keep pace with those of other parts of the state.

Table 2. Washington's population growth since 1850 and the percentage increases for each intercensal period

Census	Year	Population	Decennial Increase (%)
7	1850*	1,201	—
8	1860**	11,594	865.4
9	1870	23,955	106.6
10	1880	75,116	213.6
11	1890	357,232	375.6
12	1900	518,103	45.0
13	1910	1,141,990	120.4
14	1920	1,356,621	18.8
15	1930	1,563,396	15.2
16	1940	1,736,191	11.1
17	1950	2,378,963	37.0
18	1960	2,853,214	19.9
19	1970	3,413,244	19.6
20	1980	4,132,156	21.1

*1850 figures are for white settlers living in Oregon Territory north of the Columbia River, the majority of them in western Washington.

**1860 figures include some settlers living in what is now Idaho, which was at that time part of Washington Territory.

The importance of in-migration in population growth is particularly suggested by the massive decennial increases for the years from 1850 to 1860, 1860 to 1870, 1870 to 1880, 1880 to 1890, and 1900 to 1910, when growth exceeded one hundred percent, something not possible by natural increase alone. By contrast, the growth in the decades 1890 to 1900 and 1910 to 1920 was considerably less, even though the United States

received large numbers of immigrants from Europe during those decades. The 1893 depression, which hit Washington particularly hard, militated against high in-migration during the 1890s, and the outbreak of World War I in Europe in 1914 reduced population growth during the second decade of the century.

Since 1920 natural increase—that is, the excess of births over deaths—has played a somewhat larger role in population change, even though natural increase itself has become much more modest in these years. The lowest increase came during the 1930s, when birth rates across the nation took a notable plunge due to the Great Depression. The baby boom following World War II accounted for much of the increase between 1940 and 1950, and it continued into the 1950s while in-migration to the state soared as new opportunities in service industries and manufacturing opened up.

We have chosen to show population change by county in four separate maps, each of which covers a twenty-year period since 1900. The first two decades of the century were years of rapid growth as large in-migration continued and abundant natural resources were aggressively exploited in virtually every part of the state. In 1900 there were, it might be noted, only thirty-six counties, because Benton (1905), Grant (1909), and Pend Oreille (1911) were established after the turn of the century. Consequently, the map for 1900 to 1920 shows the growth for both the new county and the county from which this was divided. Two counties, Okanogan and Franklin, achieved astonishing growths of 2,646 percent and 1,109 percent, respectively. In western Washington fourteen of nineteen counties achieved growths of over 100 percent, the highest being King County with 254 percent. Furthermore, no western Washington county registered a decrease. In eastern Washington, however, two of the state's smallest counties, Columbia and Garfield, each declined in population, as they have continued to do to the present time.

The 1920s and 1930s saw population growth drop dramatically, and in many counties, in particular those dependent on field-crop agriculture. The exodus from the land and out of the county was high as farmers

abandoned their unrewarding and unprofitable homesteads. During this twenty-year period eight of eastern Washington's twenty counties registered declines of from eight to as much as thirty-five percent. Yet at the same time growth was well marked in three other eastern Washington counties—Grant, Chelan and Yakima—where irrigation farming had begun to flourish and demand for its products remained high. The most dramatic growth in western Washington, where only San Juan County lost population, came in Mason and Cowlitz counties, where new manufacturing industries associated with abundant forest resources and dependent on cheap electricity were established.

In the 1940s and 1950s, while most of eastern Washington made only modest gains in population, and a half-dozen of its counties continued to lose population due to increased farm size, better management, and decreased demand for agricultural labor, three other counties led the state in population growth. Benton County and adjacent Franklin County benefitted greatly from the impetus given to high-technology industries by the establishment of the nearby Hanford Reservation and the development there of nuclear power. In western Washington the rapid growth of manufacturing industries, particularly non-resource-based industries, in the SMSAS of Seattle-Everett and Tacoma resulted in marked population increases in King, Snohomish, and Pierce counties and in adjacent Kitsap County. Clark County grew in size as it became increasingly a "dormitory" suburb of Portland. At the same time the somewhat isolated and less-developed counties of San Juan, Pacific, and Wahkiakum lost some population.

In the 1960s and 1970s growth slowed considerably in the central cities, particularly in Seattle, which lost population, but it continued to grow in the suburban areas of Clark, King, Pierce, Snohomish, and Spokane counties; and counties adjacent to those experienced a good deal of suburban spillover: Kitsap (from Seattle), Thurston (from Pierce), Skamania (from Portland and Vancouver), and Stevens (from Spokane). The recent attention paid to environmentally attractive areas has resulted in notable gains for a few counties.

URBAN AND INCORPORATED POPULATION

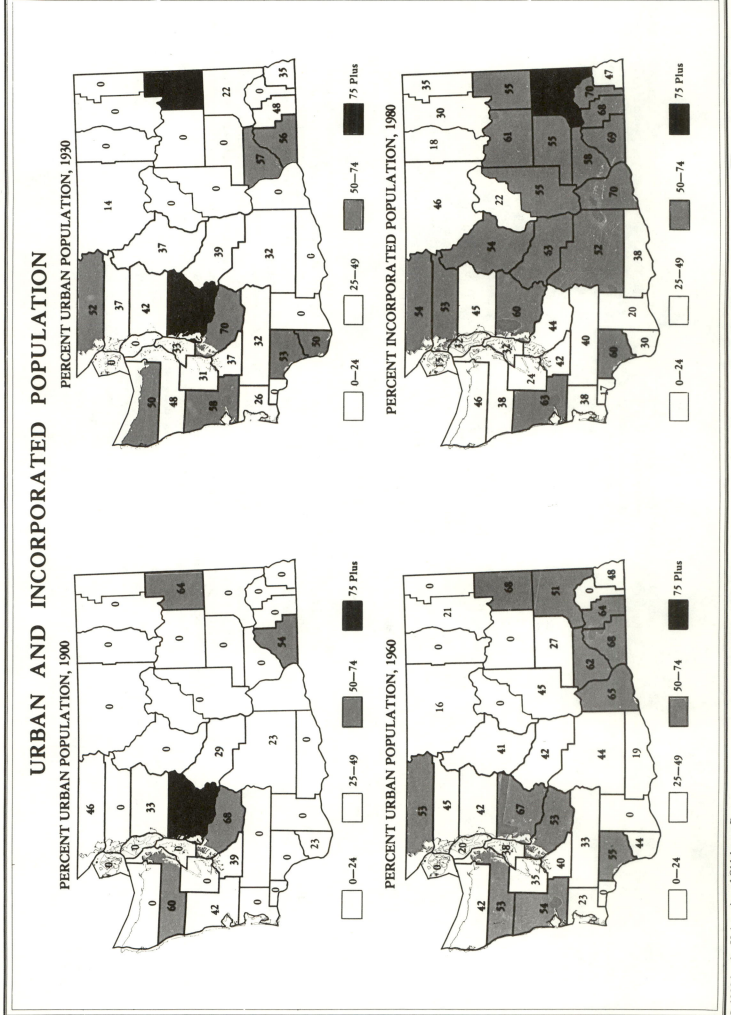

PERCENT URBAN POPULATION, 1930

PERCENT URBAN POPULATION, 1900

PERCENT INCORPORATED POPULATION, 1980

PERCENT URBAN POPULATION, 1960

0—24   25—49   50—74   75 Plus

Among the more significant social phenomena of the past 150 years has been the steady drift of population from rural areas and the accompanying growth of towns and cities. In 1790 barely 5 percent of the American population lived in urban places of 2,500 inhabitants or more; today approximately 74 percent of the American population is counted as urban.

The drift from countryside to town in earlier times produced, in almost all cases, concentrated urban settlements with high population densities and well-circumscribed rural/urban boundaries. In the past half-century or more a countervailing tendency has drawn people away from the inner city out to sprawling suburbs and to nearby but not contiguous exurbs. Although it was the streetcar that made possible this movement away from the city center at the beginning of the century, since the 1920s it has been the automobile that has enabled the suburbs to attract increasingly large segments of the urban population. Demographers are beginning to detect a reverse movement back toward the city center, as urban renewal projects and gentrification present attractive options to city workers disillusioned with the much-vaunted advantages of surburban life and the costly and time-consuming daily commute to and from the central city. Ironically, the city continues to provide the majority of jobs and the most attractive economic opportunities. The urban exodus is discernable on the maps showing urban population censuses over time. The return to the city, however, is still too tentative and limited in scale to be seen except on the largest-scale maps.

From the first days of white settlement Washington has had its urban places, even though these originally had only a few hundred inhabitants. In 1870, for example, Washington Territory claimed seven incorpo- rated places, of which the largest was Walla Walla with 1,394 inhabitants. Only two other places had more than one thousand inhabitants: Olympia with 1,203 and Seattle with 1,107. Growth came quickly, however. By 1890 there were fifty-four incorporated places, the three largest being Seattle with 42,837 inhabitants, Tacoma with 36,006, and Spokane with 19,222; and while Spokane has since surpassed Tacoma in population size, the three have remained ever since the state's largest urban places.

During the present century both urban and surburban growth have continued at a rapid pace, and the number of incorporated places has multiplied many times, from 51 in 1900 to 267 in 1980. Although incorporation is not per se a measure of size, the acquisition of official status enables a community to become responsible for its own internal government, taxation, and the provisioning of various municipal services. Most incorporated places are manifestly urban in both form and function, although some, despite early hopes, have remained small. In the 1980 census three incorporated places in Washington recorded populations fewer than 100—Krupp, in Grant County, with 87; Waverley, in Spokane County, with 88; and Hatton, in Adams County, with 90—and there were many others with populations of only a few hundred. The decade from 1900 to 1910 saw the largest number of incorporations as the number climbed from 51 to 170. Fewer than one hundred others have been added since then.

Three of the four maps on the opposite page show the urban population by county for the census years 1900, 1930, and 1960. The fourth map, by way of contrast, shows incorporated population by county. Not surprisingly, at the beginning of the century the highest percentages of urban population were registered in those counties with the biggest cities. By examining the maps for 1900, 1930, and 1960, however, we see that Seattle, King, Pierce, and Spokane counties, where Seattle, Tacoma, and Spokane, respectively, are located all increased their urban populations between 1900 and 1930 only to have these decline quite sharply by 1960 as rural and unincorporated areas increased their populations at the expense of the big cities. On the other hand, urban growth continued through 1960 in counties with a single medium-sized city and only a few other small urban places. Whatcom County (where Bellingham is the largest city), Kittitas County (Ellensburg), and Yakima County (Yakima) are good examples of this.

Today the highest densities of population in urban and incorporated places are found not in the large metropolitan counties, or even the new metropolitan counties with medium-sized cities, but in more sparsely populated areas of the state such as the southeast, where Whitman County has 82 percent of its population classified as urban, and Columbia County, 68 percent. Other sparsely populated areas, however, have some of the lowest percentages of urban population, including Wahkiakum County, with 17 percent, Ferry County, with 18 percent, and Skamania County, with 20 percent.

The importance of growth in the nonincorporated areas of the state is highlighted because, although the state's population grew by 21 percent in the 1970s, Seattle's population dropped from 530,831 to 498,000 between 1970 and 1980, and Tacoma increased by only 3,000, and Spokane by only 2,000. At the same time the population living in incorporated places rose from 1,952,901 to 2,136,101, but as a percentage of the state's population it dropped from 57.2 in 1970 to 52.8 percent in 1980.

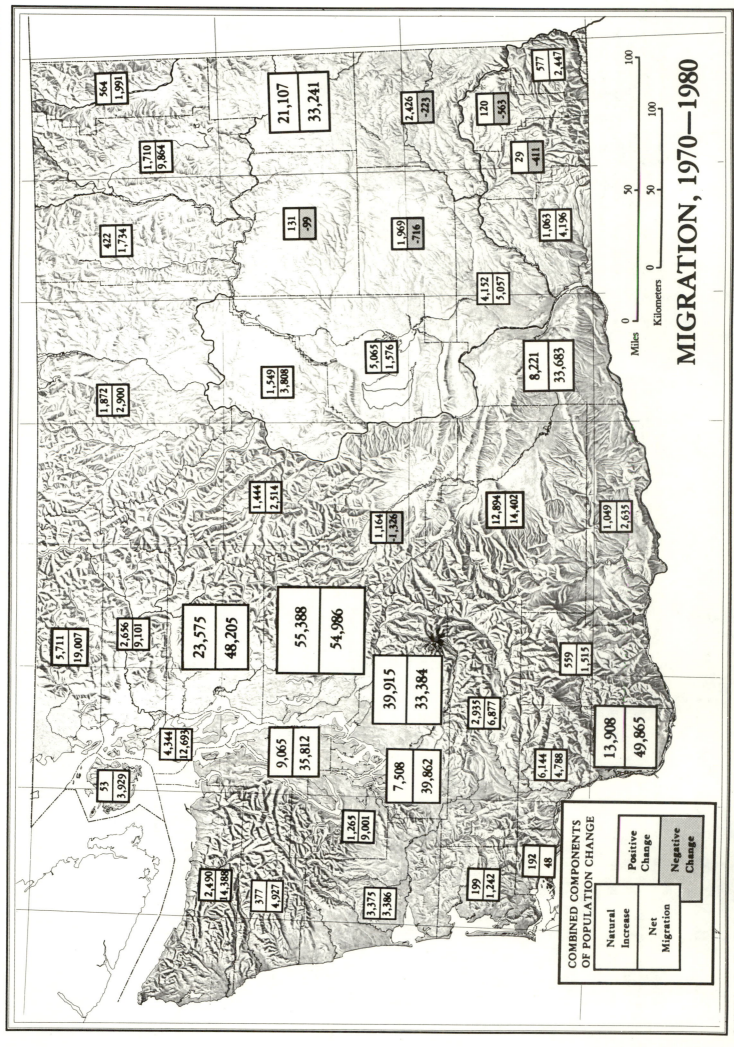

MIGRATION, 1970—1980

COMBINED COMPONENTS
OF POPULATION CHANGE

Natural Increase	Positive Change	
Net Migration	Negative Change	

Since the beginning of white settlement in the nineteenth century, migration has been a dominant, occasionally an overwhelming, factor in population change in the state of Washington. In only a few decades has the excess of births over deaths, *natural increase*, come close to or surpassed the increase caused by *net migration*, the excess of in-migrants over out-migrants.

Between 1970 and 1980, Washington's population increased from 3,413,244 to 4,132,156, a gain of 718,912, or 21 percent—a percentage increase almost half again as great as the national population increase of 13 percent during the 1970s. Approximately two-thirds of the increase was the result of continued high net migration, which came in large part from other western states. This influx increased still further the proportion of Washington's total population born out of state. Like all the western states, Washington's population contains a high percentage of such residents. Looking at the 1980 census statistics, we find that 2,150,605 persons, or 52 percent of the population, were born out of state, including 239,060 foreign-born and 41,375 Americans born abroad or at sea.

Although migration into the state continued at a high rate during the 1970s, it was not the only migratory movement affecting the region. Washingtonians proved that, like most other Americans, they were still a people on the move, even if the move was only a short distance and within the state. Of Washingtonians five years of age and older in 1980, more than 2 million of the 3.8 million total had had a different residence in 1975, and 1,059,473 had moved within the same county and 386,732 had moved from another county in the state. Such internal movements are often easier to record than to explain. It is apparent only that economic, environmental, and social factors of various sorts have entered into the decisions to relocate. "Push" factors which expel and "pull" factors which attract can generally be identified for particular places and specific dates to help explain migration.

Our map, which shows net migration statistics by county, also includes figures for natural increases. Across the state net migration rates varied during the 1970s much more than natural increase rates. All thirty-nine counties registered some natural increase, even though birth rates and death rates, which depend on the age structure of the population, varied markedly from county to county. Garfield County, for example, which registered a very small natural increase rate, had a net loss of population of approximately 20 percent due to continued out-migration—a phenomenon that has been apparent there since the beginning of the century. Five other counties in eastern Washington, all of them agricultural counties with no dominant "pull" factors present—Adams, Columbia, Kittitas, Lincoln, and Whitman—also lost population. By contrast, San Juan County in an environmentally attractive region—at the present time, a powerful "pull" factor—registered a small natural increase, which was due in large part to a much older-than-average population structure, and a very large in-migration rate. The net result was an almost 100 percent increase in population there in the 1970s. Jefferson, Skagit, Clark, and Benton were other counties that, for a variety of reasons, had considerable population increases due to rapid in-migration.

Richard Morrill has identified four prominent features of 1970s population change: (1) the deconcentration of growth from the metropolitan core of Seattle, (2) the growth of eastern Washington at a rate as fast as that of western Washington, (3) a nonmetropolitan growth that was faster than metropolitan growth, and (4) rapid growth in environmentally attractive areas. Morrill's analysis suggests that these recent migration patterns will remain significant—that population will continue to move from metropolitan to suburban areas and to rural areas that have natural beauty and necessary amenities. Revitalization of inner-city cores and gentrification of older neighborhoods, such as have occurred in other parts of the country, have not taken place to any great degree in Washington, but if and when they do occur, there could be some reversal of present migration movements and a slowing down of suburbanization and exurbanization.

POPULATION GROUPS, 1980

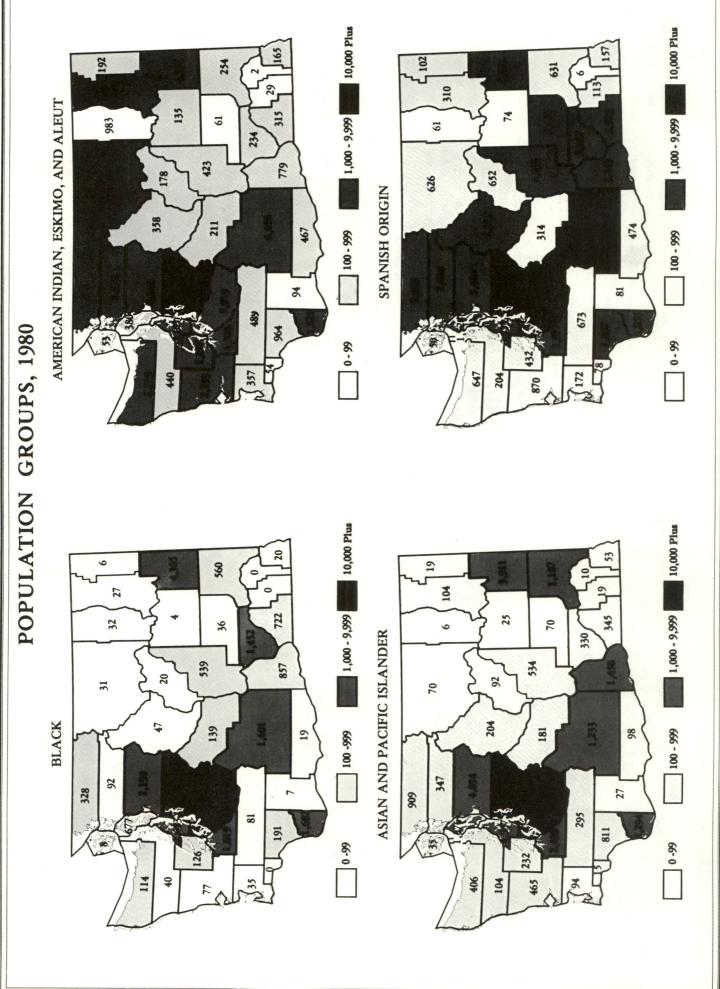

AMERICAN INDIAN, ESKIMO, AND ALEUT

SPANISH ORIGIN

BLACK

ASIAN AND PACIFIC ISLANDER

0 - 99

100 - 999

1,000 - 9,999

10,000 Plus

Although American Indians comprised the indigenous population in Washington for thousands of years, and although blacks and Asians—Chinese particularly—were among mid-nineteenth-century residents of the state, these and other nonwhite groups are today, as they have been for a century, numerically small minorities.

In 1980 the 3,790,990 whites in the state made up more than 90 percent of the population. Asians, the next largest group, totalled only 111,607 (2.6 percent), followed by blacks, with 105,604 (2.5 percent), and American Indians, who were grouped with Eskimos and Aleuts for a total of 63,808 (1.5 percent). Hispanics, a linguistic rather than a racial group, numbered 121,286, or 2.9 percent of the total.

American Indians are found in every county of the state, as might be expected. Reservations (see Map 14) were established both east and west of the Cascades, but Indians also were often allowed to take up land in rural areas and to live in urban areas. There are marginally more Indian females than males, but the difference in numbers is less than 400. Among the very much smaller groups of Eskimos and Aleuts females predominate, however. Approximately 35,000 Indians are classified as urban dwellers and 26,000 as rural dwellers, and in both types of location sex ratios are very even. Eskimos and Aleuts nonetheless tend to be found very largely in urban areas. Only in Okanogan County and Ferry County, where the Colville Reservation is located, do Indians comprise more than ten percent of the total population. In Yakima County, much of which is the Yakima Reservation, Indians make up little more than three percent of the population.

By contrast, the black population is heavily urbanized, with 101,827, or 96.4 percent, of the 105,604 blacks in the state living in urban areas, and approximately 68,000 of them in central city locations. Black males outnumber females by more than 8,000, largely because of the recent in-migration of younger, single black males. More than 50 percent of the blacks are domiciled in King County (55,950), particularly in the city of Seattle; with another 28 percent in Pierce County, most of them in Tacoma. In contrast, the other large city in the state, Spokane, has a black population less than one-tenth that of Seattle. Three counties—Columbia, Garfield, and Wahkiakum—recorded no blacks in 1980.

Asians, who numbered 111,607 in 1980, are a mixed group that in 1980 included 27,389 Japanese, 25,662 Filipinos, 17,984 Chinese, 13,441 Koreans, and smaller numbers of Asian Indians, Vietnamese, Hawaiians, and other Pacific Islanders. The Chinese are the most urbanized of the groups. All but a few hundred of them live in urban areas, and more than half live in inner-city areas, particularly the city of Seattle. The other Asians are only slightly less urbanized, and once again King County, particularly Seattle, provides the domicile for the majority of them.

Of the 121,286 Hispanics about two-thirds live in urban areas, in particular in the SMSAs of Seattle-Everett (29,482), Tacoma (12,038), Yakima (5,201), and Spokane (3,790). As with the blacks, Hispanic males outnumber females by a few thousand, and more so in the urban areas than the rural areas. Although Hispanics hail from different parts of the Spanish-speaking world, Mexico is the country of origin for approximately 65 percent of them. In 1980 every county in the state recorded some Spanish-speaking residents, although in Garfield County the total was only six. The highest percentage of Spanish-speaking residents is found in Yakima County, where the 25,455 Hispanics comprise almost 15 percent of the population.

Formerly, a large proportion of the early Hispanic population in the state consisted of migrants, who annually provided cheap field labor, particularly at harvest time, in other western states besides Washington. Over the past few decades, however, increasing numbers of Hispanics have become permanent residents. Many today are small landowners living in the Yakima valley and engaged in growing market vegetables and fruit. Others remain as casual agricultural laborers or have moved into major cities such as Seattle and Yakima.

EVOLUTION OF COUNTIES

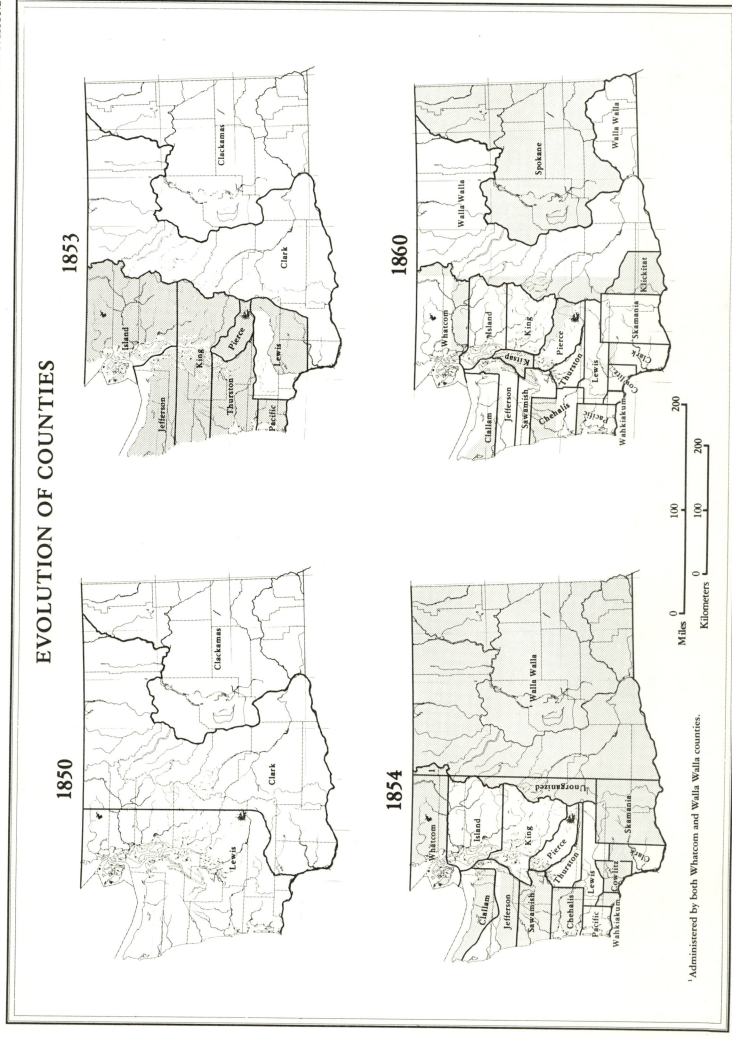

1850

1853

1854

1860

Miles

Kilometers

0 100 200

0 100 200

¹ Administered by both Whatcom and Walla Walla counties.

In the area that was to become the state of Washington, county government began with the establishment of the Oregon Provisional Government. The settlers who gathered at Champoeg in 1843 divided the Oregon Country (see Map 19) into four districts for purposes of administration, and two of these embraced Washington: Tuality District, which encompassed everything west of Oregon's Willamette River to the Pacific Ocean and north of the Yamhill River in that state, and Clackamas District, which included all that remained of present-day Washington, as well as eastern Oregon, the future state of Idaho, and western Montana. Even though the white population then in the region was sparse, the districts (redesignated counties in December 1845) were far too extensive for efficient governance, and so in August 1845 that part of Oregon lying north of the Columbia River and west of the Rockies was placed in a third district, the District of Vancouver, which, in turn, became Clark County in 1849. The Tuality District had been divided in December 1845, and the area north of the Columbia River and west of the Cowlitz River became Lewis County.

The California gold rush sent men prowling north in search of further mineral deposits and timber for the wharves and other building during the boom in San Francisco during the early 1850s. Some settled in coastal areas and on Puget Sound, while settlers seeking fertile land for farming staked out portions of the Cowlitz and Nisqually river valleys and Whidbey Island. The growth in population led, in 1851, to the designation of the southwestern corner of Lewis County as Pacific County, and in 1852, Lewis and Clark counties were subdivided to make Thurston, King, Jefferson, and Pierce counties. Island County, carved from Lewis County and including all of the coastal region north to the international boundary, was formed in 1853.

When Washington Territory's first legislature assembled early in 1854, there were eight Washington counties: Island, Pierce, Jefferson, King, Thurston, Clark, Pacific, and Lewis. Since the new territory's borders included all of the old Oregon Country that was south of forty-nine degrees north latitude but not part of the state of Oregon (see Map 21), the existing county lines required realignment and new counties had to be added. The new counties were Clallam, Chehalis, Cowlitz, Skamania, Walla Walla, Wahkiakum, Sawamish (now Mason), and Whatcom counties. In 1857 another new county was organized from portions of King and Jefferson. Originally, the legislature suggested it be named in honor of a United States Army lieutenant, W. A. Slaughter, who had died in one of the skirmishes of the Indian Wars. Voters rejected the proposal, choosing instead the name of the recently hostile Klikitat Indians' chief, Kitsap.

New population movements in response to the Indian uprisings, gold discoveries along the Fraser River, and prospecting in the eastern reaches of the territory presaged the formation of further counties. Klickitat County was established in 1859 in an area on the north side of The Dalles where population had clustered because of the U.S. Army's increased transport and supply needs. Spokane County, the eastern boundary of which was the Rocky Mountains, was authorized by the legislature in 1858, but it lacked enough interested settlers to organize it. Only in 1860, as population shifted toward Idaho's new gold camps, did Spokane County become a functioning, if cumbersome, unit of government.

EVOLUTION OF COUNTIES

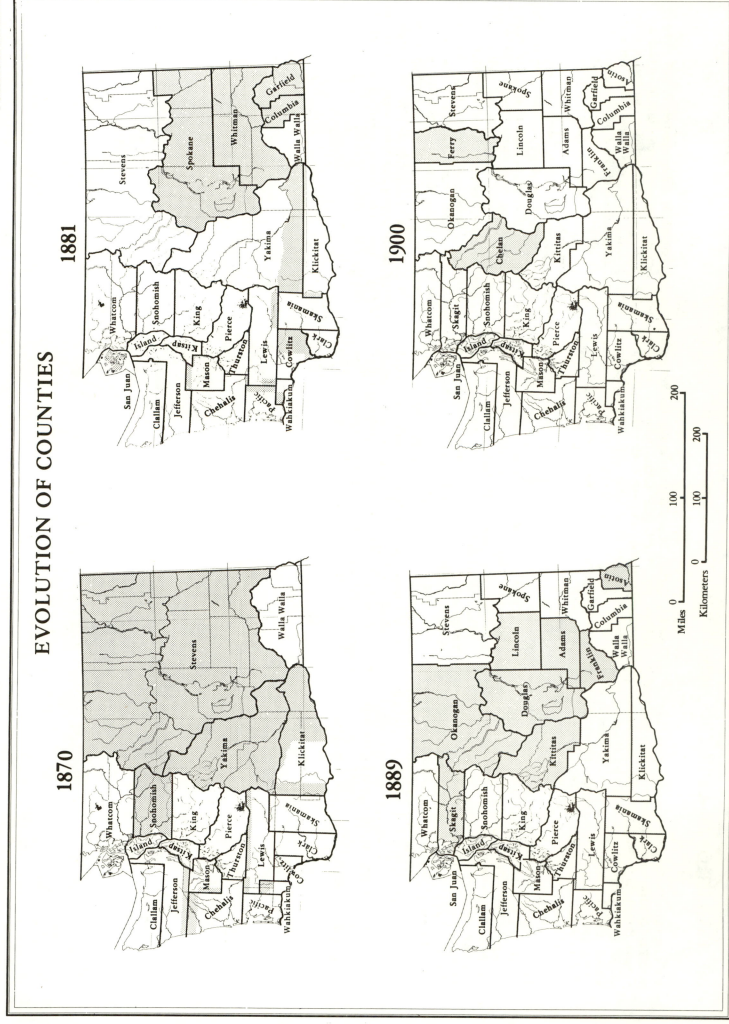

1881

1870

1900

1889

Continuing increases in population, together with the territorial legislature's habit of responding favorably and uncritically to local demands for the creation of new counties, set the pattern for the remaining years of the Washington Territory before statehood was achieved in 1889. The migration of homesteaders and would-be prospectors to northern Puget Sound led, in 1861, to the formation of Snohomish County, while gold seekers in the eastern part of the sprawling territory pressured the legislature into authorizing two counties, Missoula and Shoshone, that were never organized. Early in 1863, still reacting to the growing migration of miners and camp followers to the goldfields of Colville, Boise, Oro Fino, and the Bitter Root Mountains, legislators approved the establishment of Ferguson County, which was to be bordered by the Wenatchee River on the north, the Simcoe Range on the south, Walla Walla and Spokane counties on the east, and the Cascades on the west. Ferguson had a short life also. It vanished in 1865, its place taken by Yakima County. The easternmost counties were all either eliminated from the territory—Idaho Territory began its official life on March 3, 1863—

or were drastically redrawn. Stevens County was altered repeatedly. Spokane County disappeared completely in January 1864 and was not revived until October 1879.

Territorial assemblymen made several attempts to lessen the confusion. The substitution of surveyed boundaries for those dependent on natural features and landmarks began with the delineation of Snohomish County in 1861, and several subsequent legislative sessions, beginning in 1867, struggled with ambiguous, sometimes overlapping county lines. The 1869 legislature alone adjusted the boundaries of eleven of the territory's twenty counties. Still, legislation continued to heed local petitioners demanding further county organization. Whitman County was created from the southeast portion of Stevens County in 1871. In 1873, following settlement of the San Juan Island boundary dispute with Great Britain, San Juan County was established. A host of new counties were organized in eastern Washington, and particularly in the region between the Columbia and Snake rivers, to satisfy settlers anticipating completion of the Northern Pacific Railroad: Co-

lumbia County in 1875, Garfield in 1881, and Asotin, Franklin, Lincoln, Adams, Kittitas, and Douglas counties in 1883. On the western slope of the Cascades settlers in the Skagit River valley, beset by flood problems that Whatcom County commissioners neglected, demanded and got the partition of Whatcom County in 1883.

The free and easy policies of the territorial era did not end before, in 1888, legislators agreed to a sixth redrawing of the borders of Lewis County and established Okanogan County. Delegates to Washington's constitutional convention made sure that, henceforth, the state legislature, not local groups, would oversee county organization. Under the State Constitution no new county could be carved from an old one if it reduced the population of the existing county below 4,000 residents, and new counties were required to possess a minimum population of 2,000 persons. Such requirements appreciably reduced the creation of new counties. In the eleven years remaining in the nineteenth century, only two new counties, Ferry and Chelan (1899), were established, among eight proposed.

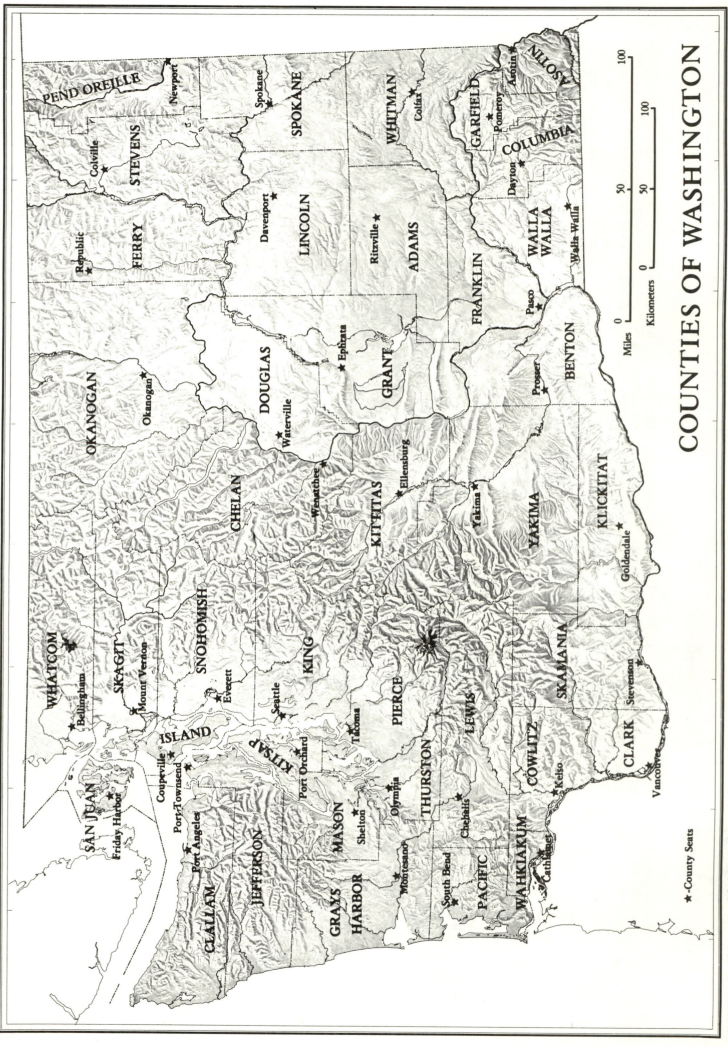

COUNTIES OF WASHINGTON

★-County Seats

Miles
Kilometers
0   50   100
0   50   100

Under the firm control of the state legislature, Washington completed most of its county building early in this century. A portion of Klickitat and Yakima counties became Benton County in 1905. A group of Chehalis County residents pressured the legislature to authorize the division of that county in order to create Grays Harbor County in 1907, and with a carelessness reminiscent of territorial days, legislators responded with tentative approval without having investigated whether such a division violated the State Constitution's population requirements. The State Supreme Court quickly rejected the authorization measure. Eventually, in 1915, Chehalis County was renamed Grays Harbor County. The state legislature in the meantime took greater care in approving the last pair of new counties, Grant and Pend Oreille, in 1909. Population requirements were complied with, the boundaries of the new counties were precisely defined, and the legislature took care to provide thorough instructions regarding the counties' fiscal obligations to their parent counties and the formation of judicial and legislative districts. The most recent attempt to create a new county, a plan to weld together the western segments of Clallam and Jefferson counties and call it Olympic County, passed the State Senate in 1984 but died in the House.

Recognizing that county realignment remains an ongoing possibility because of the ambiguity of some existing lines and shifting population and political demands, in 1967 the legislature formed a temporary County Boundary Advisory Commission, which worked with the Department of Natural Resources's Division of Surveys and Maps to seek answers to persistent questions concerning county boundaries. A County Boundary Review Board and an Annexation Review Board were established to resolve future problems. The 1969 legislature adopted a set procedure for intercounty territorial transfers: a majority of registered voters in a section must petition the county government; if the petition is accepted, a special election is scheduled within ninety days in the section requesting the change; and if the change is agreed to by at least three-fifths of the registered voters, the results are referred to the county with which combination is desired. It is left to that county's government to accept or deny the application and then notify the legislature. This process was tested virtually immediately, in 1970, when the Cliffdell area in Kittitas County sought and obtained transfer to Yakima County, a transfer that appears to have worked smoothly.

Since territorial days the legislature has stipulated the location of temporary county seats, but it has been left to county voters to make more permanent selections. Changes can be made at any general election, upon certification of a petition by at least one-third of the number of voters participating in the previous general election. A three-fifths majority is required for passage of such a petition through the legislature. In the years of rapidly multiplying counties there were numerous and often colorful contests between communities—the struggle between Spokane and Cheney, for example, and that between LaConner and Mount Vernon in Skagit County—not only because of civic pride but because of the economic advantages associated with being the center of county government.

Basing its authority upon court decisions that consistently have interpreted article eleven, section one, of the State Constitution as meaning that counties, as "legal subdivisions" of the state, lack any inherent powers, the legislature has specified county elective positions, their terms, and salaries. Such state control was somewhat curbed by passage of a home-rule amendment to the State Constitution in 1948. The amendment permits a greater degree of county autonomy in structuring government and has proved attractive to counties undergoing significant growth. Clallam, King, Pierce, Snohomish and Whatcom counties have adopted home-rule charters. Some degree of fiscal autonomy also has come about through the federal government's increased tendency in recent years to make direct appropriations to counties and cities, bypassing the state.

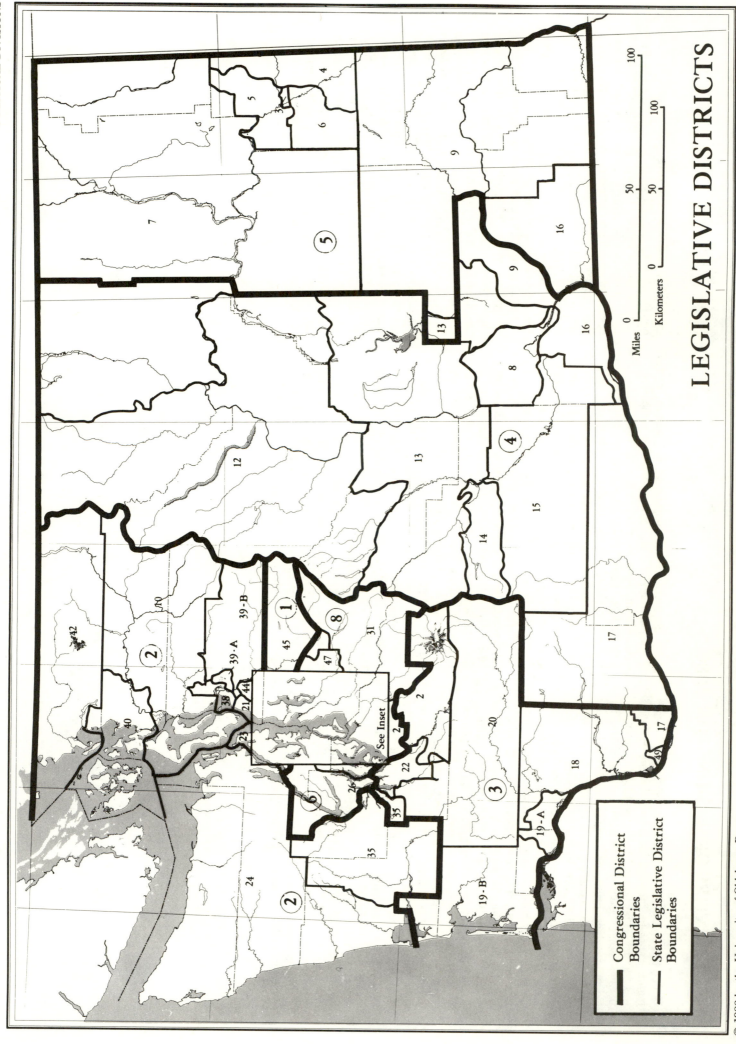

LEGISLATIVE DISTRICTS

Congressional District
Boundaries

State Legislative District
Boundaries

© 1988 by the University of Oklahoma Press

42. LEGISLATIVE DISTRICTS

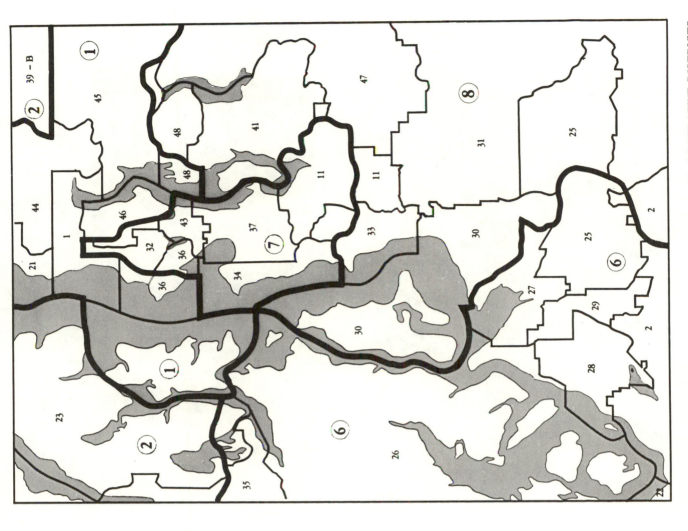

The framers of Washington's constitution set forth population as the fundamental criterion for apportioning seats in both houses of the state legislature, but political, sectional, and other pressures transformed what was intended to be a regularly performed administrative function into a complicated struggle that successive legislatures either waged for partisan advantage or neglected altogether.

The reapportionment of congressional seats, which also relied upon legislative action, proved equally troublesome. When Washington was awarded a seventh congressman in 1950, for example, the legislature allowed the seat to remain at large until 1956 because of the difficulties involved in redistricting. By 1981, when the state's population had increased by twenty-one percent, an eighth seat in congress had been added, and partisan and sectional passions were as strong as ever, the traditional reliance upon the legislature as the agency for redistricting at last proved impossible. A Republican governor vetoed a plan developed by the Republican-controlled legislature. A compromise eventually was signed into law. Then a group of Everett citizens sued to restore their area to the second congressional district, and a panel of three federal judges declared the legislature's compromise plan unconstitutional and directed that a new plan be prepared within ninety days of the beginning of the 1983 legislature's regular session. The legislature responded by establishing a temporary redistricting commission composed of five members and assisted by a staff which included a lawyer and a demographer.

This commission submitted a plan in March 1983 which was adopted by the legislature. It also recommended a permanent plan for reapportionment of legislative and congressional seats. Referred to and adopted by the electorate in November 1983, the plan amended article eleven of the State Constitution. Henceforth, redistricting is to be carried out every ten years, in the year following the federal census, by a commission consisting of four members, one each to be appointed by the two major parties' leaders in each legislative chamber, and a chairman selected by a majority of at least three of the four other commissioners. Commission members may not campaign for nor hold elective office while serving. The commission is to redistrict legislative and congressional seats according to the 1962 Supreme Court requirement of close adherence to equal population representation. The redistricting plan must be presented to the state legislature, which retains authority for approving it, by January 1 of years ending in two. The legislature may amend a plan within thirty days, but such amendments require a two-thirds majority and cannot include more than two percent of any legislative or congressional district. If the commission cannot muster a three-fourths majority for a plan, the State Supreme Court is authorized to carry out redistricting.

PRESIDENTIAL ELECTIONS

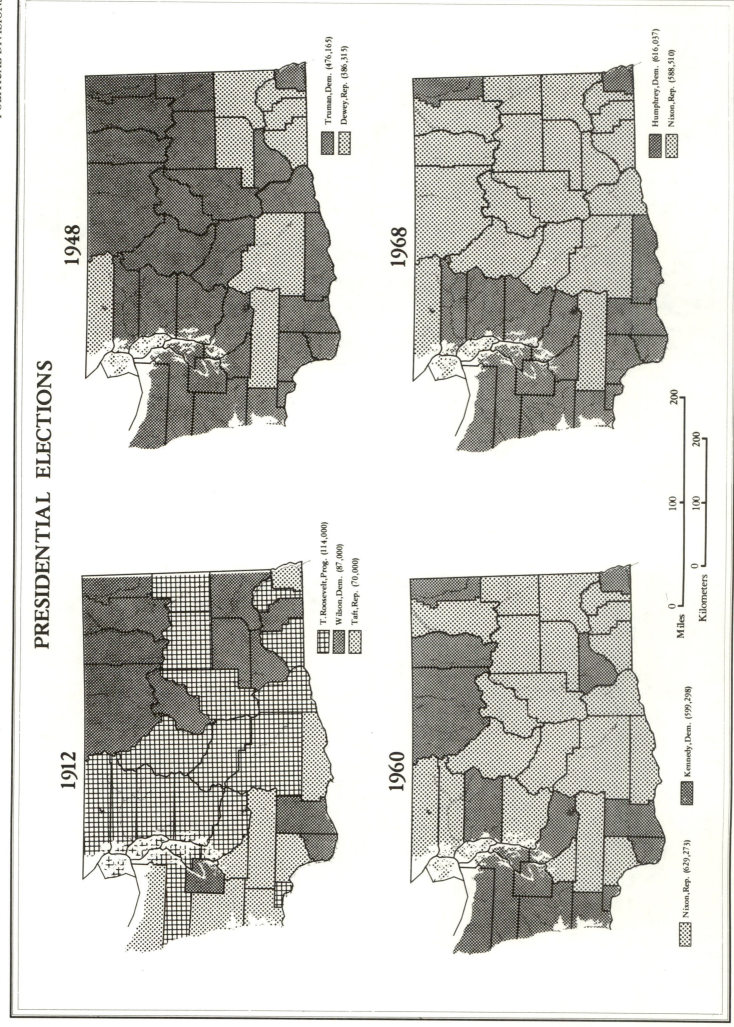

1912

T. Roosevelt, Prog. (114,000)
Wilson, Dem. (87,000)
Taft, Rep. (70,000)

1948

Truman, Dem. (476,165)
Dewey, Rep. (386,315)

1960

Nixon, Rep. (629,273)
Kennedy, Dem. (599,298)

1968

Humphrey, Dem. (616,037)
Nixon, Rep. (588,510)

Miles   0   100   200
Kilometers 0   100   200

Since its comparatively late entry into national politics as a state in 1889, Washington's reputation for seemingly aberrant political behavior has been well known. Washington voters have elected one governor who was the author of a utopian novel and another who refused to include funding in his budget for higher education. Coxey's Army of the Unemployed, the Knights of Labor, the Wobblies, and the Unemployed Citizen's League all have recruited thousands of supporters in the state, while anti-Asian riots and virulent anti-Communist witch-hunts drew adherents as well. An incumbent Seattle mayor once offered free beer for sailors as a remedy for the Great Depression, and a future Washington secretary of state campaigned for office dressed as Mahatma Gandhi, leading a goat through Seattle streets. Journalists and scholars may be forgiven for favoring the explanation of Rudyard Kipling while visiting Tacoma in 1889: "They are all mad here, all mad." In fact, the state's voting behavior has moderated considerably since the 1930s, when the writer Mary McCarthy termed it "wild, comic, theatrical, dishonest, disorganized, hopeful."

The issues in Washington's politics today are essentially those of the nation at large, though to describe them, as one political scientist has done, as "staid, mature and serious" may be overstating the case. State voters are concerned about the problems associated with industrial-urban growth, the high cost of government, the needs of education, welfare, transportation, and the criminal justice system. Abetted by a blanket primary system, they still indulge in a long-established habit of split-ticket voting; surveys suggest seventy-five percent of voting Washingtonians split tickets in both primary and general elections. Although, since 1940, a competitive two-party system has emerged, the parties are decentralized and heterogeneous, and pressure groups—business, organized labor, public and private utilities, the large wood-products companies, railroads, and professional associations—play a significant role in the decision-making process. Voters in Washington have retained the independence that once lent them regional distinctiveness, but their habits have become national characteristics.

In the years from 1889 to 1932, Republican candidates were most often successful in the state, and Democrats won most often from 1932 through 1940. Since then, although each party may dominate most elections in certain counties, real competition exists everywhere and surprises are common. For example, despite the general Republican predominance early in the twentieth century, in 1912 the GOP lost the governorship, two congressional seats, and sixty-three legislative seats, and the Republican incumbent president, William Howard Taft, ran third, with 70,200 votes, behind the Progressive Party standard-bearer, Theodore Roosevelt, with 113,400, and Woodrow Wilson, with 86,500. Certainly, local conditions played a part in the decision. The state Republican party was split at the outset by the bitter convention struggle between Taft and Roosevelt forces. The state central committee, controlled by Taft regulars, had violated tradition, which held that convention sites be alternated between the eastern and western sections of the state, by selecting Aberdeen in place of Spokane, a Roosevelt stronghold. Washington's popular United States senator, Miles Poindexter, an insurgent and later a Bull Mooser, led the convention fight for Roosevelt—and led the insurgents in a walkout and separate meeting. When the Taft regulars were seated at the national convention, the bitterness infected the presidential campaign in Washington.

By 1948 the balanced strength of the two major parties in Washington and the custom of ticket splitting had produced a result similar to what was occurring in other western states. Harry S. Truman carried the state by almost 90,000 voters, 476,165 to Thomas E. Dewey's 386,315, winning in all but ten counties, but the GOP gubernatorial nominee, Arthur Langlie, defeated a popular Democrat, Monrad C. Wallgren, 445,958 to 417,035. In 1960 pollsters predicted that in Washington, John F. Kennedy would defeat Richard M. Nixon, while the incumbent Democratic governor, Albert Rosellini, would lose to his Republican opponent. Instead, local circumstances wrought havoc with the predictions. The professionals of the state Democratic Party left the Kennedy campaign to amateurs in order to bolster Rosellini's chances. Nixon's campaign in Washington, on the other hand, was run by Mort Frazer, a seasoned former speaker of the state house of representatives. Thus in 1960 the Democrats won the state senate, 36 to 13, and the state house, 59 to 40, and reelected seven incumbents to statewide offices, and Rosellini won reelection, but Nixon defeated Kennedy by a margin of 29,926. In 1968, Democrats won control of the state senate but lost the lower house, lost all but one statewide position, but reelected United States Senator Warren Magnuson by a margin of 64.4 percent. In that year Washington was one of but two states north of Texas and west of Minnesota to choose Hubert H. Humphrey over Nixon, by a 28,000-vote margin.

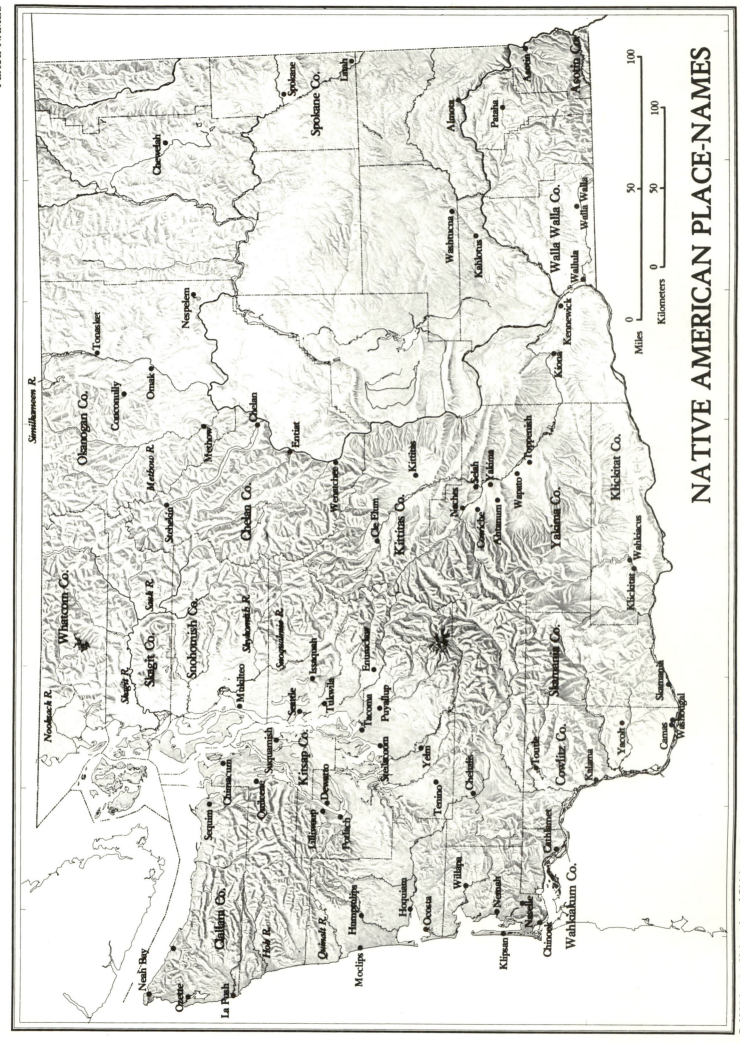

NATIVE AMERICAN PLACE-NAMES

America's heritage of Indian place-names, as George Stewart notes in his classic study, *Names on the Land,* is a rich and treasured one. Not less so is the heritage of Indian place-names in the state of Washington.

Indian tribes were usually sparing in their designation of specific names, and much more careful than later comers in their descriptive, or generic, place-naming. In general, they named only significant features in the immediate vicinity of their settlements, usually those which had special environmental and cultural associations or utility. For the most part, the Indians of the Pacific Northwest, as elsewhere, seem to have preferred generic names for places; that is, names, giving clues about resources, natural features, or environmental characteristics rather than honoring or commemorating a particular individual or tribal spirit. Hence Tukwila was the "land of hazelnuts"; Utsalady, "the land of berries"; Waiilatpu, "the place of the rye grass"; and Washougal, "the place of running water." Many of the place-names remaining today are derived from Indian personal names chosen not by the Indians but rather by newly arrived American (or European) settlers. Among these are Seattle, Steilacoom, Ilwaco, Whatcom, and Tonasket, all named for local chiefs. It should also be noted that most of the Indian place-names have suffered some degree of corruption and change as a result of poor transliteration or a contemporary error perpetrated by some clerk or settler.

Our map of Native American place-names is highly selective. No attempt has been made to locate or list the many hundreds of place-names of Indian origin.

Rather the purpose is to display the prevalence of such names in every part of the state. The bulk of the names, it will be seen, are of settlements—cities and towns—and of rivers and counties. Few mountains have retained their Indian names—Mount Shuksan, in the shadow of Mount Baker, is one of the few exceptions. Similarly, few of the state's coastal place-names and none of the larger geographical regions of the state are of Indian origin, although an occasional Indian name has been adopted, as for example the Okanogan Highlands.

It is especially noteworthy that all three of the state's major cities bear Indian names: Seattle, in honor of a local chief variously known as "See Yat" or "Sealth"; Spokane (originally Spokane Falls), for the local tribe, "the people of the sun"; and Tacoma, in honor of the mountain known today as Mount Rainier, which was known to the Indians as Tacoma or Tahoma, the mountain "near to heaven," or in other interpretations, "the nourishing breast," "the mother of waters," or "the place of frozen waters."

Of the more than thirty medium-sized Washington cities (from 10,000 to approximately 60,000 inhabitants), only six have names of Indian origin: Hoquiam, "the place of driftwood"; Kennewick, "the grassy place"; Puyallup, either "the shaded place" or "the place of generous people"; Walla Walla, "the place of running waters"; Wenatchee, the place "where the river issues from the canyon"; and Yakima, the place of "the people of the narrow river." An additional forty-odd smaller towns, most of them incorporated, have Indian names. Among them are Chewelah, Entiat, Mukilteo, Napavine,

Nespelem, Sequim, Snohomish, and Washtucna. For the most part, the meaning of each is environmental, the reference being to a river, water, grass, or shade, but occasionally the meaning is more ominous. Enumclaw, for example, is the "home of evil spirits," and Yacolt, the "haunted place." Most of the rivers of Washington have retained their Indian names, but a much smaller proportion of the creeks and few of the lakes have done so. Among the major rivers are the Okanogan, the Yakima, the Chehalis, the Snohomish, and the Skagit. It should be noted, however, that the Indians frequently employed the name that is used today for only part of the course of a river. Such a river, in fact, might have a number of names along its whole course, as did the Columbia.

Of the thirty-nine counties in the state, sixteen have names of Indian origin, usually the name that was given to one of the tribes in the immediate vicinity. These, in alphabetical order, are Asotin, Chelan, Clallam, Cowlitz, Kitsap, Kittitas, Klickitat, Okanogan, Skagit, Skamania, Snohomish, Spokane, Wahkiakum, Walla Walla, Whatcom, and Yakima. One other county, Pend Oreille, though named for a tribe of that part of the state, is, in fact, of French origin.

The interest in place-names has grown rapidly in recent years. Edmond Meany's classic 1923 volume, *Origin of Washington Geographic Names,* was the only authoritative reference work available until 1985, when Robert Hitchman's long-awaited *Place Names of Washington* was published posthumously by the Washington State Historical Society.

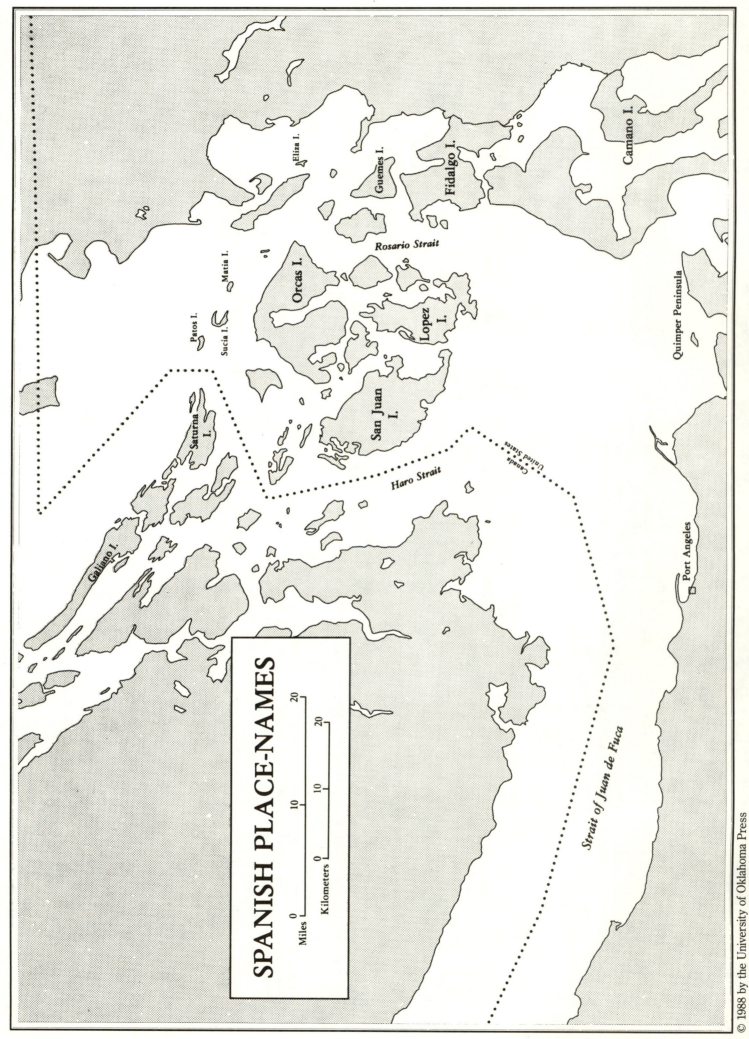

SPANISH PLACE-NAMES

Miles
0   10   20

Kilometers
0   10   20

Eliza I.

Guemes I.

Fidalgo I.

Camano I.

Rosario Strait

Orcas I.

Matia I.

Sucia I.

Patos I.

Lopez I.

Saturna I.

San Juan I.

Galiano I.

Quimper Peninsula

Haro Strait

Canada
United States

Port Angeles

Strait of Juan de Fuca

45. SPANISH PLACE-NAMES

The discovery of the Pacific Northwest by European powers—notably England and Spain—and the subsequent settlement of the region by England and the United States led inevitably to the supplanting of most American Indian place-names, and to the creation of toponyms for numerous geographical features not previously named by the Indians. It is impossible to make any precise count of the number of names lost. Certainly it must be in the hundreds, perhaps in the thousands.

Economic growth in the midnineteenth century resulted in rapid expansion of white settlement across the state, with hundreds of new names being supplied by, in their turn, explorer, surveyor, missionary, miner, settler, and, lastly, developer. A large proportion of the new settlements acquired names that commemorate such things as a native town or other birth place, a national hero, a favorite saint, a shrine of classical antiquity, or one of biblical fame. Generic names that denote some actual or perceived environmental characteristic, and specific ones that couple the name of a local settler with such suffixes as -ville, town, city, or center, were also common.

Of 2,042 separate place-names listed in Meany's *Origin of Washington Geographic Names*, 824 are those of individuals, 399 connote physical features, 386 are Indian names, 119 honor other towns, cities, or counties, 115 are named for crops, trees, animals, or birds, 33 are Spanish names, 17 are the names of American ships, and 6 are those of British ships, and another 6 are biblical names. It should be noted, however, that Meany's dictionary does not include a large number of small settlements and the names of many creeks, small lakes, and other natural features.

A considerable number of the names listed by Meany were placed on the original maps of explorers or those prepared by government surveyors or railroad officials. The Wilkes expedition is credited with 195, the United States Coast and Geodetic Survey with 73 names, and the railroad companies with at least 93 names.

Maps showing the distribution of representative American or British names would serve a limited purpose. They are ubiquitous and show no well-marked or distinctive patterns. A decision has been made, therefore, to confine our cartographic representations of place-names to American Indian and Spanish names.

The Spanish names are geographically concentrated in and around the San Juan Islands, Puget Sound, and the Olympic Peninsula. In this part of the state in the 1770s to 1790s the Spanish explorers—Heceta, Eliza, Bodega y Quadra, and others—sailed and landed, and later prepared maps containing hundreds of specific and a few generic place-names. Only a handful of the names remain today. As Warren Cook noted: "For every Spanish toponym preserved, dozens were disregarded, and the British nomenclature has prevailed." In view of the take-over of the Pacific Northwest by the Americans and British, this is hardly surprising. It is more surprising that most of the remaining Spanish names were restored in the 1840s by a British naval officer, Captain Henry Kellett, who generally gave the names to a feature other than the one for which the Spaniards had provided the name originally.

Among Kellet's "relocated" names are Fidalgo Island, Rosario Strait, and Camano Island. The name Fidalgo was given originally by Eliza to the present Rosario Strait—his Boca de Fidalgo. Rosario, in turn, was part of the original name given to the Gulf of Georgia—the Gran Canal de Nuestra Senora del Rosario la Marinera, while the name Camano was used by Eliza to designate present-day Admiralty Inlet—his Boca de Camano. The U.S. Coast and Geodetic Survey in the 1850s was responsible for yet another transfer when it restored the name of Quimper, used originally to designate present-day New Dungeness Bay, to the adjacent peninsula. The survey also restored the name Matia—originally Isla de Mata—to the group of small islands named by Wilkes the Edmunds Group.

Other places to which Spanish names were restored by Kellett are Patos Island, which had been renamed Gourd Island by Wilkes; Sucia Island, the largest of Wilkes's Percival Group; and Guemes Island, which had been renamed Lawrence Island by Wilkes. Orcas Island, renamed Hull's Island by Wilkes, received its contracted Spanish form from Kellett. Like Fidalgo Island and Camano Island, the name had been used originally for another geographical feature, Griffin Bay, the water body indenting San Juan Island, which was known to the Spaniards as the Boca de Horcasitas (Orcasitas).

The Spanish presence in Washington, fleeting though it was, is most notably and visibly commemorated in the name San Juan. The toponym is used for both the largest island of the group and for the whole archipelago that today comprises San Juan County—Spain's Isla y Archipelago de San Juan.

Today the naming of geographical features is carefully monitored by the state Commission on Geographic Names.

PART XI

THE ECONOMY: TRANSPORTATION

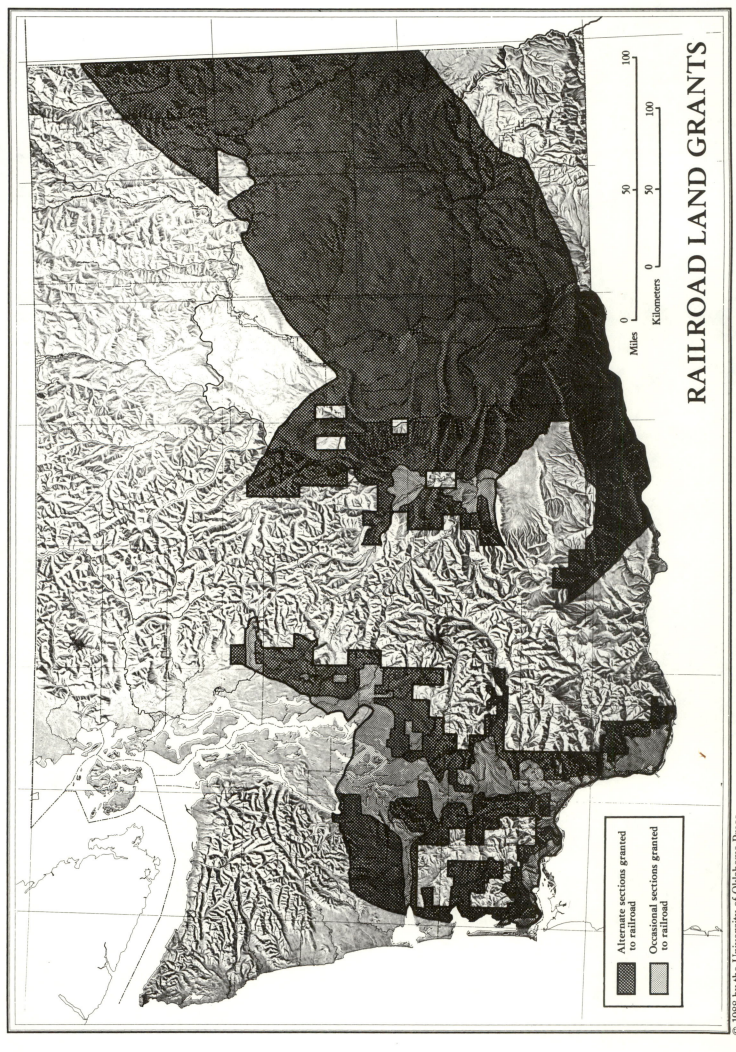

RAILROAD LAND GRANTS

Alternate sections granted
to railroad

Occasional sections granted
to railroad

Miles

Kilometers

0   50   100

0   50   100

46. RAILROAD LAND GRANTS

After years of debate, Congress agreed to subvent construction of a series of transcontinental railroads, at least in part, through the surrender of vast reaches of the public domain. Directly, by way of federal grants, and indirectly, through state and local government action, 181 million acres of public land were given to railroad companies to help finance their projects. Seventy-nine railroads obtained either federal or state grants, or both. Of the three principal land-grant railroads, it was the holdings of the Northern Pacific that had a significant impact on Washington.

The Northern Pacific Railroad originally was the pet project of Josiah Perham, who dreamed of building it as a nonprofit excursion railway. Perham was unable to raise the required capital, and control eventually fell, first, to the powerful banker, Jay Cooke, and after his failure in the 1873 depression, to Henry Villard. Cooke modified the original route in order to accommodate his recent acquisition of the Oregon Steam Navigation Company and added two million acres of forested land in alternate sections along the Columbia River and through the Cowlitz River valley. A route map was then issued, in 1870, and the General Land Office removed projected railroad lands from sale and doubled the price for federal acreage in the even-numbered sections along the proposed route. A complication soon became evident: much of the land claimed by the Northern Pacific already was occupied by earlier arriving settlers.

Further confusing matters, the railroad filed for an amended route in 1872, suggesting an entry point into Washington 108 miles north of the initial route. Although Congress sought to reduce the confusion by creating a secondary zone of so-called "lieu lands" ten miles on each side of the tracks to replace land lost to prior title, numerous disagreements over ownership found their way into court. The most important of these was the Northern Pacific's challenge to title held by Guilford Miller of Whitman County. Litigation continued for several years, until finally the U.S. Supreme Court ruled in Miller's favored and pronounced valid settlers' claims antedating 1885. Congress acted soon after to indemnify the railroad with prime timberlands. The large holdings of the Northern Pacific Railroad within the state remained a sensitive issue—there was a popular attempt to force return of the granted lands to public ownership—because the railroad remained uncompleted for so long. The land remained in Northern Pacific hands, however: 1,280,409.50 acres in original land grants and 631, 252.88 acres of lieu lands.

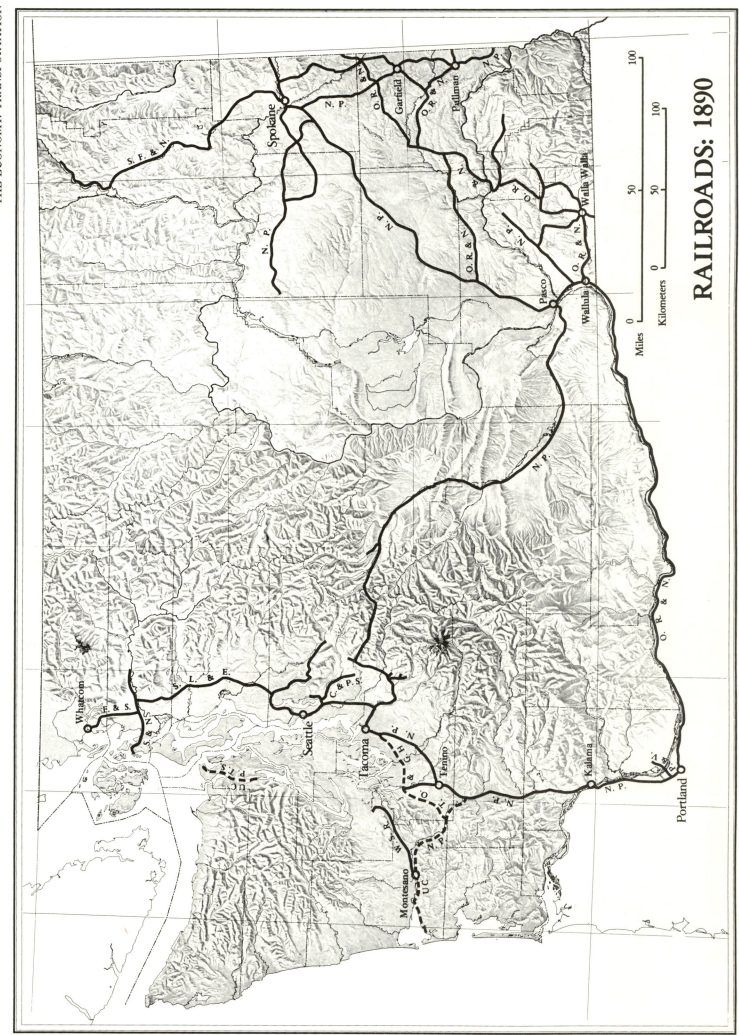

RAILROADS: 1890

Like settlers everywhere in the West, Washington's early immigrants were devout believers in the miracles to be wrought by the coming of the railroads. When that indefatigable advocate Asa Whitney succeeded in lobbying through the Congress appropriations for surveys of four potential routes, they were cheered to learn that the northernmost route would be traced by their territory's governor-designate, Isaac I. Stevens. Stevens ordered Captain George McClellan to survey a pass through Washington's Cascade Mountains while Stevens led a team of workers westward from the headwaters of the Mississippi. Since Congress took no immediate steps to authorize construction of a transcontinental railroad, in 1857, Stevens persuaded the state legislature to charter a Northern Pacific Railroad with a permissable capitalization of $15 million.

That project was stillborn, but a handful of frontier entrepreneurs did build local lines. Incorporated in 1858, the Cascade Railroad Company completed a portage tramway around the cascades of the Columbia River, utilizing wooden tracks previously installed by the military for use during Indian uprisings. The wood rails soon were encased with strap iron, and a small steam locomotive replaced animal power. The same firm extended a line between The Dalles and Celilo. The Oregon Steam Navigation Company absorbed and continued to operate these roads after obtaining a Washington charter in 1860. A second successful project was initiated by a Walla Walla physician, Dr. Dorsey S. Baker. Baker's Walla Walla and Columbia River Railroad, better known as the "Rawhide Railroad," connected Wallula and Walla Walla. The railroad was finished in 1873, but only after Walla Walla citizens provided help with funding the project's exension from Waiilatpu to their town. The first ten miles originally featured 4 × 6 fir rails, which wore out so quickly that Baker had his crews spike strap iron to the tops of the rails at curves. It was not true that the rails were covered with rawhide that the coyotes ate, as local storytellers claimed; it was true that the iron straps had an alarming tendency to wrap around the trains' wheels and sometimes spring through the wooden floor of the railroad's single passenger car.

The Oregon Railroad and Navigation Company (O. R. & N.) purchased Dorsey's line in 1881 and also acquired the Columbia and Puget Sound Railroad (C. & P. S.), which ran between Seattle and the Newcastle coalfields. In 1881 the O. R. & N. constructed a railroad from Portland, Oregon, to Wallula and branch lines from Walla Walla to Riparia and from Bolles to Dayton. It continued to extend lines in eastern Washington, connecting, among others, the communities of Connell and Moscow, Colfax, Starbuck and Pomeroy, and Pullman and Moscow, Idaho, by 1885. Through its subsidiary, the Oregon Improvement Company, O. R. & N. also controlled the Seattle and Northern Railroad (S. & N.), which skirted Samish Bay and then wound eastward along the north side of the Skagit River, serving that valley's miners and loggers.

A number of small, independent lines initiated service in the 1880s. The Bellingham Bay and British Columbia Railroad ran from the Bellingham settlements to Lynden and Glacier. The Fairhaven and Southern Railway Company (F. & S.), organized in 1888, connected Bellingham Bay residents with Vancouver, British Columbia. Port Townsend's inhabitants, hopeful that a rail link with Olympia, Tenino, and Tacoma would enable their community to cash in on its status as port of entry for the Puget Sound Customs District, organized the Port Townsend and Southern Railroad (P. T. S.) in 1887 and started construction three years later. Others—among them, the Tacoma, Olympia, and Grays Harbor Railroad (T. O. & G. H.), which was to connect Ocosta, on the southern edge of Grays Harbor, with Centralia, and the Columbia and Puget Sound Railroad (C. & P. S.), which travelled from Seattle southeast to Franklin—were acquired by the Northern Pacific Railroad (N. P.) as part of an effort to gain regional ascendency.

Armed with a federal charter and massive land grants, the Northern Pacific, under the direction of Jay Cooke, finally began construction westward from Duluth in February 1870. Workers in Washington started north from Kalama in May. Meanwhile, a fierce competition erupted over the location of the terminus of this long-awaited transcontinental railroad. Among such rivals as Olympia, Steilacoom, and Mukilteo, Seattle appeared to have a decided edge, and thus it was a rude shock to that town's citizens when the railroad chose the little village of Tacoma, on Commencement Bay, as terminal city in 1873. While Seattle attempted to build a railroad through Snoqualmie Pass to Walla Walla, the Tacoma Land Company, a subsidiary of the Northern Pacific Railroad, ballyhooed Tacoma's prospects, hiring George Francis Train, a balloonist and eccentric railroad entrepreneur who had promoted Omaha, to travel around the world in less than eighty days to advertise the new "London on the Pacific." The company also engaged the noted landscape architect Frederick Law Olmsted to design the city. (Olmsted obliged with a plan that, critics complained, featured plats shaped like fruits and vegetables—a design that was rejected as impractical by the company's profit-minded directors.)

The failure of Jay Cooke and Company in the depression of 1873 once again stalled completion of the Northern Pacific. Progress resumed in 1879, after control over the road was obtained by Henry Villard. The tracks begun at Kalama reached Spokane and continued east in 1881, while eastern crews crossed the Missouri River. The two sections were joined on the north bank of the Deer Lodge River in Montana early in September 1883. A Cascade branch was built through Stampede Pass and, after tunnelling through two miles of rock, entered Tacoma on July 3, 1887. By 1890 the Northern Pacific and the Oregon Railroad and Navigation Company were locked in a struggle to dominate rail traffic in Washington—a struggle in which they were soon to be joined by a third major force, James J. Hill's Great Northern Railroad.

RAILROADS: 1980

Miles
Kilometers

Bellingham
Everett
Seattle
Tacoma
Centralia
Portland
Wenatchee
Yakima
Spokane
Pasco
Walla Walla
Pullman

B. N.
C. M. S. P. & P.
C. F.

Washington closed out the nineteenth century in a burst of railroad building, but already the national trend toward consolidation of systems and concentration of control was evident regionally. Even before Robert Strahorn engineered the marriage of the Oregon Railroad and Navigation Company with the Union Pacific, the managers of the Oregon firm and the Northern Pacific had attempted to avoid further competition, damaging to the profits of both, by a pooling agreement that divided eastern Washington into two spheres of influence, with the Northern Pacific controlling the area north of the Clearwater and Snake rivers. Almost immediately, the Northern Pacific proceeded to violate the agreement by seizing control of the so-called Hunt System through the installation of a Northern Pacific board member, Charles B. Wright, as head of that railroad, which then constructed 123 miles of track in what was supposed to be O. R. & N. territory. The agreement broke down in 1889, but similar arrangements were clearly in the offing.

In the meantime, competition continued, and with it both consolidation of existing roads and new construction. Having penetrated the northwest, the Union Pacific gained entry to Puget Sound by acquiring control of the Port Townsend and Southern, Portland and Puget Sound, and Seattle and Northern railroads. The Northern Pacific obtained a majority interest in the Seattle, Lake Shore, and Eastern railroads in July 1890, hoping to block access to Seattle by the newest rival, James J. Hill's Great Northern Railroad, which was extended, nonetheless, through Idaho into Washington by early winter of 1893 and entered Seattle via the Fairhaven and Southern Railway Company and the Seattle and Montana Railway. Hill completed his transcontinental system in time to witness the collapse of his major rivals in 1893. He got control of the Northern Pacific during its reorganization in 1896 with help from the banker J. P. Morgan, but then found himself in a bitter struggle for railroad primacy with E. H. Harriman.

Harriman, Hill, and Morgan attempted to settle their differences by pooling their interests in a holding company, the Northern Securities Company, in 1901; but after that venture was declared illegal by the U.S. Supreme Court in 1904, they resumed their rivalry. Hill and Morgan's Great Northern and Northern Pacific built new track between Spokane and Vancouver, Washington, along the north bank of the Columbia River, creating the Spokane-Portland and Seattle Railway. The Union Pacific backed construction of the North Coast Railroad connecting Spokane to the Columbia and Yakima rivers, and also constructed the Washington Northern Railroad to Grays Harbor. In 1909 and 1910, however, the completion of another transcontinental line, the Chicago, Milwaukee, and St. Paul Railway, forced a truce between the other giants. The Union Pacific and Great Northern agreed to share the track of the Northern Pacific between Portland and Seattle for a period of ninety-nine years, and they formed, as a joint venture, the Camas Prairie Railroad, to be built along the north bank of the Snake River.

The arrival of the Milwaukee Road in Seattle, with a branch line to Tacoma, signalled an end to the era of major railroad construction in Washington. The years that followed saw the spread of consolidated control, curtailment of branch line operation, and a growing tendency toward joint use of tracks. The streamlining of service under federal management during World War I and the forced cutbacks of the 1930s furthered those trends. Although rail traffic in Washington rose to record levels during World War II, the postwar years witnessed more consolidation and shrinking service and revenues. The number of workers employed by railroads in Washington declined steadily, from 20,784 in 1953 to 12,350 a decade later. The Milwaukee Road went bankrupt in 1977, and by 1980 it had ended service on one thousand miles of track in Washington.

There remained in 1980 two major railroads, the Union Pacific (U. P.) and the Burlington Northern

(B. N.) and fourteen smaller lines, utilizing some 4,800 miles of track to carry freight. By 1984 track in use had shrunk to 4,600 miles, ninety percent of which are now used by the two principal roads. Further reductions are planned by the Burlington Northern Railroad, which wants to abandon over 433 miles of track in the state. Although passenger service also has been reduced. Although Congress created the National Railroad Passenger Corporation (AMTRAK) in 1970 to salvage rail passenger service, and national ridership has increased from 12.7 million in 1971 to 19 million in 1982, service in western states was drastically curtailed because of federal budget cuts in 1981. In Washington the original cuts proposed would have ended all but two runs: the Empire Builder (Seattle–Chicago) and the Coast Starlight (Seattle–Los Angeles), but a compromise was effected which ended service between Vancouver, B.C., and Seattle, but retained, subject to future ridership and funding levels, service on four routes utilizing over eight hundred miles of Burlington Northern track in the state. In addition to the Empire Builder and Coast Starlight, the Pioneer (Seattle–Portland–Salt Lake City) and the Mount Rainier (Seattle-Portland) were retained.

The future of Washington's railroads is uncertain. Although the number of passengers served declined from 672,078 to 450,541 between 1980 and 1982, in the face of a national increase in ridership in the same period, and the railroads' share of the intercity freight business has declined, the use of the railroads for transporting coal, grain, pulp, paper, and wood products remains at high levels. Twenty-five percent of all commodities shipped in Washington still are transported by rail. Currently, AMTRAK and the State Department of Transportation are cooperating in efforts to improve and expand rail passenger service, and a state rail plan, worked out by the Department of Transportation and administered by the Washington Utilities and Transportation Commission, has been formulated to provide a framework for rail-service planning.

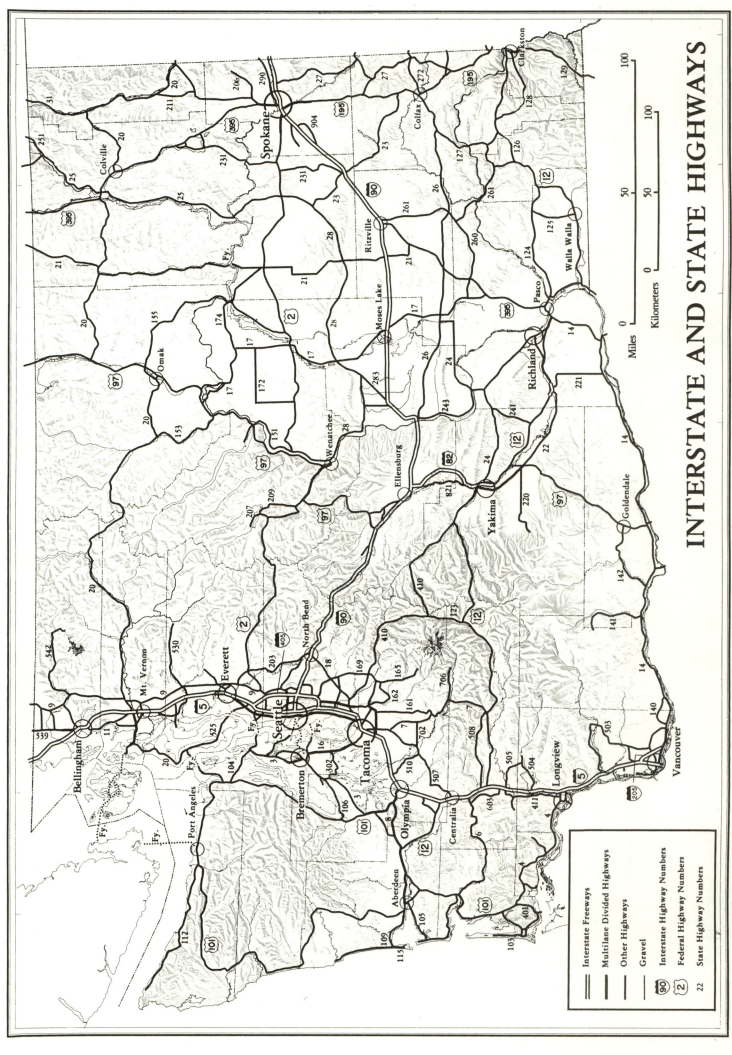

INTERSTATE AND STATE HIGHWAYS

	Interstate Freeways
	Multilane Divided Highways
	Other Highways
	Gravel
90	Interstate Highway Numbers
2	Federal Highway Numbers
22	State Highway Numbers

Miles

Kilometers

0   50   100

0   50   100

© 1988 by the University of Oklahoma Press

Washington's highway system, like those of other states today, includes part of the federal interstate network inaugurated in 1955. Representing an investment of over $10 billion, the state system includes 714 miles of interstate highways, 214 miles of other freeways and expressways, and 7,178 miles of principal and minor arterials. Together with major and minor collectors and local roadways, the system totals 95,429 miles of roads. The annual total of vehicle miles accumulated on Washington's roads continues to rise with increases in truck traffic (up 97 percent between 1950 and 1964 alone), registered vehicles in the state (which increased 60 percent between 1970 and 1982), and the tourist industry: in 1970 an estimated 11.4 billion vehicle miles were travelled on state roadways; by 1982 the total had climbed 51 percent to 17.7 billion. Despite rising maintenance and repair costs and restricted revenues, the highway system is still being extended. In 1987 a long-delayed part of Interstate 90 between Bellevue and Seattle was finally under construction; crews were completing Interstates 82 and 182 in central Washington; and Hood Canal once again had been spanned with a floating bridge. Washington's highway system, compared with those of other states, is extensive and modern.

It was not always so. During the first decade of settlement, there were no real roads, not even between early population clusters like Cowlitz Landing and Tumwater. Residents utilized waterborne transportation whenever possible. The Indian and game trails were passable routes of travel only for those on foot. The early wagon roads, in the words of one pioneer, "just growed. . . . A team would stall with an empty wagon down hill." The stagecoaches that were introduced in the 1860s, as Ezra Meeker remembered, were no more than "mudwagons in which passengers were conveyed . . . over either the roughest corduroy or deepest mud, the one bruising the muscles, the other straining the nerves in the anticipation of being dumped into the bottomless pit of mud." Not surprisingly, early petitions for territorial status seemed to rest primarily upon the need for a system of usable roads.

Before Washington's separation in 1853, the Oregon Territorial Legislature had made some effort to improve wagon roads; and in 1853, Congress had granted $20,000 for a road between Forts Steilacoom and Walla Walla. The latter was never more than a rough trail 234.5 miles long, and the first to venture forth on it nearly died of starvation. Federal monies also were appropriated for the building of the Mullan Road to connect Fort Walla Walla with Fort Benton, 624 miles east. The project cost $230,000 and took seven years, and although Lieutenant John Mullan boasted in his final report that the resulting road was as good as any turnpike through similar terrain, a local priest, Father Joseph Cataldo, summed up the views of those who used it: "The Mullan Trail wasn't much of a road. . . . We used to say, 'Captain Mullan just made enough of a trail so he could get back out of here.'"

Washington's territorial legislature moved swiftly but not always effectually to better transportation facilities. Some ten road measures became law during the first session. Roads were constructed or improved chiefly between settlements in the lower Cowlitz River area and Seattle, with branches to Grays Harbor and connections to the principal immigrant trails. Attempts failed to cut trails across the Snoqualmie and Naches passes in the late 1850s; used briefly at the height of the Indian Wars between 1858 and 1860, the unsurveyed, ungraded paths quickly vanished in the luxuriance of underbrush and undeterred saplings. Pioneer road builders tried again to build a road across Snoqualmie Pass in 1867, with $4,000 provided by the territorial legislature and King County, but the trail constructed was so steep and narrow that not even the U.S. Mail mule could use it. Few roads were surveyed, fewer still graded. Road builders sometimes left stumps in the right-of-way. The dust of summer and mud of winter were only partially allayed by using logs laid side by side (corduroy) or planks laid end to end.

Statehood witnessed gradual improvement. The first state-constructed highway connected Fairhaven (Bellingham) to Republic in the northeast quarter of the state by way of Marblemount and Twisp. When completed in 1896, this road was little better than a cattle trail, and lacking maintenance, it soon became impassable. The nationwide bicycle craze of the late nineteenth century, the increasing population's demand for better roads, and the efforts of the Good Roads lobby eventually did bring results. The more sophisticated use of blasting and the introduction of trucks and mechanized construction equipment near the close of World War I coincided with long-term federal support for the construction and repair of highways. Beginning with a congressional appropriation of $71,884 in 1916, federal funding for Washington road building grew apace with state spending, under the direction after 1905 of a State Highway Department. By 1925 the state's annual highway budget, including federal monies, had climbed to $6,688,829, compared with $111,800 allocated for the entire twelve-year period following statehood. There were 763 automobiles reported on Washington's roads in 1906, 70,000 in 1916, and the number grew rapidly every year thereafter.

The post-World War II boom, however, created an unprecedented need for new and better designed and surfaced highways. As a result Congress approved the establishment of the interstate highway system. In the single decade from 1950 to 1960 more money was spent on Washington's highways than in the previous forty years.

EVOLUTION OF WASHINGTON PORTS

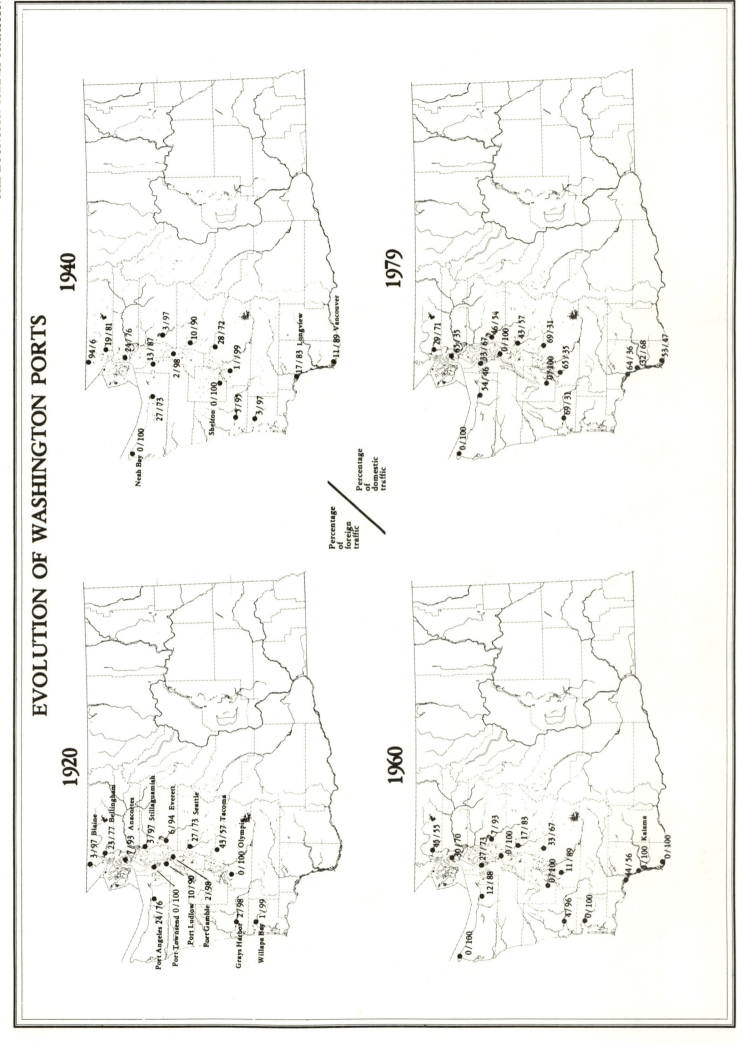

1920

3 / 97 Blaine
23 / 77 Bellingham
7 / 93 Anacortes
3 / 97 Stillaguamish
6 / 94 Everett
27 / 73 Seattle
43 / 57 Tacoma
0 / 100 Olympia
Port Angeles 24 / 76
Port Townsend 0 / 100
Port Ludlow 10 / 90
Port Gamble 2 / 98
Grays Harbor 27 / 98
Willapa Bay 1 / 99

1940

94 / 6
19 / 81
24 / 76
13 / 87
3 / 97
2 / 98
10 / 90
28 / 72
1 / 99
Shelton 0 / 100
3 / 93
3 / 97
17 / 83 Longview
11 / 89 Vancouver
Neah Bay 0 / 100
27 / 73

Percentage of foreign traffic / Percentage of domestic traffic

1960

45 / 55
30 / 70
27 / 73
7 / 93
0 / 100
17 / 83
33 / 67
12 / 88
11 / 89
0 / 100
Kalama
0 / 100
44 / 56
4 / 96
0 / 100
0 / 100

1979

29 / 71
65 / 35
33 / 67
46 / 54
0 / 100
43 / 57
69 / 31
54 / 46
0 / 100
65 / 35
69 / 31
69 / 31
0 / 100
64 / 36
32 / 68
33 / 47

The early decades of the nineteenth century witnessed a growing trade in the North Pacific, and after the settlement of the Oregon Question and the California and Fraser River gold discoveries, the waters of Washington's coastal harbors and Puget Sound sheltered bustling ports. Meanwhile, overland transportation was retarded by the huge stands of nearly impenetrable forests, the vast distances between settlements, and the Cascade Range. As a result waterborne transportation flourished and the region's numerous accessible ports prospered further. The Hudson's Bay Company steamers continued, as they had before the boundary settlement, to link Puget Sound and coastal communities as far south as the Columbia with Victoria, British Columbia, which was the principal trade center north of San Francisco until late in the nineteenth century. The steamers were joined in the coastal trade by vessels of the Pacific Coast Steamship Company (whose ships could be found from the Isthmus of Panama to Alaska) and scores of small, locally built steamboats and schooners which competed for the passenger and freight traffic of Puget Sound and its rivers. The availability of logs and lumber made early ports of Port Ludlow, Port Gamble, Olympia, Seattle, Anacortes, and Bellingham Bay. The headquarters of the U.S. Customs Bureau for the region at Port Townsend drew at least the honest shipmasters there.

The 1880s and 1890s wrought important changes. A trans-Pacific trade linked Washington ports with Hawaii, Samoa, Fiji, China, and South and Central America. A regional commerce previously notable for the large number of small, competing independent shipping lines underwent concentration and consolidation. Regularly scheduled routes bound Victoria, Olympia, and Port Townsend; Hood Canal and Seabeck; Olympia and Tacoma; Seattle and Freeport, Port Blakely, and Port Madison. Regional railroad systems reduced local reliance upon inland and river steamers. Completion of the transcontinental railroads enormously increased the port activity of terminal cities like Tacoma, Seattle, and Everett and increased, also, the volume of foreign trade at those ports. The growth of Washington's population and economy, and the dramatic impact of the railroads, permitted the expansion of the region's waterborne commerce in spite of the nationwide depression of the early 1890s.

Seattle improved on an early lead over other Washington ports in the first years of the twentieth century, partly because of her role as supplier for the Alaskan gold rush but also because of a Japanese shipping line's decision to establish regular service with Seattle. Between 1900 and 1940, Japan was the state's principal waterborne trading partner; fully 40 percent of the foreign commerce of Washington ports was with Japan. Foreign trade generally increased by 114 percent from 1910 to 1920. Yet coastal and regional domestic trade accounted for most of the traffic, and much of the growth in this trade was spurred by the opening of the Panama Canal. The growth in trade volume, and diversification of the products and services involved, demanded more

efficient harbor management. Large ports like Seattle, and even smaller ones like Bellingham, experimented with the structuring of port-district governance through commissions.

Seaborne traffic continued to grow in the years after 1920, but perhaps more important were increases both in exports by manufacturers and the variety of trade items. Since 1940 the continued importance of the wood-products industry and the increased economic roles of Washington's aerospace, petroleum refining, and aluminum industries have been reflected in trade patterns. A few Washington ports specialize in foreign trades—Longview, Vancouver, Grays Harbor, Anacortes, and Port Angeles—importing crude oil, in the case of Anacortes and Port Angeles, and exporting logs, primarily. Yet domestic traffic remains the dominant feature of port activity in Washington. In the 1980s ports like Tacoma and Seattle exemplified the extent and diversification of that traffic. Tacoma became a major shipping and receiving point with a total tonnage by 1979 of 15,192,550. Foreign imports accounted for 2,214,871 short tons and included aluminum ores and concentrates, crude petroleum, crude rubber, and iron and steel scrap. Exports in 1979 totaled 8,192,946 short tons. Logs, wood chips, agricultural commodities, and animal feeds were the main exports. Seattle in 1979 recorded foreign exports of 3,616,701 tons (primarily, lumber, paper and paperboard, wheat and other grain products, and fruit) and foreign imports of 4,983,366 tons. Domestic trade reached 11,438,363 tons.

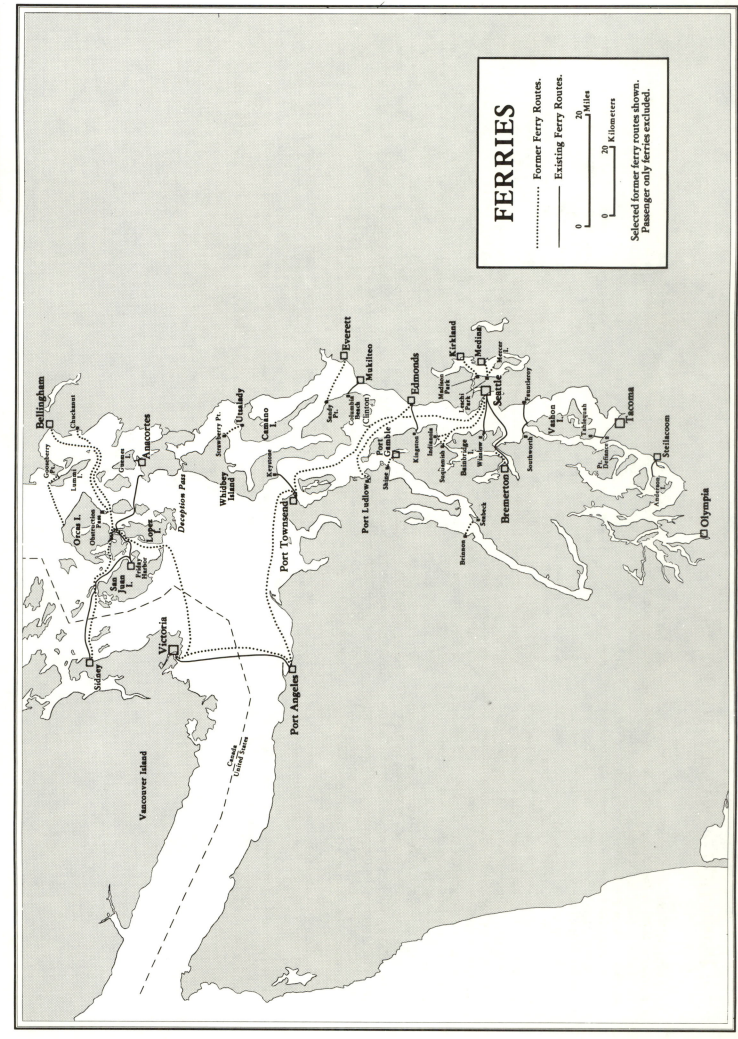

FERRIES

.... Former Ferry Routes.

——— Existing Ferry Routes.

Selected former ferry routes shown.
Passenger only ferries excluded.

Equipped with thirty-eight ferries worth an estimated $200 million, Washington claims to operate the world's largest ferry fleet. Nine coordinated routes, employing twenty ferries with a daily capacity of 30,000 passengers and 2,100 vehicles, crisscross Puget Sound. From Seattle's ferry terminal in Elliott Bay, ferries carry thousands of commuters to Winslow and Bremerton; the Fauntleroy Terminal in West Seattle provides service to Vashon Island and Southworth on the Kitsap Peninsula. A small ferry, in recent years *Hiyu*, connects Tahlequah at the southern end of Vashon Island with Point Defiance Park and Tacoma. Another runs between the historic town of Steilacoom and McNeil and Anderson islands. Puget Sound's other routes—between Edmonds and Kingston, and Mukilteo and Clinton on Whidbey Island—are serviced by large ferries making frequent runs, as is the route connecting Anacortes with the San Juan Islands and Vancouver Island. There is considerable traffic also on ferries serving the route crossing between Keystone, at the midpoint of the west coast of Whidbey Island, and Port Townsend and the Olympic Peninsula. During summer months, when tourists join the state's commuters, the ferries average four hundred trips and eighteen hundred miles a day.

This impressive system had its origins in the Mosquito Fleet, a collection of sail- and steam-powered vessels that linked Washington's port towns in the years before the completion of a regional network of railroads and highways. The advent of automobiles encouraged modification of some of the steamers so that vehicles could be carried on the open decks. Often, sponsons were attached, additional deck space was constructed, and automobile-sized ports cut above the water line of the hull. In 1903 a side-wheeler, *City of Seattle*, initiated ferry service between the main docks of Seattle's waterfront and West Seattle, and soon after cross-sound service was inaugurated. From various points on the eastern shore of Puget sound, ferries soon made scheduled stops at Bremerton, Port Orchard, Port Blakely, and other places on the Kitsap Peninsula. By 1919, Seattle was connected by regular service with Harper, on Vashon Island. Small vessels also ferried passengers across Lake Washington, tying Seattle to Kirkland, Medina, Bellevue, and points east.

By the mid-1920s an improved road system had robbed the Mosquito Fleet of a once-profitable coastal business on the sound, and the rapidly increasing volume of automobile and truck traffic rendered the passenger steamers' makeshift ferrying efforts a losing proposition as well. Operating ferries designed to carry vehicles and comparatively large numbers of passengers, the Puget Sound Navigation Company's Black Ball Line inexorably tightened control over the business between the 1920s and the 1940s, driving out the small, independent operators. State regulation of ferry service increased also, however; and in 1948 a confrontation ensued when the Black Ball Line insisted on a thirty percent rate increase, supposedly to offset workers' wage demands, and the Washington's Public Utilities Commission refused any more than a ten percent increase. A shutdown of ferry service was followed by negotiations, which in December 1950 resulted in state purchase of the company's intrastate facilities and sixteen of its twenty-one vessels. Since then the state system of ferry services, together with the bridges later built across Lake Washington and Hood Canal, has grown and has become increasingly integrated.

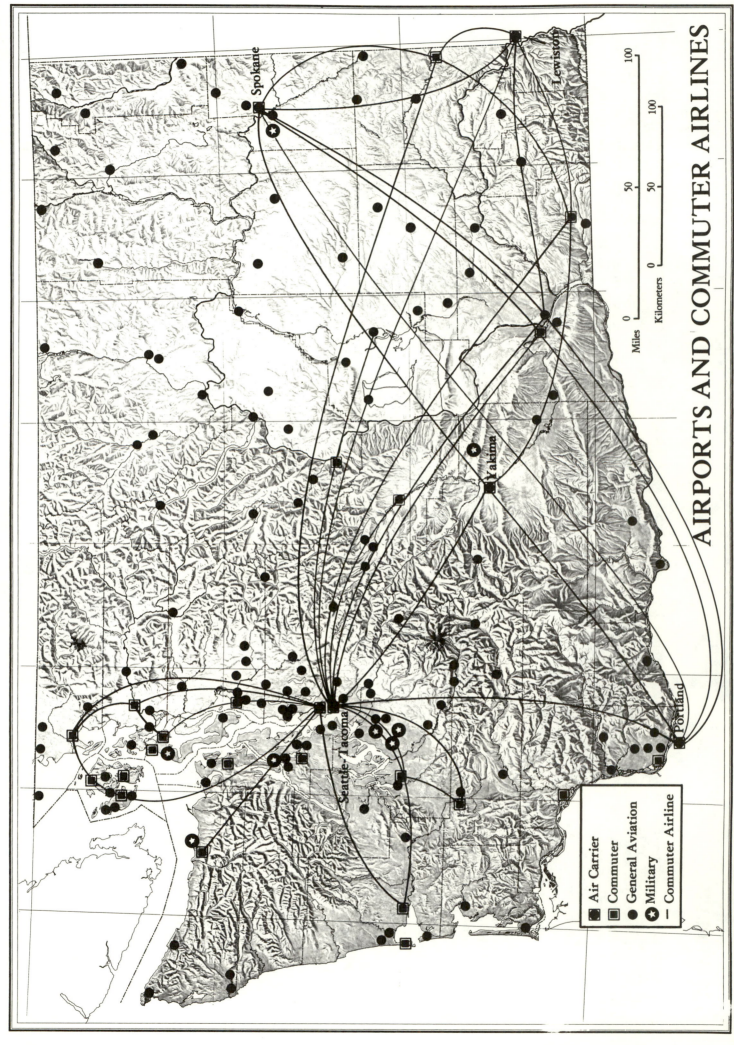

AIRPORTS AND COMMUTER AIRLINES

Spokane

Lewiston

Yakima

Seattle-Tacoma

Portland

■	Air Carrier
◼	Commuter
●	General Aviation
✪	Military
—	Commuter Airline

Miles 0   50   100

Kilometers 0   50   100

In the early years of this century Washington shared the nation's unrestrained fascination with human flight. By 1910 a small nucleus of daredevils like L. Guy Mecklem flew biplanes on a regular circuit of fairs, amusement parks, and circuses in the Pacific Northwest. World War I demonstrated the practical potential of the airplane, and by the early 1920s an increasing number of aircraft used northwest skies, many of them war-surplus planes that sold for an average of $300. Although the need for regulation was fiercely debated, there were no requirements or restrictions concerning air travel until 1926, except for a period between February 1918 and July 1919 when President Wilson imposed a ban on civilian flights over war zones.

The federal government was the first to exert some influence over the nature and direction of air travel. The Air Mail Act of 1925, which resulted in U.S. Post Office contracts with the infant air carriers to transport domestic mail, spurred the systemization of the industry, particularly in regard to airport ground operations and airways. This trend was abetted further by the passage in 1926 of the Air Commerce Act. At that time there existed, throughout the United States, barely two thousand miles of airways equipped with the ground-based navigational aids necessary for night and all-weather flying in the years before in-flight instrumentation and radios. In the late 1920s the federal government undertook the installation of lighting at and between airstrips. The airway between Portland, Oregon, and Spokane lay partly up the Columbia River gorge between Cape Horn, which is east of Washougal, and Lyle, Washington, northwest of The Dalles, Oregon. The area was susceptible to dense fog; airplanes often had to fly below 250-foot ceilings. Technicians had to find a way to fasten lights along the steep walls of the gorge, twelve on the Washington side, eleven on the Oregon side. At one location workers used a logging company's flume to get equipment to the selected site. A large sled was built to carry the materials a half mile down the gorge.

By 1927, when the U.S. Postal Service's Airways Division was transferred to the Commerce Department, the future appeared bright for commercial aviation. Air passengers and freight services increasingly were available in most sections of the country, offered by such pioneers as Seattle's William Boeing, who had begun manufacturing airplanes in 1915 and operated the Boeing Air Transport System from 1927 until 1934. As air traffic grew, so too did governmental involvement. The federal government assumed control over airway traffic control stations in 1937, and this role was strengthened with the establishment in June 1938 of the Civil Aeronautics Authority, which was destined to grow into first the Federal Aviation Agency and later, as part of the Department of Transportation, the Federal Aviation Administration. The agency was charged with sole responsibility for the regulation of the nation's air space and the development of a common civil and military system of air navigation and traffic control. Federal monies also became available, beginning in 1946, for the construction and improvement of airport runways and facilities. Federal aid between 1947 and 1970 totaled $1.7 billion nationally. Matching grants since 1970, with increased funding levels since 1981, have been utilized in the state of Washington as elsewhere. Between 1971 and 1981, Washington received $88 million.

Washington's airport facilities received no state assistance until 1947, when the legislature passed the Aeronautics Commission Act. Before 1945 only cities and counties possessed the authority to finance and operate airports. The Municipal Airports Act of 1945 legalized the formation of county airport districts for the same purpose, but this instrument has been used only once, in the case of Vashon Island's airport district. A more popular recent option has been the use of port districts, and twenty-five Washington airports are operated under their aegis. For the first two decades of the State Aeronautics Commission's existence annual state appropriations for airport use averaged $75,000. Most of this

money was spent on search-and-rescue operations, safety-education programs, and publication of maps and pilots' guidebooks. Then in 1967 the legislature established a pilot registration fee and an aviation fuel tax, the revenue from which is made available to the commission for distribution. The State Airport Aid Program allotted $2,650,300 between 1967 and 1982.

Currently about 26,000 pilots and 6,500 general aviation aircraft are registered in Washington, and state officials have estimated that this represents one-third of the actual number of pilots and two-thirds of the planes in use. There are 390 airports in the state, including ten military fields, thirteen seaplane landing sites, and eighty-eight heliports. In addition, the state owns eighteen emergency fields. Passenger air travel in Washington is increasing about 6 percent per year. Ninety percent of the state's population resides within sixty minutes' drive of an airport providing major airline service and within thirty minutes' drive of one with commuter service. Almost everyone lives thirty minutes away from a field offering unscheduled air taxi service. As one of the nation's top twenty passenger terminals and five busiest cargo airports, Seattle-Tacoma International Airport accounts for 85 percent of all scheduled enplanements in the state, and in the two decades since 1962 there has been a 479 percent growth in the number of passengers there. Economy moves by the scheduled airlines reduced the number of Washington airports serviced by them, between 1970 and 1982, from eleven to four: Seattle-Tacoma, with ten passenger airlines and three cargo airlines; Spokane, with four airlines; and Pasco and Yakima, with one each. Many of the communities that have lost certificated airline service since 1970 are served by four commuter airlines which use twelve regional airports, the four major airline airports, and two reliever airports. The State Department of Transportation reports that approximately 400,000 persons now fly on commuter airlines each year.

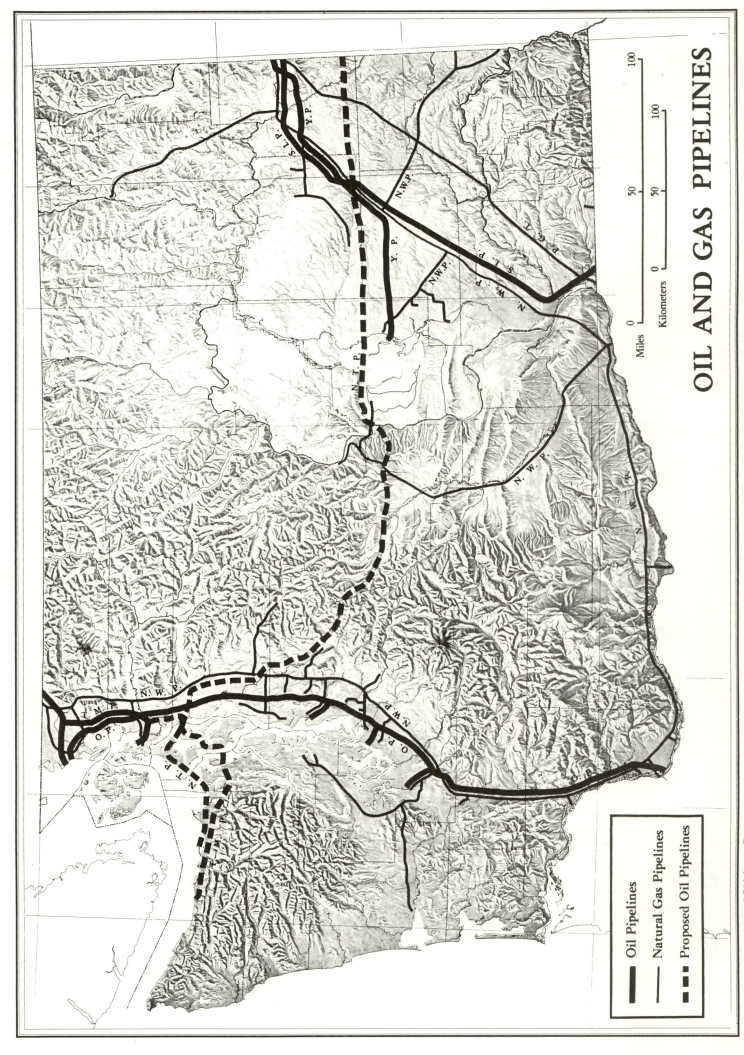

OIL AND GAS PIPELINES

Oil Pipelines
Natural Gas Pipelines
Proposed Oil Pipelines

53. OIL AND GAS PIPELINES

Washington is not a producer of crude oil or natural gas, but it does possess eight refineries and several large terminals for receiving, processing, and storing crude oil. Petroleum supplies more than half, and natural gas supplies twenty percent, of the total energy used in the Pacific Northwest, and thus pipelines play an important role in providing the region's energy needs. Four natural gas companies and three petroleum pipelines serve the state. Natural gas first was introduced to Washington following approval by the Federal Power Commission of an application by Pacific Northwest Pipeline Corporation to bring it to the area through a 1,466-mile pipeline from New Mexico. Later natural gas from Canada's Peace River region was made accessible by a connection with Canada's Westcoast Transmission Company pipeline. The most recent gas pipeline, completed in De-

cember 1961 by the Pacific Gas Transmission Company, taps Alberta's reserves and traverses Washington's southeastern corner en route to the Oregon-California border. Most of this gas is delivered to Pacific Gas and Electric Company's California market, but some is distributed to Washington customers through an agreement with Pacific Northwest Pipeline Corporation. The state's oil pipelines include the Olympic, which begins on Puget Sound and extends south to Portland and Eugene, Oregon; Chevron's Salt Lake City pipeline, which originates in Utah and penetrates eastern Washington and Oregon by way of southern Idaho; and the Yellowstone pipeline, which connects refineries in Wyoming and Montana with Spokane via northern Idaho.

Nationally, pipeline development only became a significant enterprise in the 1870s, and long-range, large-

dimension systems came in the 1920s, supplanting the coal gas manufactured earlier. Washington's network is even more recent. The first successful venture was launched in 1954. Government regulation, too, is a comparatively new phenomenon. Vested in the Federal Power Commission, it began at the national level in 1938. Washington also has its own regulatory agency, the State Utilities and Transportation Commission, which is empowered to oversee facilities, rates, and service.

Among the serious proposals for additional pipelines in the 1980s were the Northern Tier Pipeline (N.T.P.) and the Transmountain Pipeline (T.M.P.). Part of the N.T.P. would be under Puget Sound, a proposal that has alarmed environmental groups.

PART XII

THE ECONOMY: PRODUCTION

FARMS AND FARM ACREAGE

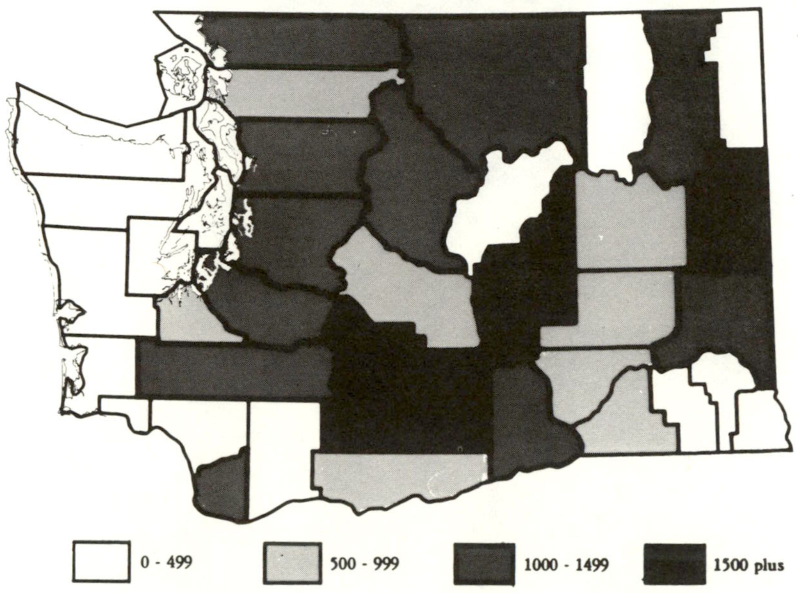

TOTAL LAND IN FARMS ('000 acres)

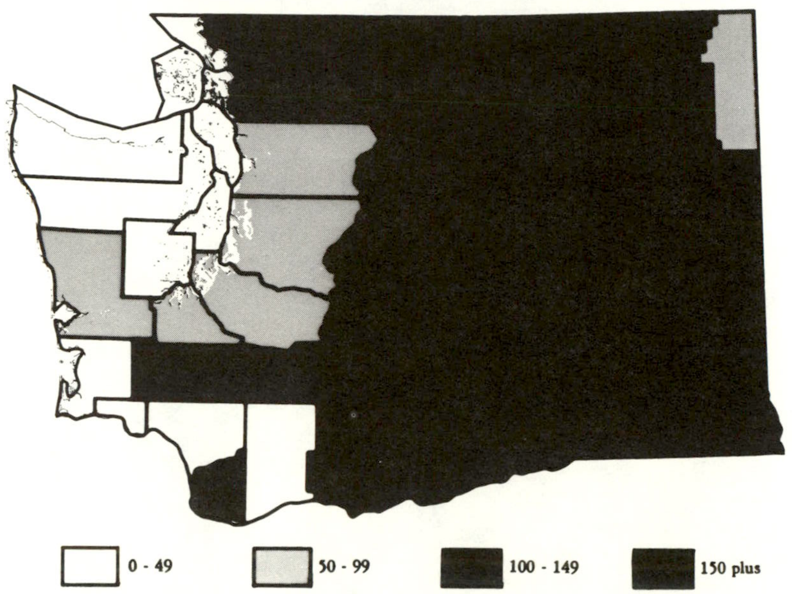

150 plus

100 - 149

50 - 99

0 - 49

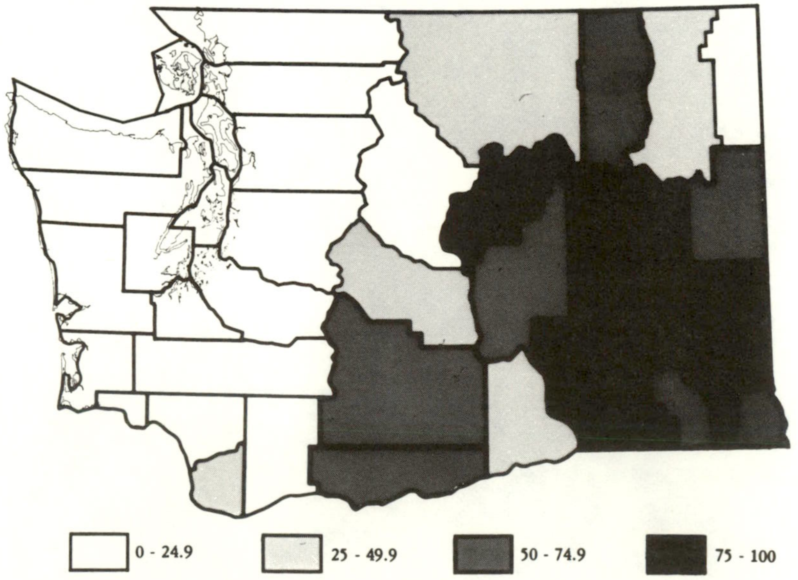

WOODLAND AS A PERCENTAGE OF COUNTY AREA

45 plus

30 - 44.9

15 - 29.9

0 - 14.9

TOTAL NUMBER OF FARMS

1500 plus

1000 - 1499

500 - 999

0 - 499

FARM ACREAGE AS A PERCENTAGE OF COUNTY AREA

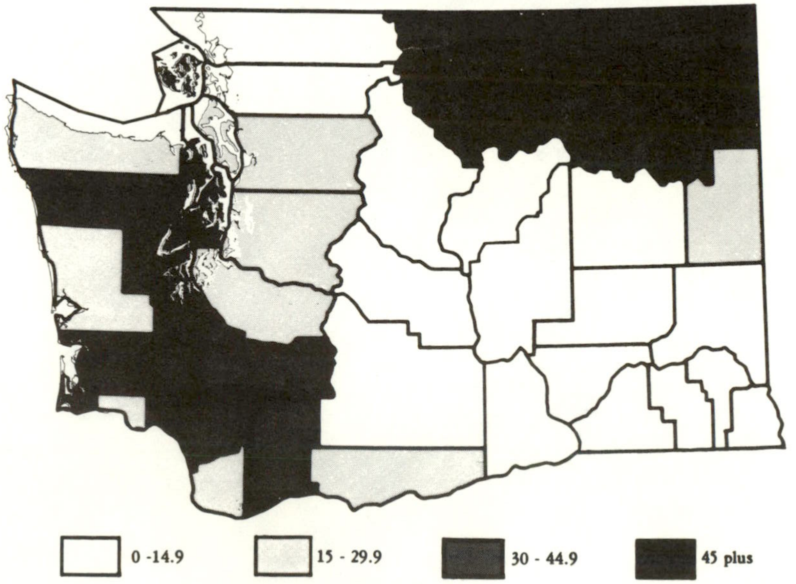

75 - 100

50 - 74.9

25 - 49.9

0 - 24.9

54. FARMS AND FARM ACREAGE

During the past century the farm acreage of Washington has soared from about four million acres in 1890 to more than seventeen million in 1978. The area farmed increased regularly and continuously until the mid-1960s. Since then there has been some decline because of factors such as the spread of urban areas, increased land devoted to parks and wilderness areas, and the demand for land for transportation purposes, including airports.

The most dramatic increase in farm acreage came in the 1890s, coinciding with the opening of new markets in the eastern United States and elsewhere as a result of the initiation of transcontinental rail routes and greatly expanded freighter traffic from Washington ports to the Orient, Alaska, and Europe. The total acreage increased from 4.2 million to 8.5 million between 1890 and 1900, and the improved acreage from 1.8 million to 3.4 million. The following decade saw further great increases from 8.5 million to 11.7 million acres, but thereafter the absolute and proportional increases were smaller. By 1930, 13.5 million acres were being farmed, about half of that amount as cropland. At the end of World War II the farm acreage totalled close to 17 million, and it continued to increase into the 1960s, when in 1964 it topped 19 million acres. This amount has since dropped to about 17 million acres once more.

During the same period, from 1890 to the present, the number of farms has fluctuated more dramatically. From 18,056 farms in 1890, the numbers increased rapidly in the next few decades: 33,262 in 1900; 56,192 in 1910; 66,288 in 1920; and 73,202 in 1930. Despite the Great Depression and the accompanying collapse of businesses in other sectors of the economy, the number of farms remained fairly steady, although production declined as demands dropped and profits plummeted. Then increased demands for food and other agricultural products during World War II led to a rapid revival of farming, and by 1945 79,887 farms were in operation. Since then the numbers have dropped sharply as the smaller family farms have been sold and the land combined in ever larger holdings. By 1950 there were 10,000 fewer farms in operation, and twenty years later the total had dropped to approximately 40,000, barely half what it had been in 1945. In 1978 there were 37,730 farms in the state.

The size of farms has changed also during the past century. In 1890 the average farm was 231.4 acres in size, rising to 256 acres in 1900. Thereafter for the next few decades it dropped slowly in size, until in 1930 it was 190.9 acres. Since World War II there has been a marked reverse trend—as the number of farms has dropped, the size of farms has increased. In 1978 the average Washington farm covered 451 acres. Averages for a state as varied in its physical qualities as Washington are largely meaningless. In 1978, Ferry County, with only 200 farms and most of its acreage in pasture or mixed woodland-pasture, averaged 3,974 acres per farm. Nine other counties, all of them in eastern Washington and all of them important crop-producing counties, had farms that averaged more than 1,000 acres:

Lincoln (1,888), Asotin (1,844), Adams (1,680), Garfield (1,652), Columbia (1,533), Klickitat (1,472), Douglas (1,158), Whitman (1,090), and Walla Walla (1,028).

By contrast, farms in western Washington were very much smaller. Kitsap County's 260 farms averaged only 31 acres. Others with average acreages less than 100 were King (45), Pierce (59), Snohomish (68), Clark (80), Whatcom (88), Island, (89), and Mason (95). Chelan County (97) was the only eastern Washington county with an average of less than 100 acres.

The importance of agriculture in eastern Washington's land use and, by inference, its economy is clearly indicated in the map at the lower left, which shows farm acreage as a percentage of the county area. Seven of the twenty counties of eastern Washington have more than 75 percent of their acreage in farms, and another seven have between 50 percent and 74 percent. Of the remaining six counties only two—Chelan and Pend Oreille—have less than 25 percent in farmland. By contrast, the only western Washington county with more than 25 percent in farmland is Clark County.

The last of the four maps shown here concerns woodland as a percentage of total county acreage. In two areas of the state woodland comprises a considerable portion of the total: northeastern Washington, where Pend Oreille, Stevens, and Ferry counties each have more than 45 percent of their land area in woodland; and in a group of southwestern counties, including part of the Olympic Peninsula, where 30 percent to 44.9 percent of the land is woodland.

MAJOR AGRICULTURAL PRODUCTS

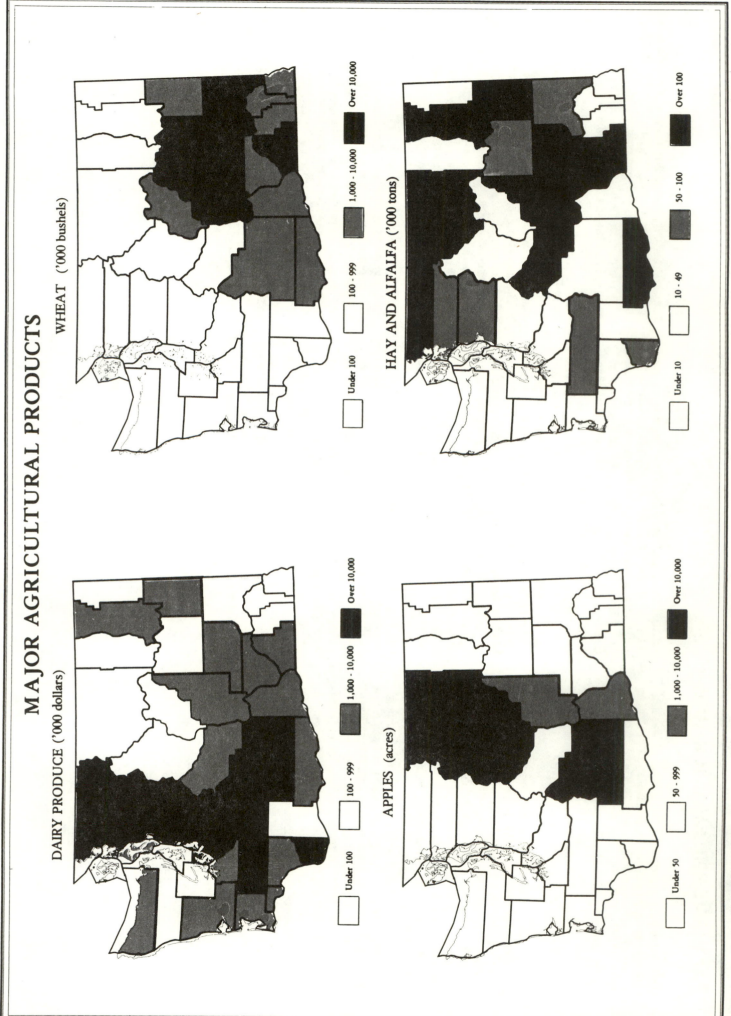

WHEAT ('000 bushels)

Under 100

100 - 999

1,000 - 10,000

Over 10,000

HAY AND ALFALFA ('000 tons)

Under 10

10 - 49

50 - 100

Over 100

DAIRY PRODUCE ('000 dollars)

Under 100

100 - 999

1,000 - 10,000

Over 10,000

APPLES (acres)

Under 50

50 - 999

1,000 - 10,000

Over 10,000

55. MAJOR AGRICULTURAL PRODUCTS

Although during the past century there have been great changes in the relative importance of a large proportion of the agricultural products grown or processed in the state of Washington, each of the products shown in these maps had achieved statewide significance by 1900, and each has maintained a high ranking ever since.

The rise of dairy farming as one of the state's principal agricultural activities is closely linked to improvements in the technologies of transportation, refrigeration, and processing and packaging. Before 1890 relatively small amounts of fresh milk were sold more than a half dozen miles from the farm, and many urban dwellers, like virtually all rural dwellers, depended for their milk on the family cow. Butter and cheese enjoyed wider hinterlands, especially after the establishment in the 1880s and 1890s of many commercial creameries in or close to the major urban settlements of the Puget Sound region. Rail transportation—especially electric railways, including the interurbans—helped speed up the transfer of milk from farm to dairy or creamery, and the distribution of dairy products from factories to retail outlets, but it was the advent of motor transportation that had the most widespread impact. As the numbers of vehicles multiplied so did the number and mileage of roads in rural areas. Thus by the end of World War I the metropolitan milksheds of Seattle, Tacoma, and Spokane reached far into the adjacent counties, and with the introduction of refrigeration tankers the growth in the size of regions from which the milk could be collected

for processing at the larger creameries—Carnation and Darigold among them—resulted in the demise of many small dairies and creameries. Today the dairy industry is heavily concentrated in a tier of counties on the west side of the Cascades—from Whatcom County, long the number-one producer, in the north to Clark County in the south. Processing is even more concentrated, with a half dozen plants serving all of western Washington and some eastern Washington counties as well.

Wheat, which was grown in Washington as early as the 1820s, did not become a major crop until more than a half century later, when the rolling Palouse Hills—hitherto used, if used at all, for range farming—began to be plowed under and planted to wheat. Good transportation was the key to growth in this, as in all economic development. In the early years the Columbia River and its tributaries were used to move the grain to urban markets in western Oregon and Washington, as well as for shipment overseas, but it was the expansion of railroads throughout the Palouse region that triggered the explosive growth of production that occurred in the 1880s and 1890s. Wheat sacks and transshipment by barge in the early years were replaced by grain elevators for storage and railcars that could move large quantities quickly to the ports of Portland, Tacoma, and Seattle. Meanwhile, in the rolling wheatfields with their often precipitous slopes, special techniques were being developed to plow and harvest the crops, and at Washington State University (then the State College of Wash-

ington) researchers were developing new and improved strains of wheat to increase yields and to resist disease and the vagaries of climate, among other things. The wheat region, which remains most concentrated in southeast Washington, especially in Whitman County, was extended northwards and westwards beyond the Palouse region as reclamation of the dry steppe of the Columbia Basin was achieved.

Washington's most famous crop, if not its most valuable in terms of value of production, is apples, of which the state produces a third or more of the nation's total. The industry is the product largely of twentieth-century investments in irrigation improvements and storage technology. Although the orchards are confined largely to the irrigated benchlands along the Columbia, Yakima, Okanogan, and Wenatchee rivers, many other counties east and west of the Cascades produce modest harvests. Many varieties of apples are grown, but two of them dominate production—red delicious and golden delicious.

Although hay is produced in some quantity in all thirty-nine counties, alfalfa is grown largely on irrigated lands in the Columbia Basin. A large proportion of the alfalfa crop and a much smaller proportion of other hay crops are shipped out of their counties of production, in particular to the dairy counties of western Washington.

Together these four agricultural products had a total value in 1985 of approximately $1.5 billion, slightly less than 50 percent of the state's total agricultural product.

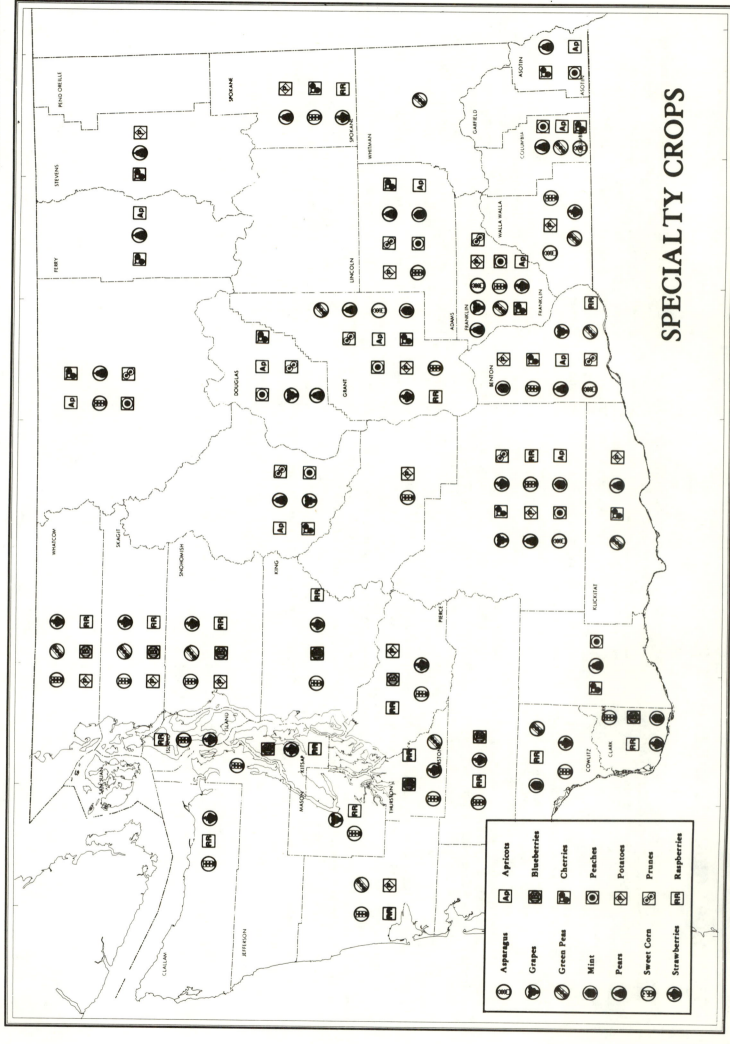

SPECIALTY CROPS

Long gone are the days when virtually every farmer produced, or tried to produce, a little of everything—both crops and livestock products. The subsistence farming of Washington's pioneer era had begun to give way to a modest degree of specialization well before the turn of the nineteenth century. New crops were introduced, and new methods of transportation, handling, and marketing, as well as production, provided incentives to concentrate on fewer crops and reach the ever-widening markets that first the railroads, then paved roads and trucks made it possible to reach.

One of the earliest specialty crops was hops, which were publicized and popularized by Ezra Meeker, one of Washington's most famous pioneers and himself a hop farmer. At that time, in the 1890s, the crop was grown exclusively in western Washington, in particular in the Green River valley of King County and the Nooksack valley of Whatcom County, but by 1900 it had made inroads among farmers east of the Cascades. Today the crop is grown exclusively in the eastern part of the state, most of it in Yakima County. Similar accounts may be found for the score or more of specialty crops grown in the state today, not to mention the many others, such as flax, that were introduced and boosted only to fail because the market or climate proved unsuitable for further experimentation.

Although well behind such states as California and Texas in total agricultural production, and even the range of its crops, Washington has long ranked high in the United States both in total production and the number of crops for which it is the first or second producer. In 1980, for example, Washington ranked first in the nation in the production of apples, hops, spearmint oil, dry edible peas, sweet cherries, currants, and red raspberries. The state was second in potatoes, peas, prunes and plums, apricots, asparagus, green peas, black raspberries, and blackberries.

The map shows production in the counties of fourteen specialty crops selected from a list of more than twice that number. Missing are specialty crops produced exclusively in one or two counties, as for example hops (grown mainly in Yakima County) and cranberries (grown exclusively in Pacific and Grays Harbor counties).

The crops shown include representatives of each of four of the five classes used by the Washington Crop and Livestock Reporting Service. Two *field crops* are mint and potatoes. Mint, of which two varieties are produced—spearmint and peppermint—is grown today almost exclusively in eastern Washington: 29,170 acres are there of the 1979 total of approximately 30,000, 22,000 of them in Yakima County alone. Potatoes, on the other hand, have a much wider distribution, but even so the preponderance of the acreage in the eastern region is well marked: 98,000 out of a state total of 102,000 acres in 1979. Grant, Benton, and Franklin counties each grow more than 20,000 acres of potatoes. Noteworthy also is the dramatic increase in the state's production in the past quarter century.

Production in 1979 totalled 48 million hundredweights, even though it was not until 1956 that a total of 10 million was first reached, and for most of the previous thirty years production had fluctuated between 4 and 7 million hundredweights.

Fruit crops are separated into two classes, tree fruits and berries, and here there are some interesting locational contrasts. Whereas the *tree fruit* crops are overwhelmingly important east of the Cascades on irrigated lands along or close to the Columbia, Yakima, Snake, and Okanogan rivers, the berry crops are particularly important in the Puget Sound region, except for cranberries, which are restricted to two southwest Washington counties, Pacific and Grays Harbor. Major changes have come during the past few decades in production and productivity, varieties grown, harvesting, handling, and marketing—most notably in the production of grapes. Today grapes are grown increasingly for wine, particularly in Yakima, Benton, and Franklin counties. In 1920 the state's grape harvest amounted to only 1,800 tons; in 1978 it totalled 166,000 tons. Increases in the production of other fruits have been less dramatic, and some have declined in production. During the same period apple production increased by only modest amounts, while peach production declined markedly—the record peach harvest of 1947 was more than three times those of 1978, 1979, or 1980.

For the *vegetable crops* the importance of irrigation is clearly evident. Asparagus and sweet corn are produced mainly in eastern Washington, especially in Yakima, Franklin, Walla Walla, Grant, and Benton counties, although green peas are grown both east and west of the Cascades, in Skagit, Snohomish, and Whatcom counties on the west and Walla Walla and Columbia counties on the east. The increase in asparagus production has been as spectacular as that of grapes. In 1927 total production was less than 1,000 tons; in recent years it has been well above 20,000 tons. Production of green peas and sweet corn also has risen rapidly. Pea production went from less than 10,000 tons before 1930 to more than 139,000 tons in 1979. Statistics for sweet corn are not available before 1949, but production increased from 32,000 tons in 1949 to almost 330,000 tons in 1979.

Although population increases, both regionally and nationally, account for much of the increase in agricultural production in the past century, changes in dietary preferences are undoubtedly also responsible for many of the more dramatic increases in many of these specialty crops. Yet new technologies, especially in the quick freezing and packaging of vegetables and fruits, have done much to encourage these dietary changes.

COMMERCIAL FORESTS AND FOREST PRODUCTS

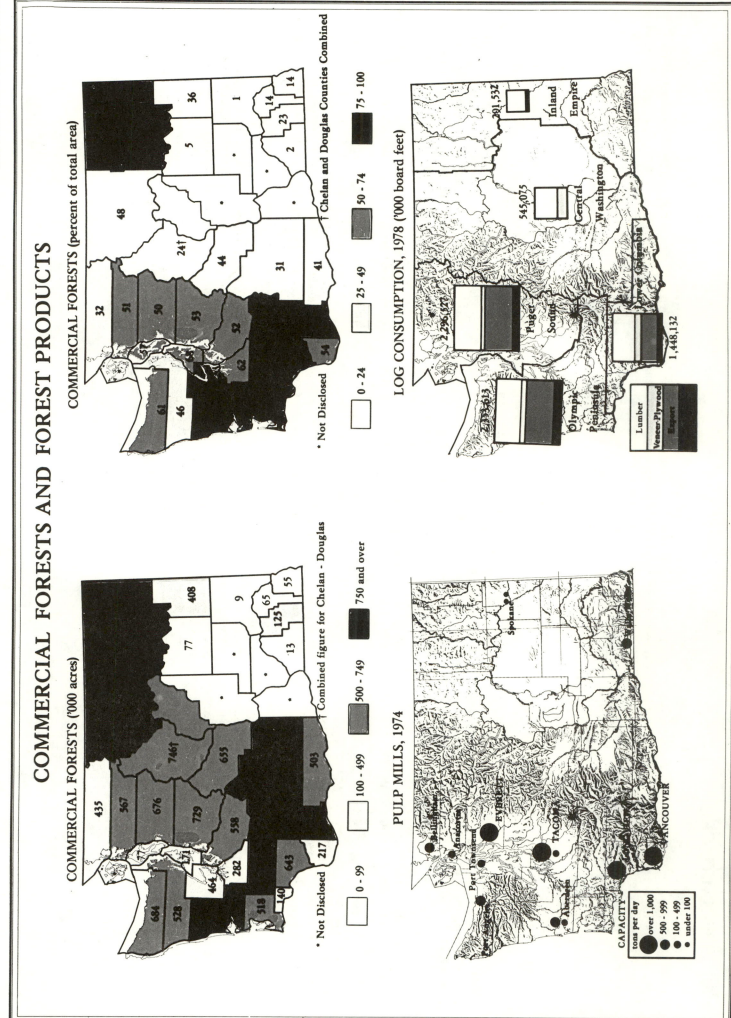

COMMERCIAL FORESTS (percent of total area)

† Chelan and Douglas Counties Combined

75 - 100

50 - 74

25 - 49

0 - 24

☐ Not Disclosed

COMMERCIAL FORESTS ('000 acres)

† Combined figure for Chelan - Douglas

750 and over

500 - 749

100 - 499

0 - 99

* Not Disclosed

LOG CONSUMPTION, 1978 ('000 board feet)

Inland Empire

Central Washington

Puget Sound

River of Columbia

Olympic Peninsula

Lumber

Veneer-Plywood

Export

201,532

545,075

2,296,327

1,448,132

PULP MILLS, 1974

Spokane

Bellingham

Anacortes

Port Townsend

EVERETT

TACOMA

Aberdeen

VANCOUVER

CAPACITY
tons per day

● over 1,000

● 500 - 999

● 100 - 499

· under 100

During the more than 150 years that Washington has maintained a commercial forest industry, it has undergone several major locational and technological changes. The pioneer industry has already been dealt with in Map 33; the modern industry is considered in the series of eight maps here and the following page.

Commercial forests are those stands of forest deemed to be of suitable quality and of sufficient quantity to be commercially valuable. In Washington they are heavily concentrated in the western half of the state, but also extend along the eastern foothills of the Cascades and, particularly, in the northern tier of counties along the United Sates–Canada border. The Columbia Basin by contrast is almost treeless, apart from thin stands of cottonwoods and poplars lining the valley bottoms.

The area of commercial forest in 1980 was estimated to be 17,805,000 acres out of a total state area of 43,608,960 acres. This means that more than 40 percent of Washington can be classified as commercial forest, one of the highest percentages in the nation. Of the total forest area slightly more than one-half (50.6 percent) is in the public domain. The ownership of the rest is about equally divided between the property of industrial giants such as Weyerhaeuser, Georgia-Pacific, I.T.T. Rayonier, and Simpson (4,279,000 acres, or 24.0 percent) and that of miscellaneous land owners (4,528,000 acres, or 25.4 percent). The National Forest Service controls by far the largest area of forest in the state with 5,057,000 acres, or 28.4 percent of the total. Not all the forests under federal control are readily accessible, however; and included in the total is almost half of the old-growth forest in the state. The other public owners include the various state agencies, notably the

Department of Natural Resources (1,833,000 acres, or 10.3 percent) and Indian forest lands administered by the Bureau of Indian Affairs (1,577,000 acres, or 8.9 percent). Map 76 should be consulted for the location of the national forests. No attempt has been made in this atlas to show the wide distribution of state lands, including a great many small, as well as a few more extensive, forested areas. Indian forest lands are heavily concentrated on the Olympic Peninsula (especially on the Quinault and Hoh reservations), in Yakima County (on the Yakima Reservation), and in Okanogan and Ferry counties (on the Colville Reservation). (See map 14, "Indian Reservations, 1960.")

In the midnineteenth century the forest industries eventually spread from tidewater on the lower Columbia River and upriver on Puget Sound, by means of logging railroads, to areas with no natural routeways. By the end of the nineteenth century forest resources were exploited in virtually every part of the state except the high mountain areas. Today a large proportion of the inaccessible high forest is included in the wilderness areas and is no longer classified as commercial forest.

Sawmills, shake and shingle mills, plywood and veneer mills, and pulp mills came into existence as economic conditions dictated. The thousands of small businesses of earlier days, however, have been reduced to a fraction of the original number as a result of technological advances and economic exigencies. Gone are the so-called glory days of logging, including the romantic but lice-ridden lumber camps, the ricketty logging railroads, and the spluttering steam donkey engines. Gone also for the most part are the host of tiny mill

towns or settlements with their beehive furnaces and company houses. Both logging and wood processing have become increasingly concentrated in the hands of a dozen or so large companies. Likewise, wood production is now located in a relatively few major centers, particularly in the western half of the state.

Log Consumption. The most obvious fact that emerges from the graphic representations in Maps 57 and 58 is that the export trade in logs is confined to the western part of the state. The Olympic Peninsula region, with its major ports of Aberdeen-Hoquiam and Port Angeles, and the Puget Sound region, with Everett, Seattle, Tacoma, and Bellingham as its major ports, vie with one another for the maritime trade in logs with Japan and other Asian countries. Somewhat less important is the lower Columbia region, where Longview is the main port.

Pulp Mills. Generally, the wood pulp industry is more concentrated than any of the other forest industries because it requires high initial capital investment, a large nearby market or requisite transportation to regional, national, or international markets, and supplies of suitable roundwood. Only a dozen sites, ten of them in western Washington, were engaged in the production of wood pulp in the mid-1970s, and at the present time it seems likely that the next decade will see the reduction of those dozen sites perhaps to fewer than ten, because of increasingly rigid antipollution controls, changing economies of scale, and shifting markets. Among the major companies presently engaged in pulp production in Washington are Weyerhaeuser, Crown Zellerbach, Georgia Pacific, and Potlatch.

FOREST PRODUCTS

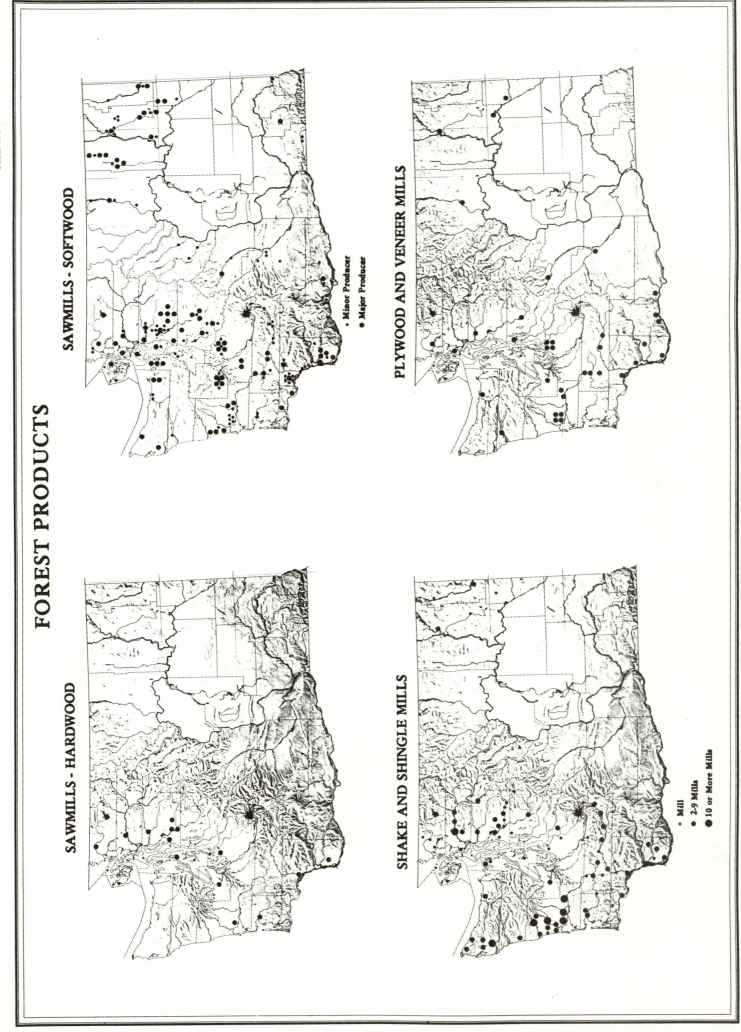

SAWMILLS - SOFTWOOD

· Minor Producer

● Major Producer

PLYWOOD AND VENEER MILLS

SAWMILLS - HARDWOOD

SHAKE AND SHINGLE MILLS

· Mill

● 2-9 Mills

● 10 or More Mills

The earliest processing industry in the Pacific Northwest, not including the various crafts practiced by Indian tribes, was sawmilling. The first sawmill in Washington was constructed by the Hudson's Bay Company in 1827 at La Camas, six miles upstream from Fort Vancouver. The mill was water-driven, and the labor was provided by Kanakas from the Sandwich Islands (Hawaii). The output, about 3,000 board feet a day, was minuscule by modern standards but more than enough for local requirements, and it even provided a surplus for export to the Sandwich Islands and other places served by the company. With the arrival of American settlers at Tumwater in the mid-1840s, sawmilling was introduced to the Puget Sound region.

The early mills were small, and although water-driven, they relied on a good amount of hand labor. The first steam mill was erected in 1853 by Henry Yesler in Seattle, close to today's Pioneer Square. By the end of the 1850s, Yesler's mill had been joined by a score of others up and down the Sound, and at points along the Lower Columbia. As yet the Olympic Peninsula, which later became one of the most important lumber-producing regions in the world, was totally undeveloped.

Sawmills, some concentrating on softwoods, some on hardwoods, but most using both, became the most ubiquitous of the pioneer industries, although they were certainly outnumbered by the many hundreds of shake and shingle mills. The latter sprang up all over western Washington wherever western red cedar was available; elsewhere they were rarely found. Requiring less in the way of capital than sawmills, the shake and shingle mills were often flimsily built, and through reckless-

ness or carelessness they were frequently destroyed by fire.

In the larger settlements of western Washington especially, other forest-products industries flourished, notably sash and door factories and a wide array of furniture-making industries. Toward the end of the century, however, with the opening up of eastern markets, and after the recovery from the 1893 depression, considerable changes began to be made in the wood-processing industries. As industrial giants such as Weyerhauser and Simpson moved in, many of the smaller operations began to disappear, either driven out of business by the competition or else swallowed up in amalgamations with larger firms. Various technological changes in the industry came with the introduction of new machinery and the discovery of new ways of utilizing wood and wood wastes. Transportation changes also, particularly in road vehicles, led to further localization and concentration of manufacturing operations.

The 1978 *Washington Mill Survey* recorded more than 600 mills, excluding log export operations. This was an increase of more than 100 mills in the previous ten years. With the notable exception of shake and shingle mills, however, all other types of shingle mills decreased in number. Shake and shingle mills increased from 158 to 337, reflecting an interesting change in tastes as more and more householders installed cedar shake roofs when they could.

Only a dozen mills in the state were more than ninety percent dependent on hardwoods for their raw materials in 1978, and another thirteen used, but were not dependent on, hardwoods. All the hardwoods mills, it will

be seen, are located in western Washington, where ample supplies of alder, maple, and birch are available.

Sawmills that depend mainly or entirely on softwoods are many times more numerous than hardwood mills. They are found in most parts of the state. The 182 sawmills that existed in 1978 were classified in four categories: class A, with a single-shift capacity of more than 120 MBF (120,000 board feet), was the largest; and class D, with less than 40 MBF capacity, was the smallest. During the previous decade both the largest- and the smallest-capacity mills increased in number and in production, while the two intervening categories lost ground. Roughly 20 percent of the mills are in class A, but their capacity is approximately 60 percent of the total single-shift capacity of 12.368 MBF. The Olympic Peninsula, with fifty-seven mills, leads in the number of mills, and Snohomish County, with twenty-two mills, is the leading county.

Shake and shingle mills outnumber sawmills almost two to one, 337 compared to 182. Approximately two-thirds of the shake and shingle mills are located on the Olympic Peninsula, where Grays Harbor County had in 1978 more than 100 of them.

Plywood and veneer mills, which use both softwoods and hardwoods, are fewer in number than either saw-mills or shake and shingle mills. All but four of the thirty-six veneer-plywood mills in existence in 1978 were located in western Washington. The Olympic Peninsula was the leading area, with sixteen mills; and Grays Harbor County and Lewis County, each with five, were the leading counties.

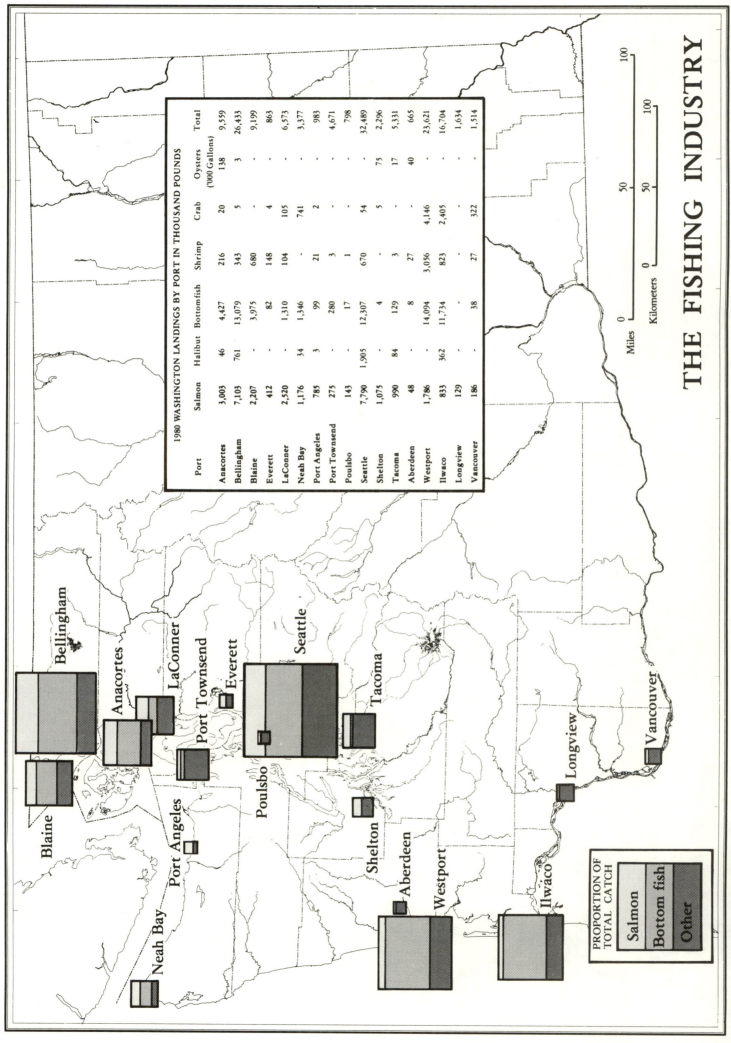

THE FISHING INDUSTRY

1980 WASHINGTON LANDINGS BY PORT IN THOUSAND POUNDS

Port	Salmon	Halibut	Bottomfish	Shrimp	Crab	Oysters ('000 Gallons)	Total
Anacortes	3,003	46	4,427	216	20	138	9,559
Bellingham	7,103	761	13,079	343	5	3	26,433
Blaine	2,207	-	3,975	680	-	-	9,199
Everett	412	-	82	148	4	-	863
LaConner	2,520	-	1,310	104	105	-	6,573
Neah Bay	1,176	34	1,346	-	741	-	3,377
Port Angeles	785	3	99	21	2	-	983
Port Townsend	275	-	280	3	-	-	4,671
Poulsbo	143	-	17	1	-	-	798
Seattle	7,790	1,905	12,307	670	54	75	32,489
Shelton	1,075	-	4	3	5	17	2,296
Tacoma	990	84	129	-	-	-	5,331
Aberdeen	48	-	8	27	-	40	665
Westport	1,786	-	14,094	3,056	4,146	-	23,621
Ilwaco	833	362	11,734	823	2,405	-	16,704
Longview	129	-	-	27	-	-	1,634
Vancouver	186	-	38	27	322	-	1,514

PROPORTION OF TOTAL CATCH
- Salmon
- Bottom fish
- Other

Miles 0 50 100
Kilometers 0 100

Bellingham, Anacortes, LaConner, Port Townsend, Everett, Seattle, Blaine, Neah Bay, Port Angeles, Poulsbo, Tacoma, Shelton, Aberdeen, Westport, Ilwaco, Longview, Vancouver

59. THE FISHING INDUSTRY

Of all the industries of Washington fishing is the most venerable, its origins lost in the dim recesses of Indian prehistory. There can be no doubt that the Indians of Washington exploited the fisheries of the ocean littoral and the state's rivers and lakes. At archeological sites throughout the state excavated middens abound in fish and shellfish remains. By the time of the first white-Indian culture contacts Indian trade in fish and fish products was widespread. Points along the Columbia—The Dalles, Celilo Falls, Kettle Falls—were particularly important centers of this trade.

The earliest fur trading companies were vitally interested in the sea otter and other marine mammals, but fishing per se was of no great concern apart from periodic purchases or exchanges of fish for immediate consumption. The Hudson's Bay Company, however, and particularly Dr. John McLoughlin, superintendent of the Columbia District, recognized the salmon fishery's great potential; and at Fort Vancouver, on the Columbia River, and Fort Langley, on the Fraser, efforts were made to process the salmon for overseas markets. Salmon, like pelts, were obtained from the local Indians and, after drying or salting, were packed in large barrels made on the spot by company coopers. Although the British public was largely unappreciative of the product, and that market never developed on any scale, other markets were found in Hawaii, California, and China. From time to time "Boston men," such as Nataniel Wyeth, and other American traders attempted unsuccessfully to develop the Columbia fishery, although it was not until some decades after the departure of the Hudson's Bay Company that any great changes were effected in what was then a very limited operation.

Although the 1860s witnessed successful early attempts to establish a salmon canning operation on the Sacramento River in California, it was not until the 1870s that such operations were firmly established along the lower Columbia and on Puget Sound. The first cannery on the sound was built in 1876 at Mukilteo.

By the end of the nineteenth century the demand for canned salmon had increased enormously in Europe, as well as across the United States, and this in turn had resulted in the introduction of new technologies that revolutionized the industry, both in the catching of the fish and in its canning. The primitive methods that had long been employed by the Indians, which were the methods followed in large part by the early white fishermen, were replaced. The new, vastly more efficient methods eventually were so successful that the resource was severely depleted and certain species were threatened with extinction.

In the fishing operation, canoes were replaced by small sailing trollers, and in turn these gave way to gas- and diesel-powered vessels after 1900. Dip nets, spears, and reef nets continued to be used until the end of the century, but gill nets, which had been used as early as 1851, quickly took over after a net-weaving machine was invented in the late 1870s. While gill-netters continued to fish the estuaries and rivers of the state, larger purse seiners were introduced on the open waters of Puget Sound and the straits of Georgia and Juan de Fuca. Today these vessels dominate the industry. Close to shore, fish traps were used with great effect in the later years of the nineteenth century, and they continued to be employed in Washington waters until outlawed in 1934. Photographs of thousands of salmon impounded in such traps are numerous and are among the best-known illustrations of the early commercial fish industry.

In the canneries also, technology improved dramatically with the introduction of tin-plated metal cans and new vacuum-packing methods. Labor costs were drastically cut, and efficiency of operations was accelerated as hand cleaners and hand packers ere replaced by machines such as the so-called Iron Chink, one of which, it was said, could replace as many as fifty workers.

The depletion of the fisheries during the first few decades of the present century and the opening of the Alaska fisheries at the same time led to a series of changes that were to have widespread effects. Among these were the controls instituted by state and federal

governments, agreements with Canada regarding the salmon of the Fraser River, other international agreements regarding the halibut catch, and the involvement of the universities (in particular, the University of Washington) in research programs and the development of state hatcheries in many parts of the state.

At the present time the fisheries contribute only a small proportion of the state's gross product, and they provide jobs for an even smaller proportion of the state's population. And while the number of large vessels over fifty tons has changed little in recent years, the number of smaller vessels has declined dramatically. The U.S. District Court's Boldt decision of 1974, which allocated one-half of the catch to Indian fishermen, has had important consequences. Not only has the number of non-Indians in the industry declined markedly, the dominance of one tribe, the Lummi of Whatcom County, has become a matter of statewide interest and contention.

The value of the state's total production in recent years has varied from less than $60 million a year to almost $100 million. Salmon continues to fetch the highest prices, and it accounts for more than half the total value of the state's fish production. For many fishing ports, however, salmon constitutes a much smaller percentage of the tonnage handled. Two Puget sound ports—Seattle and Bellingham—and two Pacific ports—Westport and Ilwaco—dominate the industry. In none of the four is salmon the number-one catch landed so far as tonnage is concerned: bottom fish predominate in all four. Elsewhere salmon predominates in the tonnage landed only in LaConner, Port Angeles, and Shelton—all of them sites of Indian reservations.

Apart from salmon and bottom fish, shellfish, in particular, crab, oysters, and shrimp, are of great importance; and these have been the focus of much research and investment in recent years. The possibilities of fishmeal production, utilizing little-used and poorly regarded species, have also been investigated, but little development has taken place.

MANUFACTURING INDUSTRIES

VALUE OF SHIPMENTS (million dollars)

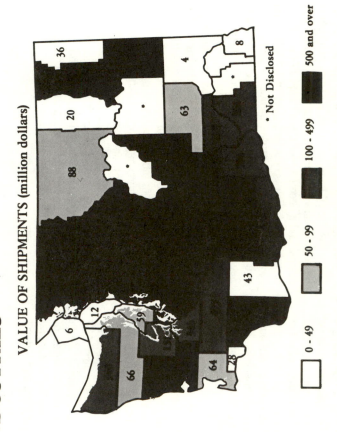

□ 0 - 49
▨ 50 - 99
▩ 100 - 499
■ 500 and over
· Not Disclosed

VALUE ADDED BY MANUFACTURE (million dollars)

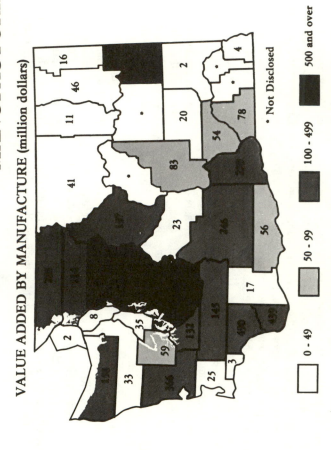

□ 0 - 49
▨ 50 - 99
▩ 100 - 499
■ 500 and over
· Not Disclosed

SELECTED MANUFACTURING INDUSTRIES (except forest products)

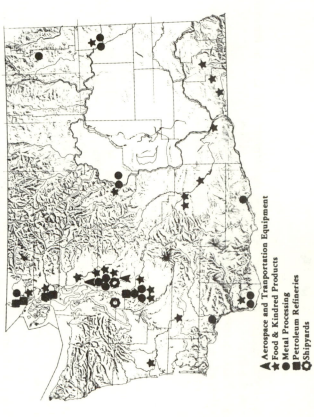

▲ Aerospace and Tranportation Equipment
★ Food & Kindred Products
● Metal Processing
■ Petroleum Refineries
○ Shipyards

MANUFACTURING EMPLOYMENT (percent of total employment)

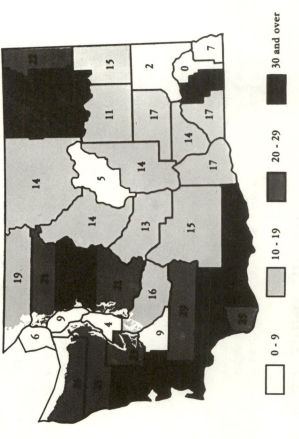

□ 0 - 9
▨ 10 - 19
▩ 20 - 29
■ 30 and over

Manufacturing, including both primary processing and secondary production, has been part of the Washington scene since 1827 when the Hudson's Bay Company established the first sawmill in the Pacific Northwest at La Camas, east of Fort Vancouver. Yet, examined from the point of view of the numbers employed, magnitude of production, value added, or any other financial aspect, manufacturing did not become a major component of the region's economy until the 1850s. Essentially, it began when the speculative shipping of sawn lumber to the California market sparked rapid development of the wood-processing industries. Fish canning became important only in the late 1870s, and shortly after that metal processing was added as a third group of resource-based industry. The access to eastern markets after the opening of the Northern Pacific Railroad in 1883 led to both the growth of various agriculturally based industries and the rapid expansion of the previously established resource industries.

By the beginning of the twentieth century the combined manufacturing industries provided the largest share of jobs in the state. At the same time manufacturing provided a greater proportion of the state's gross product than any other sector, even the service industries. Manufacturing has continued its growth, and a broad array of new, space-age industries have joined the older, but still very significant, resource industries. Manufacturing's relative position in the Washington economy has declined, however, as the service industries, particularly government service, have risen in importance. Today services make up the principal sector of the state's economy, accounting for approximately half the labor force and a little more than half the gross wages and salaries. Manufacturing accounts for about one-half of the rest.

In the late nineteenth century western Washington assumed a dominance that it has retained in the manufacturing sector and for a number of reasons. Not least of these was the early establishment of the forest-products industries around Puget Sound and the other lowland areas of western Washington, and the growth there of most of the largest cities, as well as all the major ports.

The maps on the upper left and the upper right show, respectively, the value added to each county by manufacturing and by value of shipments. Whereas in 1980 six western Washington counties registered total values exceeding $1 billion, in eastern Washington only Spokane County had that value, and this eastern county was well behind King, Snohomish, and Pierce counties, about equal with Cowlitz County, and only slightly ahead of Whatcom County and Clark County. On the other hand, in terms of value added by manufacture, interesting contrasts occur between those seven leading counties, while two other counties—Benton County and Yakima County—each with a fraction of the value of manufactures shipped from the others, registered a total value added in excess of Whatcom County, sixth of the seven. These two sets of statistics show that, whereas in King County the value added by manufacture amounted to 47.6 percent of the value of shipments, in Whatcom County the value added by manufacture was only 22.5 percent of the value of shipments. In Benton County, however, the percentage is a very high 73 percent, and in Yakima County 36 percent. The principal reasons for these anomalies lie in the types of industries contributing to the totals. Counties with a high proportion of resource-based industry registered a lower value added than those counties in which raw materials were a relatively minor factor in the cost of production. In other words, industries such as electronics, pharmaceuticals, metal fabrication, and aerospace, and other high-tech industries that rely heavily on skills that

convert low-cost items into high-priced products, are those with the highest value-added totals. And in the location of these industries external markets, large local markets, a skilled and well-trained labor force, and the most efficient transportation facilities and linkages have long been the major factors contributing to economic success. Consequently, it has been the large metropolitan counties—King, Snohomish, Pierce, and Spokane—that hitherto have been able to attract to their areas the majority of these high value–added footloose industries.

As William Beyers has demonstrated in a recent report, industries such as electrical machinery and scientific instruments, which have registered strong growth in the state in the past two decades, had most of that growth concentrated in the Seattle-Everett SMSA—with 85 percent of the growth in electrical machinery and 67 percent in scientific instruments.

Just as with decentralization of population, there has been some decentralization of industry, especially of the footloose sort, but in general the concentration of manufacturing industry in the greater metropolitan regions remains strong, even though some of the newer metropolitan areas, especially the Tri-Cities, have registered great gains in recent years. The rise of Benton County as a major manufacturing region has occurred in the past twenty-five years, and it owes much to the development of the Hanford Reserve and the location nearby of high-tech industries, some of them related to nuclear power. By way of contrast, aluminum smelting, the newest of the state's metal-processing industries, has been located at several places away from the central metropolitan areas, where the promise of cheap electric power and advantageous water sites encouraged the establishment of the industry in the 1960s.

MINERAL RESOURCES

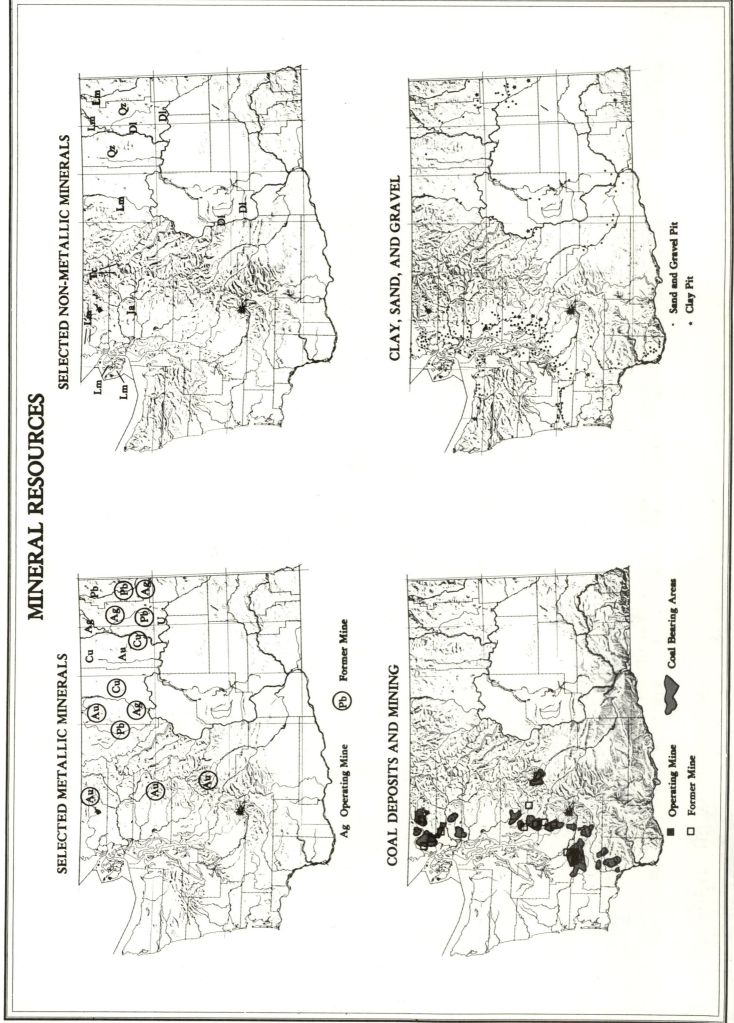

SELECTED METALLIC MINERALS

Ag Operating Mine

(Pb) Former Mine

SELECTED NON-METALLIC MINERALS

COAL DEPOSITS AND MINING

■ Operating Mine

□ Former Mine

Coal Bearing Areas

CLAY, SAND, AND GRAVEL

• Sand and Gravel Pit

٭ Clay Pit

61. MINERAL RESOURCES

Since the 1850s minerals have played a valuable but never a dominant role in the economy of Washington. Mineral exploitation has provided incentives for investors, profits for promoters, and jobs, directly or indirectly, for thousands of citizens.

The first significant commercial activity involving minerals was the shipment of 150 tons of coal from Bellingham Bay to San Francisco in 1853. Since that date more than thirty minerals—among them gold, silver, copper, lead, and zinc, plus limestone, sand, and gravel—have been mined successfully. The total value of mineral production between 1853 and 1980 was estimated by Wayne Moen to be approximately $4 billion, $2.5 billion of it since 1950 and in recent years averaging more than $200 million annually.

Washington, despite its success in mining, can boast no great gold rush, no Comstock, or Klondike. The lure of gold—or some other metal—did draw miners from far afield to northeast Washington in the 1850s, and to the Okanogan River and to Monte Cristo and other spots in the North Cascades in later decades. And in the development of the placer gold of the Fraser River, the lode deposits of British Columbia's Cariboo Mountains, the silver-lead-zinc deposits of southeast British Columbia, and the silver-lead deposits of Idaho, Washington has played a far from insignificant role, the Spokane region in particular.

The state's major metalliferous minerals include gold (au), silver (ag), copper (cu), and lead (pb). The map on the upper left shows a few of the more important locations of past and present metal mining. It should be noted that few of the deposits were worked for long periods, and only a few of the known sites are presently active.

Although the most glamorous of the minerals is gold, its overall contribution to the total value of minerals produced is quite modest. In 1981 about $6 million out of a total mineral production of $218 million was contributed by gold. Nonetheless, many of the best-known mines were connected with gold. It first attracted attention in northeast Washington near Fort Colville in 1855, and although the discovery led to a small gold rush, the placer deposits there were soon exhausted. Other placer deposits were discovered along the Similkameen River in Okanogan County in 1859, and in later years along many rivers both east and west of the Cascades. Few of them proved to be winners, and all of them were short-lived. Lode mining, however, when it began in the 1880s, uncovered many quite rich seams, and in a few locations mines were sunk that became highly remunerative. In the Mount Baker district there was the Lone Jack mine; around the flanks of Chopaka Mountain, a cluster of successful mines; and in the Monte Cristo district and the Okanogan Highlands, various others. Most of the mines produced little gold, however, and no returns for their stockholders. Today a half dozen mines are in production, although only the Knob Hill mine near Republic has had prolonged success.

Silver, copper, lead, and zinc mines have been operated in various parts of the state from the North Cascades eastward to the Rockies. The Holden Mine, near Lake Chelan, has been the most successful of the copper ventures, while northeast Washington has had a score of mines that have produced sizeable quantities of lead and zinc, the lead ores frequently mixed with silver. Other metals that are now being mined are tungsten and uranium. Iron, barium, and molybdenum are among the metalliferous deposits being considered for development. All in all, metals have been considerably less important, both in terms of value and in workers employed, than have coal and the various non-metalliferous deposits that are widely distributed across the state.

Most of the state's coal deposits lie west of the Cascades, from the Canadian border almost to the Columbia River. These coal deposits vary markedly in their quality, their quantity, and their ease of access. High-quality anthracite is found in only a few localities, such as Glacier in Whatcom County, and mining it is difficult because of thin and contorted seams. Thicker, more horizontal, and more easily worked seams of less valuable coal are found in Whatcom, Skagit, King, Pierce, Kittitas, and Lewis counties. Some of these have been extensively worked, notably those of the Roslyn–Cle Elum area. Today the only operational coal mines are those of Lewis County, near Centralia, where the coal is mined by open-pit methods and used on the spot for the production of electricity.

Among the non-metallic minerals used at present are limestone (Lm), quartz (Qz), diatomite (Dl), and jade (Ja). The locations of the workings are shown on the upper righthand map. Limestone, used in the production of portland cement, is by far the most important of them. Its value in the years 1979 to 1981 averaged more than $95 million annually, which was approximately 45 percent of the total value of mineral production in the state. Sand and gravel workings are numerous and widely distributed, with the highest concentrations in the lowland areas of the Puget Sound region. The value of these products for the same three-year period was approximately $50 million annually, or approximately 24 percent of the total. Clay, which was formerly widely used in brickmaking, has declined in importance in recent years, while oil and gas, though much sought after, have been produced only in miniscule amounts.

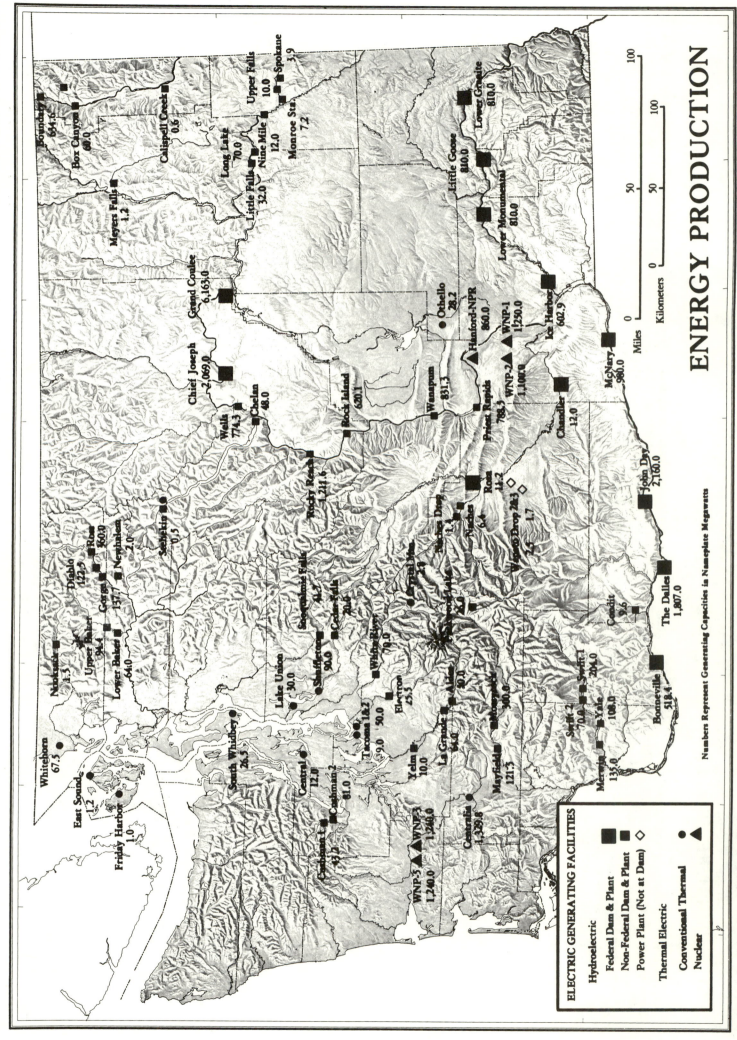

ENERGY PRODUCTION

ELECTRIC GENERATING FACILITIES

Hydroelectric

■ Federal Dam & Plant

■ Non-Federal Dam & Plant

◇ Power Plant (Not at Dam)

Thermal Electric

▲ Conventional Thermal

▲ Nuclear

Numbers Represent Generating Capacities in Nameplate Megawatts

Whitehorn 67.5
Nooksack 4.5
Upper Baker 94.4
Diablo 122.5
Ross 360.0
Gorge 157.7
Lower Baker 64.0
Noqualum 2.0
East Sound 1.2
Friday Harbor 1.0
Sedro 0.5
South Whidbey 26.3
Central 12.0
Cushman 2 81.0
Cushman 1 43.0
WNP-3 1,240.0
WNP-5 1,240.0
Centralia 1,329.6
Mayfield 121.3
Mossyrock 300.0
Yale 108.0
Swift 1 204.0
Swift 2 70.0
Merwin 135.0
Bonneville 518.4
The Dalles 1,807.0
Condit 9.6
John Day 2,160.0
McNary 980.0
Chandler 12.0
Ice Harbor 602.9
Lower Monumental 810.0
Little Goose 810.0
Lower Granite 810.0
Priest Rapids 788.5
WNP-2 1,100.0
WNP-1 1,250.0
Hanford-NPR 860.0
Othello 28.2
Wanapum 831.3
Rock Island 620.1
Rocky Reach 741.6
Wells 774.3
Chelan 48.0
Chief Joseph 2,069.0
Grand Coulee 6,163.0
Monroe Sta 7.2
Spokane 3.9
Nine Mile 12.0
Upper Falls 10.0
Little Falls 32.0
Long Lake 70.0
Meyers Falls 1.2
Calispell Creek 0.5
Box Canyon 60.0
Boundary 654.0
Lake Union 30.0
Shuffleton 90.0
Cedar Falls 20.0
Snoqualmie Falls 44.0
White River 70.0
Electron 25.5
Tacoma 1&2 50.0
Tacoma 1 50.0
Yelm 10.0
La Grande 64.0
Alder 50.0
Nisqually 2.8
Buckley 2.4
Naches 6.4
Wynoochee 2&3 12.3
Wynoochee 3 1.7
Roza 11.2
Rocky Brook 1.1

© 1988 by the University of Oklahoma Press

Probably in no other aspect has Washington undergone such changes in the past half century as in energy production, which until the 1930s still depended heavily on thermal sources, particularly coal and coal gas. In the 1980s, Washington has depended more on hydroelectricity than any other state. And while in the past energy production was strictly a local matter, today a statewide grid ensures that all regions can be supplied with energy produced within the state. In addition, pipelines bring oil and gas from places outside the state, including British Columbia. Fuels are used predominantly, however, in transportation and industry and for domestic and commercial heating, rather than for energy production.

The harnessing of the state's vast water resources began in the 1880s, when domestic and industrial users still depended on traditional methods of lighting and heating. Coal, to be sure, had been supplementing wood and animal fats and oils since the 1850s, and in a few urban areas gas companies were producing coal gas for local use. Water power, where used, was restricted to gristmills and lumber mills; its utilization for hydroelectricity was still in its infancy.

Many of the initial attempts to harness Washington's water power were made by transit companies intent on establishing street railways and interurban rail lines, or by companies that were keen to reduce their reliance on purchased coal or coal gas. Before 1900 the establishment of municipal light companies in Seattle, Tacoma, and other cities had resulted in the rapid electrification of many towns and cities, even though the power was used primarily for domestic and commercial lighting rather than heating. Elsewhere private utilities, such as Puget Sound Power and Light Company in western Washington and the Washington Water Power Company in eastern Washington, provided similar services for larger areas. In the early years much of their production came from coal-fired generators, but as the potential of nearby rivers was assessed, and suitable properties were acquired, small dams and hydro generating stations were constructed. Rivers like the Skagit and Lewis in the west and the Spokane in the east were among the earliest in the state to be harnessed for electricity production. Yet the transmission lines seldom carried the resulting power more than a dozen or so miles to a larger urban center nearby.

With the growing demand for rural electrification during the 1920s and 1930s, and with proposals to irrigate large segments of the Columbia Basin, came opportunities to develop public utilities outside the cities. Public Utility Districts (PUDS) were formed in approximately half the counties of Washington, and plans were made to develop the hydroelectric potential of various rivers and creeks within their areas. In a dozen other counties public cooperatives came into being to do the same for their service areas.

Although these public utilities proved to be important, their combined efforts eventually were dwarfed by the achievements of the Bonneville Power Administration (BPA), established in 1935 during President Franklin D. Roosevelt's first term. Since then BPA has brought into production more than a dozen major generating plants along the Columbia and Snake rivers. Among the most notable are the Grand Coulee (the largest electrical generating plant in the world), the Chief Joseph, and the John Day, all of which are capable of producing millions of megawatts. BPA is also responsible for a transmission grid that covers the state and connects it with grids across the United States and in British Columbia.

The state's electrical generating capacity has increased so rapidly during the past twenty-five years that virtually all the potential sites for large-scale generation have already been developed. Although small hydro projects are presently under way or under construction on a score of rivers, most of them in western Washington, these will add only slightly to the present capacity. And so, with most of the potential realized, the state's once-vaunted energy surplus has shrunk to minuscule proportions. Thermal sources of electric power—coal, oil, natural gas, and nuclear fuels—which have been used on a large scale in other states, are now figuring more prominently in Washington's power planning.

Nonetheless, hydropower still accounts for more than 80 percent of the state's total energy production, compared to little more than 10 percent in the United States as a whole. On the other hand, coal, which produces just under 50 percent of the country's electricity, accounts for less than 10 percent of Washington's. Oil is used only in very small quantities for this purpose in the state—accounting for less than 1 percent of production, compared to about 15 percent for the country as a whole—and natural gas is not used at all. Nuclear power (the only other important source of electricity at the present time), wind power, tidal power, wave power, and geothermal power are still of little or no importance, accounting for about 5 percent of the state's electricity, compared to more than twice that proportion in the whole country.

The public utilities, of which BPA is by far the most important, account for about 90 percent of the state's total energy output, and of this amount more than 90 percent is hydro power. The private utilities by contrast depend more heavily on coal (which produces over 40 percent of their power) and oil (about 10 percent), but even so hydro production is the single most important contributor to their total output. With the future of nuclear power stations in doubt—four of the five Washington stations are, or likely soon will be, in "mothballs" (the term applied widely in the industry)—it seems that the state will continue, until the year 2000 at least, to depend almost entirely for its electricity on conventional hydro and thermal plants.

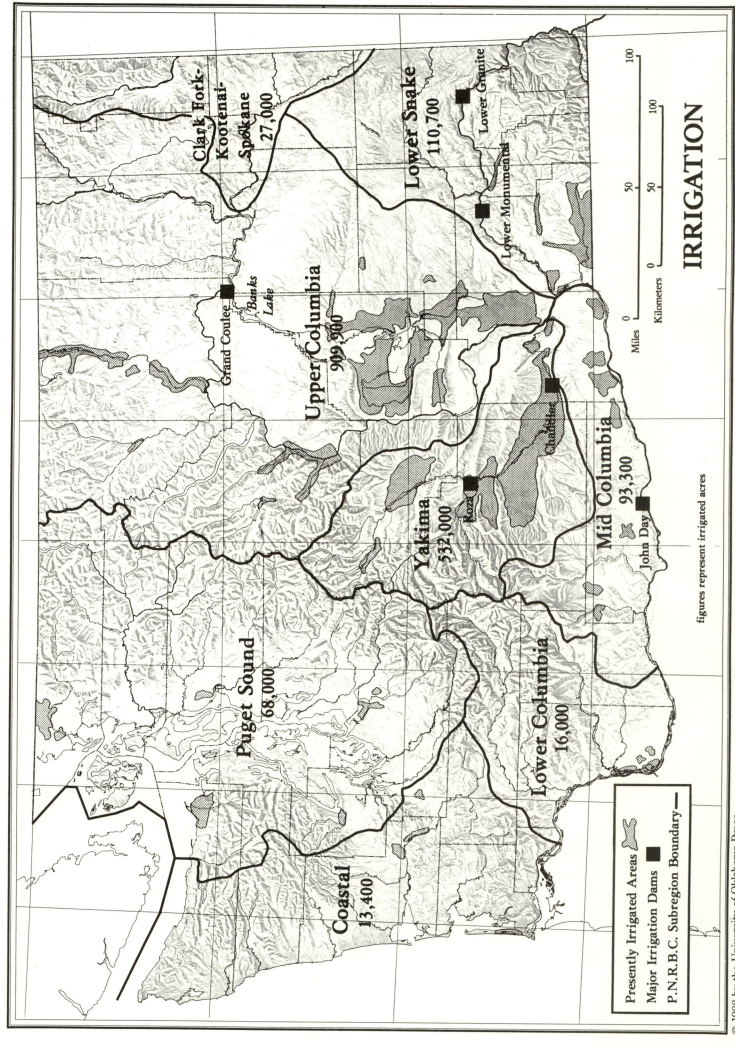

Clark Fork-
Kootenai-
Spokane
27,000

Lower Snake
110,700

Lower Granite

Lower Monumental

Grand Coulee

Banks
Lake

Upper Columbia
909,900

Little Goose

Ice Harbor

Yakima
532,000

Mid Columbia
93,300

Puget Sound
68,000

John Day

Lower Columbia
16,000

Coastal
13,400

figures represent irrigated acres

Presently Irrigated Areas
Major Irrigation Dams
P.N.R.B.C. Subregion Boundary

Miles
Kilometers

IRRIGATION

63. IRRIGATION

Of the major developments that have helped to transform Washington's agriculture in the twentieth century, none is more important than the spread of irrigation across the Columbia Basin.

The first successful irrigation in the region was undertaken by the Hudson's Bay Company on land near Wallula Gap in 1826, and by the late 1830s missionaries living east of the Cascades were using irrigation to improve yields, as they in turn encouraged the nearby Indians to settle down and do the same. Yet it was not until a half century later that irrigation was developed on more than a small and very localized scale.

During the 1880s settlers in the Yakima and Kittitas valleys along the eastern slopes of the Cascades made the first concerted efforts to direct water from those rivers onto lands along the valley floors and to adjacent benchlands. Costs were high, and the problems to be overcome were frequently beyond the means of the individual landowner. As a result, large and well-capitalized companies were formed to undertake canal digging, aquaduct building, and other technical activities. One of the first of these was the Yakima Canal Company, organized in 1889 with backing from the Northern Pacific Railroad, which itself was vitally interested in encouraging settlement of lands in the region. Other companies were the Yakima Irrigation and Improvement Company and the Spokane Falls Irrigation Company.

The first federal support of such projects came with the passage of the Cary Act in 1894, but the state of Washington, unlike Idaho, made no effort to take advantage of the measure. Hence it was not until passage of the National Reclamation (Newlands) Act in 1902 that federal support became a major factor in Washington's development of irrigation. One of the stipulations of the Newlands Act was that settlers who acquired land under the Homestead Act—from a minimum of 40 acres to a maximum of 160 acres—must make repayments to the revolving fund established at the time in each state for the cost of constructing the necessary irrigation works.

Payments, however, could be made over a period of ten years. In turn, the revolving fund could be used for further works. The result was the creation, especially in the Yakima valley, of a landscape of relatively small farms, engaged for the most part in truck farming and fruit growing.

In 1902 there were approximately 150,000 acres under irrigation; by 1910 the area under irrigation had doubled to 334,000 acres. Among the projects undertaken were those of the Okanogan valley, with 7,700 acres provided for near Omak, and of the Yakima valley, which came to incorporate the private undertakings of the Washington Irrigation Company, making feasible comprehensive development of the whole valley. With the completion of the Sunnyside and Tieton units and the construction of dams along the Yakima River and in the Cascades, an area of half a million acres was eventually brought into cultivation.

Despite this support, increasing costs of construction during the first few decades of the century led to reductions in the total area under irrigation. By 1930 less land was being irrigated than in 1920, although the number of farms using irrigation had increased considerably.

Remaining untouched by irrigation was the Big Bend Country along the Columbia River, although not from want of trying. The prospects for irrigating this region had been discussed as early as 1900, but the infeasibility of funding such a massive and expensive undertaking led to repeated delays and the rejection of all the earliest proposals. In 1918 prospects were reviewed once more, and two different plans proposed. The first called for the diversion of water from Lake Pend Oreille in northern Idaho, via a series of tunnels and siphons, and the use of an extended canal of about 100 miles in length. The second plan, which was proposed by William Clapp and James O'Sullivan of Ephrata and Rufus Woods, editor of the *Wenatchee World*, called for a dam across the Columbia at Grand Coulee, and the lifting of water hundreds of feet into a reservoir to be created along the

post-Pleistocene channel of Grand Coulee. It was the second scheme that eventually was chosen, an undertaking that has since been recognized as one of the supreme achievements of the Roosevelt administration.

Begun in 1933, Grand Coulee Dam produced its first power in 1941, but not until nearly a decade later did the irrigation channels leading from Banks Lake bring water to vast areas of the Big Bend Country. Since that time additional reservoirs on the Columbia—notably those above the John Day and McNary dams—and on the Snake River have provided water for irrigation of other parts of the Columbia Basin.

By the mid 1970s close to eight million acre-feet of water was being diverted from Washington's rivers and from underground aquifers to irrigate more than 1,770,000 acres of farmland. Although the Big Bend Country, with more than 800,000 acres, and the Yakima region, with more than 500,000 acres, are the chief beneficiaries, it is not only the dry eastern parts of Washington that have been served by these undertakings. Further extension of irrigation in both eastern and western Washington is possible, but in general it will have to be on a much smaller scale than in previous decades.

Not only has the area under irrigation been greatly enlarged, but also there have been great advances in irrigation technology in recent years. In turn, these have had considerable impact on the landscape of the state. Movable linear sprinkling systems did much to enlarge the area under irrigation in the early years, and they are still in use in many places; but it is center-pivot irrigation, with slow-moving radial arms up to a quarter-mile in length, that has helped create quite different—often spectacular—geometrical patterns in the steppelands of eastern Washington.

The boundaries shown on the map are those drawn by the Pacific Northwest River Basins Commission.

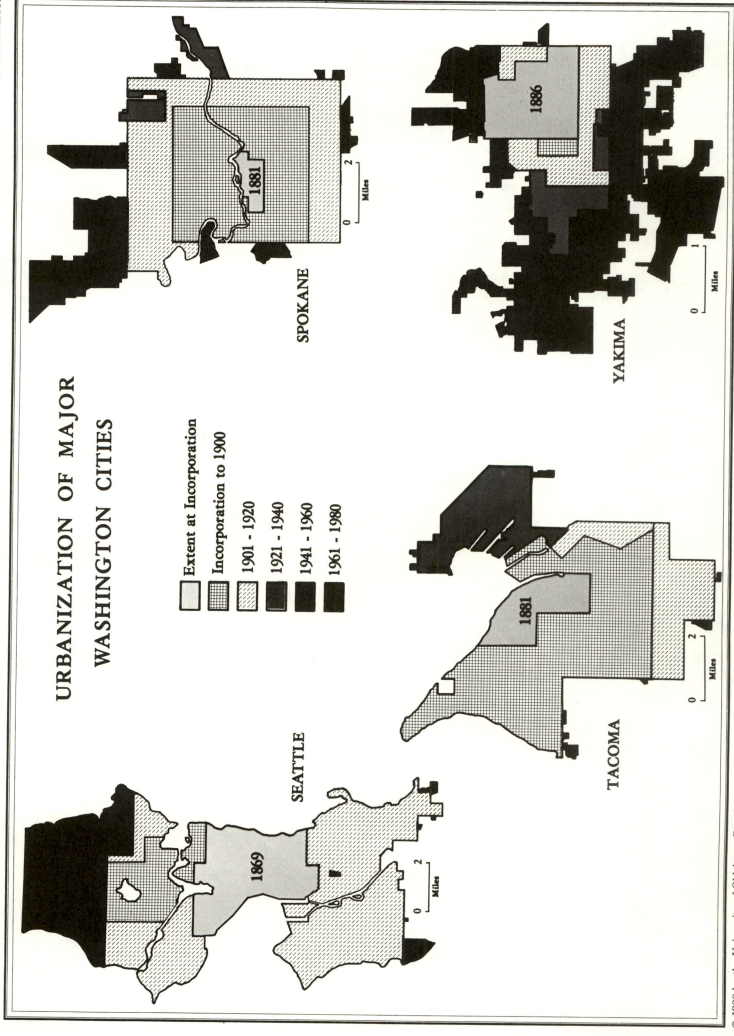

URBANIZATION OF MAJOR
WASHINGTON CITIES

Extent at Incorporation
Incorporation to 1900
1901 - 1920
1921 - 1940
1941 - 1960
1961 - 1980

SPOKANE

YAKIMA

SEATTLE

TACOMA

1881

1886

1869

1881

Miles
0   2

Miles
0   1

Miles
0   2

Miles
0   2

Richard C. Wade's comment that "the towns were the spearheads of the frontier" is nowhere more true than in the state of Washington, where after the midnineteenth century virtually all economic activity was initiated, and to a considerable extent controlled, by the business leaders of its major cities. Lumbering, fishing, mining, and even agriculture—the four basic resource industries of the Pacific Northwest—were all to a greater or lesser degree dependent upon the capital that flowed through, if it did not always derive from, the major northwest cities. And it was the cities themselves that became the principal regional markets, the major pools of labor, and the entrepots for national and international trade.

In this process of urban growth in the later nineteenth century Seattle, Tacoma, and Spokane emerged as the state's leading cities. Seattle and Tacoma, the termini, respectively, of the Great Northern and the Northern Pacific railroads, already were two of the three major Pacific Northwest ports (Portland was the third). Spokane, hub of the Inland Empire, was the major interior Washington center of mining activity, transportation, and commerce. Other cities, like Yakima, Wenatchee, Bellingham, and Walla Walla, continued to have aspirations for challenging and even surpassing the three leaders, but none was to acquire the regional or national importance of these three early metropolitan centers.

In the accompanying map we show the spatial growth of Seattle, Tacoma, and Spokane, the three largest cities, and that of Yakima, the city that became Washington's fourth SMSA in the 1970s. All four cities were incorporated within a few years of one another, beginning with Seattle in 1869, followed by Tacoma and Spokane in 1881, and Yakima in 1886. The original incorporated areas of all four were relatively small, less than eight square miles in the case of Seattle, and not much more than one square mile in the case of Spokane. At that time population in cities everywhere in North America tended to be highly concentrated in and around the downtown areas, where streets were usually narrow, and houses and commercial buildings always closely packed. Only in the peripheral areas of the cities were domestic building lots at all spacious, and these outlying areas frequently included small farms, dairies, and market gardens.

Suburban development began in the late 1880s, but occurred mainly in the 1890s. Electric street railways were built in a half dozen of the state's largest towns and cities, including Seattle, Tacoma, and Spokane. With the street railways came the so-called streetcar suburbs at the journey's end or at points along the route. Once this initial suburbanization was successfully accomplished, cities began the process that has continued to the present time of *municipal annexation*, which brings under the city's jurisdiction, either by direct legislative action or by legal procedures established by the legislature, contiguous areas closely connected to the city economically and culturally. By 1900, Seattle had expanded northwards into the Green Lake area and

the University District, in so doing adding almost as large an area as that comprising the city at the time of its incorporation. The growth of Tacoma and Spokane during the same period was much more expansive. By contrast that of Yakima was miniscule.

After 1910 the automobile began to compete with the streetcar as the principal means of commuting between downtown and suburb, but it was not until the 1920s that explosive growth of suburbs, occasioned by widespread adoption of the automobile by the middle classes, really got under way. By 1940, Tacoma had expanded to something close to its present size. Seattle, however, added considerably to its size between 1940 and 1960, moving northwards from the Greenwood/University District toward the Snohomish County line, and encompassing the burgeoning Blue Ridge, Broadview, Northgate, and Lake City suburbs. Small additions were also made in the extreme southwest (Arbor Heights) and the extreme southeast of the city. Between 1960 and 1980, Spokane added several tracts on all sides of the city. Many of these were along developed, or about to be developed, transportation corridors, most notably the Division Street tract along Highway 195.

Yakima is the city that in recent years has had the most complex history of land annexation. Most of this has been achieved since the 1940s north, south, and west of the city, but particularly, close to the river and its tributaries and the adjacent benchlands. The result is by far the most intricate boundary of any city in the state.

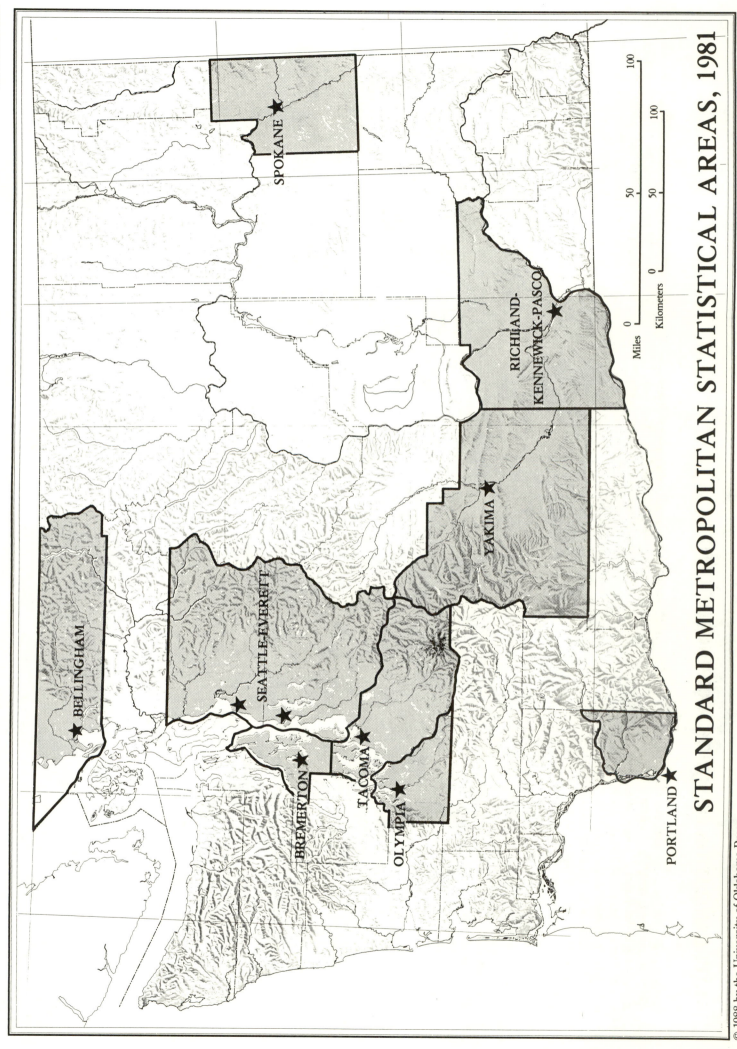

STANDARD METROPOLITAN STATISTICAL AREAS, 1981

SPOKANE

RICHLAND-
KENNEWICK-PASCO

YAKIMA

BELLINGHAM

SEATTLE-EVERETT

BREMERTON

TACOMA

OLYMPIA

PORTLAND

Miles

Kilometers

100

100

50

50

0

0

65. STANDARD METROPOLITAN STATISTICAL AREAS, 1981

Unlike counties, cities, towns, villages, and various minor civil divisions, which serve a variety of administrative and political functions, Standard Metropolitan Statistical Areas (SMSAs) are the creation of the U.S. Bureau of the Census. In the words of the *1980 Census of Population*, "the general concept of a metropolitan area is one of a large population nucleus, together with adjacent communities which have a high degree of economic and social integration with that nucleus." In other words, the SMSA is a well-defined statistical region for which census information is made available in many different forms for use by government agencies, economists, demographers, and other interested parties. Certain types of information are collected and released for SMSAs only, as for example, statistics on the journey to work.

New standards for the designation of SMSAs were adopted early in 1980, prior to the Twentieth Census of that year. Each SMSA must have one or more central counties that contain the area's main population concentration and an urbanized area with at least 50,000 inhabitants. Outlying counties that have close social and economic ties with the central area may also be included in the SMSA. The total population of the area designated, including that of the central urbanized area, must be not less than 100,000.

Before 1970 the state of Washington included three entire SMSAs—Seattle-Everett with adjacent King and Snohomish counties, Tacoma with Pierce County, and Spokane with Spokane County. In addition, Clark County was designated part of the Portland (Oregon)

SMSA. During the 1970s, Yakima with Yakima County, and Richland-Kennewick-Pasco (the Tri-Cities) with adjacent Benton and Franklin counties, were designated as SMSAs. Three more SMSAs were designated in 1980: Bellingham with Whatcom County, Bremerton with Kitsap County, and Olympia with Thurston County.

One further standard statistical area was introduced recently, the Standard Consolidated Statistical Area (SCSA), designated by the U.S. Office of Management and Budget. An SCSA consists of two or more adjoining SMSAs that are closely tied economically and socially. Within the state of Washington the Seattle-Everett and the Tacoma SMSAs are now joined for certain statistical purposes as the Seattle-Tacoma SCSA.

65. STANDARD METROPOLITAN STATISTICAL AREAS, 1981

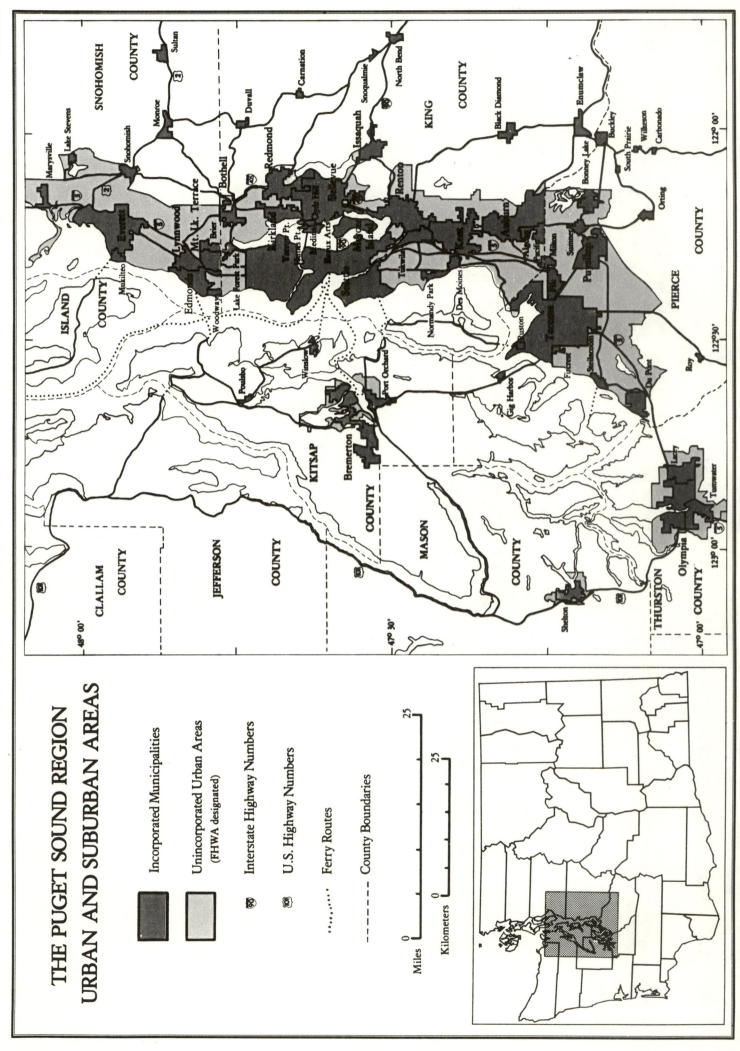

THE PUGET SOUND REGION
URBAN AND SUBURBAN AREAS

Incorporated Municipalities

Unincorporated Urban Areas
(FHWA designated)

Interstate Highway Numbers

U.S. Highway Numbers

Ferry Routes

County Boundaries

Miles

Kilometers

No part of the Pacific Northwest has moved so far toward the formation of a giant megalopolis as the Puget Sound region. During the past fifty years the rapid spread of towns and cities into the surrounding rural hinterland has resulted in a well-marked north-south string of towns and cities, plus overlapping urban fringes, with little truly rural land separating them. From well north of Everett to well south of Tacoma the sprawl has continued unabated, and there are indicators that Olympia on the south and Bellingham on the north may eventually become part of this elongated urban-suburban continuum, perhaps before the end of the century.

Threading its way through this embryonic megalopolis is Interstate 5, which has eased some of the problems of commuting for workers in the central cities of Seattle, Tacoma, Everett, and Olympia. In that respect the highway has encouraged the urban sprawl, but it cannot be pinpointed as the cause of it. The principal reasons for the rapid suburbanization of the southern Puget Sound region in the past thirty to forty years are the attractions of suitable building sites on the undulating lowlands of the eastern Puget Sound shoreline,

nearby water bodies on the west and east (Puget Sound, Lake Washington, Lake Stevens, and others), and the snow-clad mountains of the Cascades on the east and the Olympics across the sound on the west. Ferries across the sound from Seattle, Mukilteo, Edmonds, and Steilacoom also have encouraged suburban developments on the western shore of Puget Sound, particularly around Bremerton, and on some of the islands, notably Bainbridge Island and southern Whidbey Island.

North-south state and county highways east of Interstate 5 and its spur Interstate 405 have been somewhat less built up than those west of the freeway and closer to the shore of Puget Sound. Likewise, the two principal east-west highways—Interstate 90 from Seattle to Spokane, and State Highway 2 from Everett to Spokane—have been only moderately built up as yet, and only in the vicinity of Seattle and Everett.

Table 3 gives population statistics showing the growth since 1960 of the five central cities of the Puget Sound region and twenty-seven smaller towns and suburbs, all of them incorporated places, that have become part of what might be called "Pugetopolis."

Table 3. The growth of the Puget Sound megalopolis, 1960–80

	1960 Population	1970 Population	1980 Population
Central Cities			
Seattle	557,087	530,831	493,846
Tacoma	147,979	154,407	158,501
Everett	40,304	53,622	54,413
Olympia	18,273	23,296	27,447
Bremerton	28,922	35,307	36,208
Suburbs and Towns			
Auburn	11,933	21,653	26,417
Bellevue	12,809	61,196	73,903
Black Diamond	1,026	1,160	1,170
Bothell	2,237	5,420	7,943
Carnation	490	530	913
Dupont	354	384	559
Duval	345	607	729
Edmonds	8,016	23,684	27,679
Enumclaw	3,269	4,703	5,427
Issaquah	1,870	4,313	5,536
Kent	9,107	17,711	23,152
Kirkland	6,025	14,970	18,779
Lake Stevens	—	1,283	1,660
Marysville	3,117	4,343	5,080
Mercer Island	—	19,047	21,522
Monroe	1,901	2,687	2,869
Mukilteo	1,128	1,369	1,426
North Bend	945	1,625	1,701
Port Orchard	2,778	3,900	4,787
Puyallup	12,063	14,742	18,251
Redmond	1,426	11,020	23,518
Renton	18,453	25,878	30,612
Shelton	5,651	6,515	7,629
Snohomish	3,894	5,174	5,294
Steilacoom	1,569	2,850	4,886
Sultan	821	1,119	1,578
Winslow	909	1,461	2,196

Seattle
1884

Olympia
1879

67. PANORAMIC MAPS: SEATTLE, 1884, AND OLYMPIA, 1879

One of the most popular and successful forms of late nineteenth-century cartography was the panoramic map, also known as the bird's-eye view, perspective, panorama, or aero view. More than a thousand such maps were completed for cities in both the United States and Canada between 1870 and 1910. Eastern and midwestern cities were particularly well served; by contrast, southern and western cities were somewhat neglected.

Fortunately, more than a score of panoramic maps exist for the cities and towns of Washington. In addition to two or more panoramic maps for Seattle, Tacoma, Spokane, Olympic, and Whatcom, there are others for Chehalis, Cheney, Dayton, Fairhaven, North Yakima, Port Townsend, and Walla Walla. Eight of these maps are reproduced in this atlas.

Sponsored by chambers of commerce, boards of trade, and real estate companies, such maps were aimed primarily at boosting the fortunes of the particular town or city, playing up its natural surroundings—by prettification or dramatization—and highlighting its social amenities and business opportunities. In so doing, varying degrees of artistic license were employed. Scenes of natural beauty might be carefully relocated to bring them into the picture, while railroads and harbors frequently were shown as far busier than they ever were at the time or were ever likely to be. Nonetheless, the basic geography of the town is there to be

checked against the original plat maps or later cadastral surveys, and the topography of the surrounding area, although sometimes dramatized, is generally recognizable. The draftsmen who made the maps were artists as well as skilled cartographers, and many of them enjoyed a national reputation and pursued their craft for a half century or more. As many as 2,000 prints might be published of some maps, but 500 is thought to have been the average run. Consequently, many of the maps are now rare collectors' items.

For most of the maps issued, and for all eight of the maps reproduced here, the perspective is from an elevation between 2,000 and 3,000 feet. In the majority of the maps such an oblique aerial perspective could only be simulated by the artist, there being no means available to see the view at firsthand. That so many of the maps are convincing is a tribute to the artistic skills of the cartographers.

SEATTLE 1884

This 1884 view is one of five panoramic maps of Seattle in the Library of Congress and the second of the five to be completed. The artist was H. Wellge, who completed a drawing of Tacoma the same year. The map was published in Madison, Wisconsin, by the firm of J. J. Stoner, and the lithography was done in Milwaukee

by the firm of Beck and Paulli. The original print measures seventeen by thirty-two and a half inches.

Shown is Seattle before the fire of 1889 and before the creation of the Denny Regrade and other cosmetic changes that transformed the face of the city. The year before, in 1883, the Northern Pacific Railroad had connected Tacoma to eastern United States markets, and so various railroad projects were busily underway to connect Seattle with a transcontinental railroad. Shown also are Yesler's Mill (in the lower right of the map) and various industrial activities at or near the waterfront, as well as the various piers there and flotillas of ships. In the distance can be seen Lake Union and Lake Washington.

OLYMPIA 1879

This 1879 view of Olympia by E. S. Glover of Portland, Oregon, shows clearly the hilly topography of the Olympia area. One of the earliest-settled American communities in Washington, Olympia had been for a quarter of a century the territorial capital. Efforts to relocate the capital were still being made at the time, but eventually Olympia prevailed, and in 1889 it was chosen as the state capital. The industrial activities of Olympia—the lumber mills and associated forest industries—and the busy port and railroad make the town look somewhat more successful than it actually was.

67. PANORAMIC MAPS: SEATTLE, 1884, AND OLYMPIA, 1879

Tacoma
1884

Spokane
1905

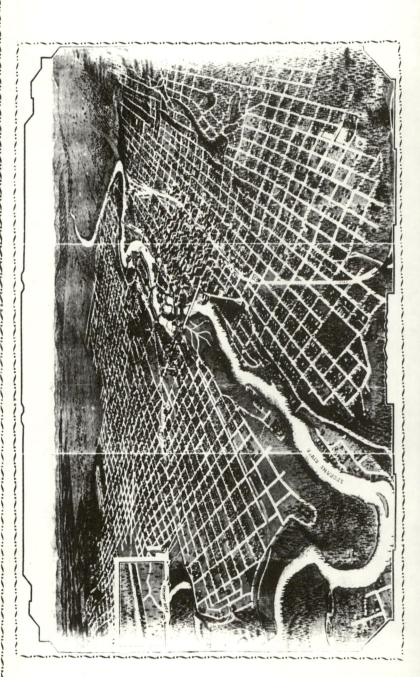

68. PANORAMIC MAPS: TACOMA, 1884, AND SPOKANE, 1905

TACOMA, 1884

This panoramic map, like that of Seattle in the same year, was drawn by H. Wellge and published by Beck and Paulli of Milwaukee.

Having rejected the plan prepared by the famous landscape architect Frederic Law Olmsted, who proposed a street grid that would have blended well into the heavily forested and rugged terrain, the Northern Pacific Railroad opted for a regular rectangular grid. The result was a host of problems, not the least of which were the steep gradients on many of the streets and the need to build a roadbed for the railroad that would reduce these gradients to negligible proportions. By 1884 the forest had been pushed back and the present street grid was established, although the gradients remained, as do many of them today. The Northern Pacific Railroad tracks are clearly shown, as are the various lumber mills, piers, and other activities that made Tacoma a city of more than regional importance. The small inset sketch depicts Tacoma's presiding presence, the nearby volcano of Mount Ranier or, as many residents called it, Mount Tahoma.

SPOKANE, 1905

This relatively late panoramic map of Spokane in 1905 was produced in the city and published by John W. Graham and Company. The artist and the lithographer are not indicated on the map.

In 1905, Spokane was firmly established as the premier city of eastern Washington and, indeed, of a much larger territory—the Inland Empire, as it was called— that stretched into Idaho and western Montana and even included part of southeastern British Columbia. Mining and agriculture were the twin sources of this dominance, and both contributed to the commercial and manufacturing activities of the city.

The significance is apparent of the Spokane River and its falls, adjacent to which were a number of manufacturing plants, including the Spokane Flour Milling Company. Less emphasized, for some reason that is not clear, are the railroads that passed through the city. The inset map shows the United States Army's Fort Wright.

Walla Walla
1876

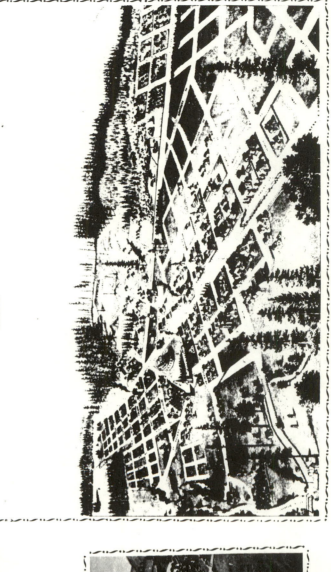

Chehalis
1890

Whatcom and Sehome
(Bellingham)
1889

Dayton
1884

69. PANORAMIC MAPS: WHATCOM AND SEHOME (BELLINGHAM), 1889; WALLA WALLA, 1876; DAYTON, 1884; AND CHEHALIS, 1890

WHATCOM AND SEHOME, 1889

One of the Puget Sound's earliest settlements, Whatcom on Bellingham Bay, was in 1889 the largest of four settlements that today comprise Bellingham. Sehome, the neighboring town on the south, joined with Whatcom in 1891 to form the city of New Whatcom, while the two other settlements, Bellingham and Fairhaven, joined together in 1890 to form the city of Fairhaven. In 1903, Whatcom (which had dropped the "New" a few years before) and Fairhaven joined together to bring into being the present city of Bellingham.

Shown in the panorama are Whatcom in the foreground and Sehome in the middle distance. Also shown, but with artistic license, are Lake Whatcom and Mount Baker, neither of which it would be possible to see from such an aerial perspective. The drawing is noteworthy in that it was not prepared by one of the professional artists usually engaged for such work. Instead, it was the work of a talented amateur, Jimmy Pickett, the half-Indian son of General George Pickett, who had been commander of Fort Bellingham more than thirty years earlier.

WALLA WALLA, 1876

This map drawn by E. S. Glover of Portland, Oregon was published by the artist. At the time, 1876, Walla Walla was still the largest settlement in the state, with a population of about 2,500, nearly double the number recorded in the 1870 census. The city had become a booming industrial town with lumber mills, flour mills, a furniture factory, and several breweries. Nearby was the U.S. Army's Fort Walla Walla. In the previous year the Walla Walla and Columbia River Railroad—also called the Baker Railroad—was completed. This connected Walla Walla with the Columbia River at Wallula, and was an important factor in the economic development of the wheatlands of the Palouse.

DAYTON, 1884

Another of H. Wellge's panoramic maps, completed in the same year as his maps of Seattle and Tacoma, is this map of Dayton, the county seat of then-booming Columbia County. Set in rolling countryside south of the Snake River and the Palouse Hills, with the Blue Mountains south of the town, Dayton was a small but up-and-coming market center for one of the most flourishing farming areas of the territory. Dayton remains to this day a small market and administrative center occupying a grid little changed from that shown in the map. The inset shows "west-side of Main Street."

CHEHALIS, 1890

This bird's-eye view of the smallest, and at the time the least-developed, of the towns included in our selection of panoramic maps, was the work of the artist E. S. Moore. Moore had been responsible some sixteen years earlier for a similar map of the town of Preston, Minnesota, but so far as we have been able to ascertain, he drew no others that were published.

The Chehalis map was sponsored by the town's board of trade, which also appears to have been the publisher. Although the single-street downtown area is shown as being well developed, many of the outlying blocks of the grid were still unoccupied, or at least not built upon. The clearing of the surrounding forest had been largely completed.

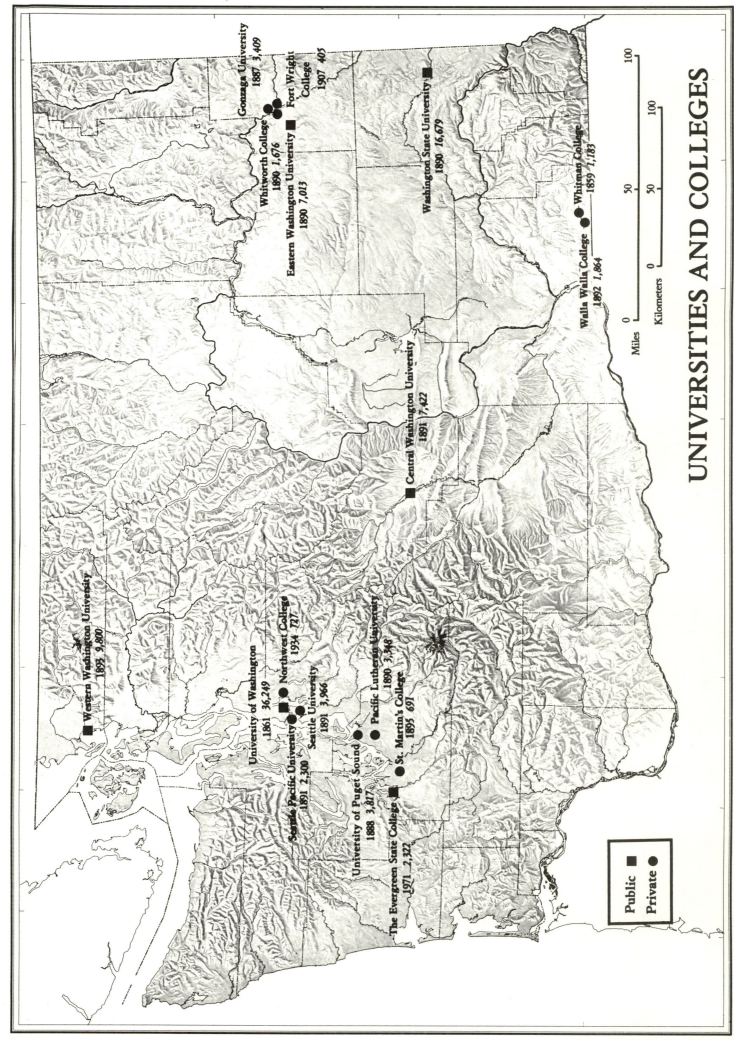

Gonzaga University
1887 3,409

Fort Wright
College
1907 405

Whitworth College
1890 1,676

Eastern Washington University
1890 7,013

Washington State University
1890 16,679

Central Washington University
1891 7,422

Whitman College
1859 1,183

Walla Walla College
1892 1,864

Western Washington University
1893 9,800

University of Washington
1861 36,249

Northwest College
1934 717

Seattle Pacific University
1891 2,300

Seattle University
1891 3,966

University of Puget Sound
1888 3,817

Pacific Lutheran University
1890 3,348

St. Martin's College
1895 697

The Evergreen State College
1971 2,322

Public ■
Private ●

UNIVERSITIES AND COLLEGES

Miles
0   50   100

Kilometers
0   50   100

Although poorly funded and equipped in the early years, Washington's private colleges, in the words of historian James Hitchman, "preserved educational opportunity and cultural heritage before public education took root." Most of the private schools were organized initially by church groups. The first of these, and the oldest institution of higher learning in Washington, was Whitman Seminary, chartered in 1859 and renamed Whitman College in 1882. Located in Walla Walla, the college, which was nondenominational from the beginning, experienced lean times in the early decades, but has survived to become a prestigious liberal arts institution.

The University of Puget Sound which shares with Whitman a reputation for academic excellence and stability, began even less auspiciously. The Methodist Episcopal Church had established a committee to explore the organization of a college in 1884, but it was not until 1888 that Puget Sound University was incorporated, and it was 1890 before classes began. Beset by financial and other problems, the school grew slowly. After a severe retrenchment and a name change, the College of Puget Sound settled on a permanent campus in north Tacoma in 1924, and in 1960 it became the University of Puget Sound. Also in Tacoma, the Pacific Lutheran Academy was organized by the Norwegian Evangelical Lutheran Synod in 1890. The college opened in 1894, moved briefly to Everett in 1918, combined with Columbia Lutheran College, and returned to Tacoma in 1921. It attained university status in 1960.

In December 1892 the Seventh-Day Adventists founded Walla Walla College at College Place, Washington. Soon afterwards, in 1893, the Free Methodist Church established Seattle Seminary, which later was renamed Seattle Pacific College and is today Seattle Pacific University. The history of Whitworth College, founded as a Presbyterian academy in Sumner in 1883 and elevated to college status in 1890, is probably the most adventurous of any of the Washington Protestant schools. In 1897 its location was moved to Tacoma, and

in 1914 it moved east of the mountains to Spokane. Other Protestant foundations included Spokane University, chartered by the Churches of Christ in 1913, and Northwest College, sponsored by the Northwest Council of the Assemblies of God in 1934 and located in Kirkland. Spokane University was a victim of the Great Crash of 1929, but Northwest College has continued into the 1980s.

Catholics, too, actively supported the development of higher education in Washington. The Holy Names Academy and Normal School opened in Seattle in 1881, but it ended college-level course work in 1930. Also in 1881, Father Joseph Cataldo, S.J., initiated the establishment of Gonzaga University, which opened formally in Spokane in 1887. Seattle College, another Jesuit foundation, was organized in 1892 and opened in 1894. Today it is Seattle University. St. Martin's College in Lacey was founded by the Benedictine Order in 1895. Less fortunate were three other Catholic foundations: Forest Ridge Convent, established in Seattle in 1907; St. Edward's Seminary, established in 1930 by the Sulpician Fathers in Seattle; and Fort Wright College, Spokane, which began its existence as Our Lady of Lourdes School in 1888. All have since been closed.

The first chartered public institution of higher learning was the University of Washington. Acting upon Congress's promise of two townships of land for university purposes—given in Washington Territory's Enabling Act of 1854—the territorial legislature in January 1855 directed construction of a main university campus in Seattle and a branch campus in Lewis County. The territory's county school superintendents, who were empowered to select the land and notify the legislature, failed to do so, and in 1858 the legislature decided to relocate the university on Cowlitz Farm Prairie. The next legislative session saw the university returned to Seattle, and lest the politicians change their minds again, the school's supporters quickly erected a building and appointed Asa Mercer to act as both president and faculty.

The university opened in November 1861, but its growth was slow and fitful. There were closures from 1867 to 1869 and in 1874 and 1876. But by the close of the 1880s, under the vigorous leadership of President Thomas Gatch, the institution had become truly a university. Moved to its present location in Seattle in 1895 and reorganized, the University of Washington has grown steadily to become a major center of learning and research.

Washington State University, at Pullman, resulted from the national impetus for college-level instruction in agricultural and industrial knowledge, and the passage of the Morrill Act of 1862, which resulted in the creation of the various state land-grant universities. The territorial legislature, anxious to establish an agricultural college, decided in 1865 that it should be located in Vancouver, but no further action was taken until 1890 when Pullman was chosen as the site. Classes began there in January 1892. The school was fortunate in having two long-term presidents in the formative years—Enoch Bryan and Ernest Holland.

Since the preparation of teachers was a need only partially met by private colleges and the University of Washington, normal schools were chartered in Ellensburg and Cheney in 1890, in New Whatcom in 1893, and in Centralia in 1919. The Centralia school was opened, but it operated for only one summer. The other three made slow but steady progress, and in 1933 they were permitted to grant the baccalaureate in education. All three became colleges of education in 1937 and in 1959, state colleges. Regional university status was conferred in 1977 on Western Washington University at Bellingham, Central Washington University at Ellensburg, and Eastern Washington University at Cheney.

In response to the findings of a 1966 Temporary Advisory Council on Public Higher Education, a new four-year liberal arts college, The Evergreen State College, was chartered. Located on the western edge of Olympia, the college opened in 1971.

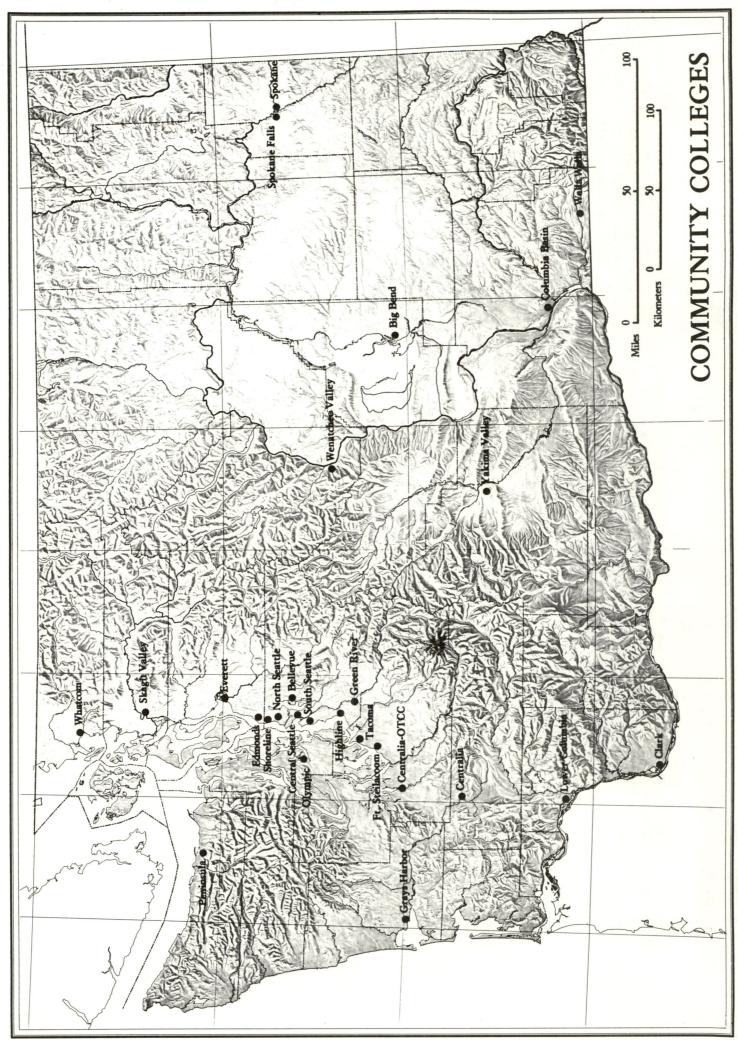

Whatcom

Skagit Valley

Peninsula

Edmonds
Shoreline
Central Seattle
Olympic

Everett

North Seattle
Bellevue
South Seattle

Green River

Highline

Wenatchee Valley

Big Bend

Spokane Falls
Spokane

Tacoma
Ft. Steilacoom

Centralia-OTCC

Grays Harbor

Centralia

Yakima Valley

Lower Columbia

Clark

Columbia Basin

Walla Walla

COMMUNITY COLLEGES

Miles
Kilometers
0   50   100
0   50   100

The two-year college movement in the United States is, excepting a scattering of private experiments, a twentieth-century phenomenon, and Washington was among the first half-dozen states to have such institutions. Champions of the idea, such as William Rainey Harper, president of the University of Chicago, Alexis Lange, a professor in the University of California, and William Folwell, the University of Minnesota's first president, advanced several reasons in its support. Harper favored junior colleges as a means of removing the burden of general educational instruction from increasingly specialized universities. Others believed that separating higher education in this way was sound on pedagogical grounds—that the introductory courses of the freshman and sophomore years were more appropriately extensions of high school studies, a transitional middle ground between common schools' curricula and those of universities. Still others, especially in western states like California and Washington, perceived the open-door two-year college as providing greater educational opportunities for large numbers of citizens who might not otherwise attend a college or university.

Washington's first such institution was opened to forty-two prospective students on the top story of the Everett High School Building in 1915 by the high school's energetic principal, Alexander C. Roberts. Working with University of Washington professor Frederick Bolton, Roberts was able to arrange university transfer credits for the course work offered by the Everett Junior College. The school failed in 1923 because of sparse enrollment, but two years later a two-year college opened (and stayed open) in Centralia. Several more followed: Mount Vernon Junior College in 1926, Yakima Valley Junior College in 1928, Grays Harbor Junior College in 1930. On the eve of World War II there were eight two-year colleges, with a total enrollment of about one thousand, in the state.

Until 1941 the junior colleges had subsisted without state funding, helped sometimes by local school districts' in-kind contributions of loaned facilities but largely dependent on student tuition and fees—tuition and fees that often were higher than those charged by the University of Washington or Washington State College. The 1941 legislature attempted to improve matters by officially acknowledging the schools as part of the state system, providing support at a rate of $75 per year for general education students and $100 per year for vocational education students, with an annual institutional maximum of $10,000. The number of possible junior colleges was restricted to twelve, and subsequent legislation in 1943 and 1945 prescribed the modes of local governance while establishing the State Board of Education's general supervisory authority. Unfortunately, a 1945 statute also forbade establishment of junior colleges in counties where four-year state institutions existed, thus depriving the state's three most populous counties of junior colleges.

Thereafter the number of two-year colleges grew slowly until, in 1961, the legislature redefined the mission of such schools to include a greater emphasis on vocational, technical, and semiprofessional education and community outreach. The junior colleges became community colleges, and they were given authorization to locate anywhere that a need could be documented. In the six years following, the number of community colleges doubled, most of the new ones being organized in King, Pierce, and Spokane counties, and enrollment tripled. In 1967, after statewide hearings and preparation of a long-range plan, the legislature created a state community-college system under the general supervision of the State Board for Community Education. Twenty-seven state-funded institutions, organized within twenty-two community college districts, serve approximately half of the students enrolled in higher education in Washington.

Enrollment had reached 204,782 by the fall of 1980 before a 10.4 percent budget cut forced serious reductions in faculty, staff, and available courses and programs and raised tuition and fees. In the fall of 1983 enrollment stood at 152,814. In 1983 the legislature increased the community college appropriation and passed a High Technology Education and Training Act directed at encouraging cooperation among the community colleges and the state's regional universities in developing and expanding high-technology degree programs. These pieces of legislation bode well for the system's immediate future.

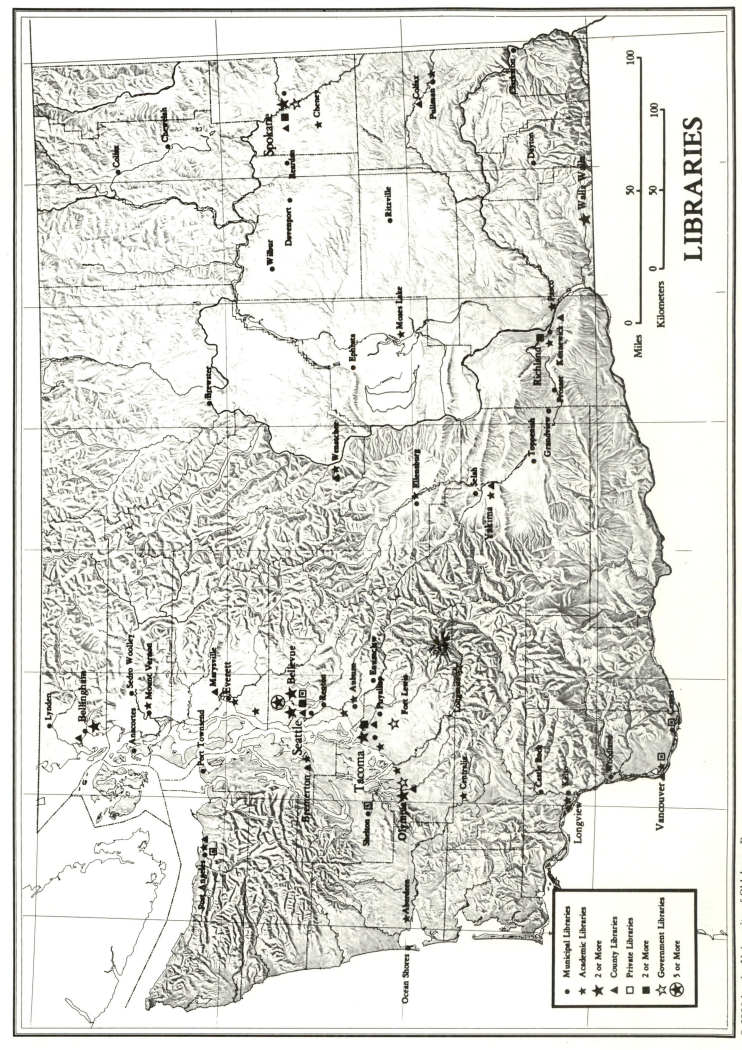

LIBRARIES

Municipal Libraries
Academic Libraries
County Libraries
2 or More
Private Libraries
2 or More
Government Libraries
5 or More

Public libraries have had a long and generally successful history in the state of Washington, dating back to the beginning of the territorial period when the Congress authorized the expenditure of $5,000 for the creation of the Territorial Library. The approximate two thousand books ordered by Governor Isaac Stevens form the core of the Washington State Library. At the commencement of statehood in 1889 the library's collection numbered more than 10,000 volumes, by 1979 this number had increased to more than 430,000 volumes, and the State Library continues to grow by an additional few thousand volumes annually.

Five years after the creation of the Territorial Library, citizens of Steilacoom organized the first subscription library in the state. Other such libraries were formed in the next two decades in Vancouver, Walla Walla, Seattle, and other towns and cities. Many of these libraries folded a short time later, but a few, like that at Walla Walla, later became public libraries.

The first free public library in Washington was established by the city of Dayton in 1876, and in the next decade public libraries were established in Spokane (1884) and Tacoma (1886). The Seattle Public Library dates from 1891, and the Everett Public Library from 1894. Over the next half century such libraries became the rule rather than the exception in almost every part of the state. Support for the establishment and mainte-

nance of the libraries, including the payment of professional salaries and the purchase of books, came directly from local taxes. Since World War I the state's settlement pattern has stabilized, many of the more isolated towns have declined, and the larger cities have spawned myriad suburbs. Meanwhile, county and regional libraries have been organized to serve these more dispersed communities, by means of either branch libraries or mobile units. The earliest of these was the Fort Vancouver Regional Library founded in 1910.

As important as the public libraries in the cultural evolution of the region have been the libraries of the state's seventeen four-year universities and colleges and its twenty-seven community colleges. Largest by far of the academic libraries, and the oldest, is that of the University of Washington, which dates from 1862. The university's library holdings in 1985 numbered approximately 4.3 million books and bound periodicals. And that figure did not include a diverse array of special collections, such as the Pacific Northwest History and Literature Collection, which includes thousands of rare pamphlets and other published materials of local and regional interest. Washington State University, established thirty years after the University of Washington, also possesses a major research library, which in 1985 totalled more than 1.4 million volumes. As for the other public four-year institutions, the state's three regional

universities, which were founded as normal schools between 1890 and 1899, all have sizeable libraries numbering between 290,000 volumes (Eastern Washington University) and 417,000 volumes (Western Washington University). The Evergreen State College, founded only in 1969, had built up a library of more than 183,000 volumes by 1979.

Largest of the private colleges and the earliest—dating from 1882—is Whitman College with more than 300,000 volumes. The University of Puget Sound, also dating from the 1880s, has a library of over 245,000 volumes; and Seattle University, one of 200,000 volumes. Other large private college libraries are at Gonzaga University, Walla Walla College, Seattle Pacific University, Pacific Lutheran University, and Whitworth College.

In general the community college libraries are smaller than those of the four-year colleges. Their libraries range in size from less than 10,000 volumes to more than 60,000 volumes, the largest being that of Tacoma Community College, founded in 1965.

In addition to the state's public and academic libraries, there are numerous libraries attached to government agencies—both federal and state—and to hospitals, manufacturing companies, commercial organizations, and various private clubs and cultural organizations. The location of some of these, as of the public and academic libraries, is shown on the adjacent map.

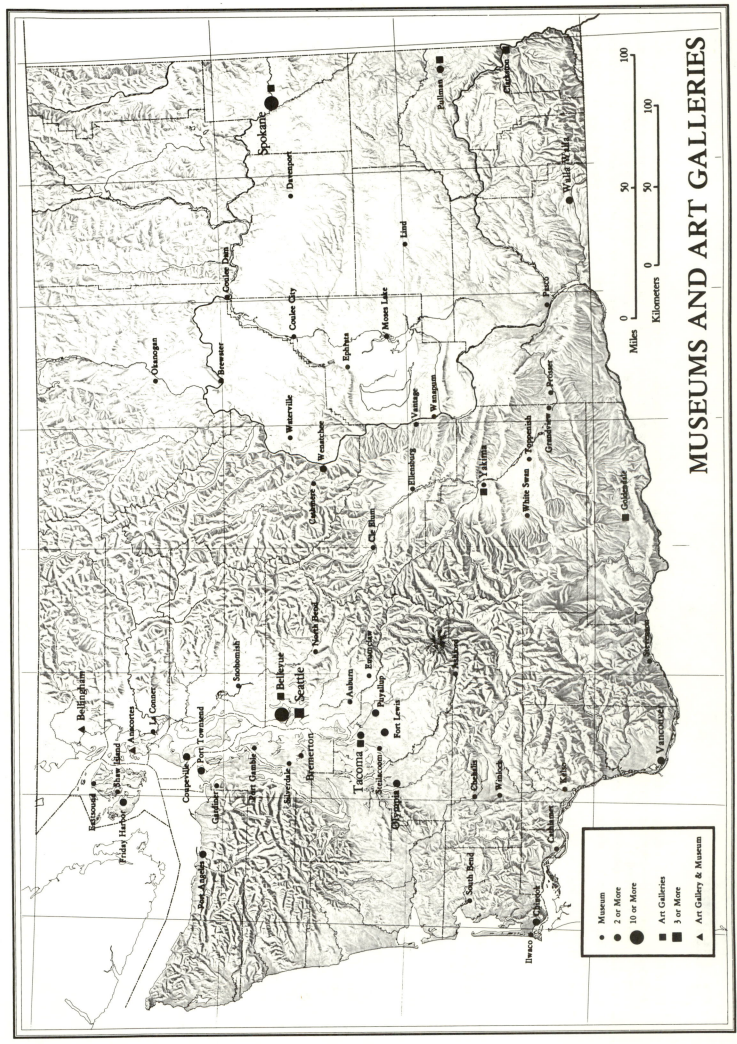

MUSEUMS AND ART GALLERIES

Spokane
Davenport
Coulee Dam
Brewster
Coulee City
Okanogan
Ephrata
Moses Lake
Lind
Waterville
Wenatchee
Wenatchee
Prosser
Grandview
Goldendale
Toppenish
White Swan
Yakima
Ellensburg
Cashmere
Cle Elum
North Bend
Snohomish
Bellevue
Seattle
Bellingham
Anacortes
La Conner
Shaw Island
Port Townsend
Friday Harbor
Coupeville
Gardiner
Port Gamble
Silverdale
Bremerton
Port Angeles
Olympia
Steilacoom
Tacoma
Fort Lewis
Puyallup
Auburn
Enumclaw
Chehalis
Winlock
Kelso
Cathlamet
South Bend
Chinook
Ilwaco
Vancouver
Stevenson
Wenatchee
Pullman
Clarkston
Walla Walla
Pasco

Museum
2 or More
10 or More
Art Galleries
3 or More
Art Gallery & Museum

Miles
Kilometers
0   50   100
0   50   100

Museums and art galleries—the latter often included as part of the former—have been a notable facet of settled American life since at least the late eighteenth century. Although not the earliest in America, Charles Willson Peale's museum in Philadelphia (eventually taken over by the American Philosophical Society) became the first of a long line of great American museums that today includes the Smithsonian Institution in Washington, D.C., and the Metropolitan Museum of Art in New York.

Progress during the nineteenth century was sporadic and rarely spectacular; by the end of the century there were many large towns that could boast neither a museum nor an art gallery. Public support of such ventures was infrequent, and it was seldom enough to cover the cost of operations. Rather, support depended largely, if not exclusively, on the donations of wealthy patrons or on the fund-raising activities of local groups interested in the arts or in the preservation of the area's pioneer heritage.

Change came quickly only with the rapid expansion of leisure time in the early twentieth century, and with the advent of the modern media—glossy magazines, motion pictures, radio, and eventually, television. Then increased public demand for cultural outlets, as well as the physical amenities needed to provide these, resulted in the establishment in most parts of the country of city and county museums that enjoyed generous, if not total, support from their local authority.

At the same time came renewed efforts at museum building and the expansion of collections by local historical societies, art guilds, and other more specialized groups. Today more than five thousand museums and art galleries exist to provide the residents of all fifty states access to and interpretation of their cultural heritage: the art treasures, crafts, and ways of life of the cultural groups that inhabit, or once inhabited, not only the United States but also many other parts of the world.

Like most states, Washington's pattern of distribution of museums and art galleries is markedly hierarchical. The largest number of such institutions are located in the state's major cities. Seattle, Spokane, and Tacoma are especially well served. Exhibits in all three cities tend to be, more often than not, of statewide, even nationwide, significance, rather than of purely local interest.

Seattle has more than one dozen public museums and art galleries. Among them is the renowned Seattle Art Museum, the recipient of generous gifts since its establishment in 1933, including, for example, the Oriental treasures of the Fuller family and paintings from the Samuel H. Kress Foundation. Also outstanding are the Seattle Art Museum Pavilion and the Pacific Science Center, the 74-acre site developed for the 1962 Seattle World's Fair; the University of Washington's Henry Art Gallery and its Burke Museum of Anthropology; and

the Seattle and King County Historical Society's Museum of History and Industry. Tacoma's principal museum is that of the Washington State Historical Society, while Spokane can boast two major museums: the Eastern Washington State Historical Society Museum and the recently established Museum of Native American Cultures adjacent to Gonzaga University, its sponsoring organization.

Regional museums of more than local importance outside of the state's three major metropolitan cities include the Bellevue Art Museum, the Capitol Museum in Olympia, and the Whatcom Museum of History and Art in Bellingham.

Among the federally supported museums are those at the state's National Historic Sites: the Whitman Mission at Waiilatpu in the Walla Walla valley, the Fort Vancouver fur trading post of the Hudson's Bay Company, English Camp and American Camp on San Juan Island, and the Klondike Gold Rush National Historic Site in Pioneer Square, Seattle. The State of Washington also has established historic sites, some of which include museums. Among the best known are the museums at Dry Falls; Fort Okanogan, near Brewster; Spokane House, west of Spokane; Fort Stevens, at the confluence of the Spokane and Columbia rivers; Fort Simcoe, in the Yakima valley; and Fort Columbia near the mouth of Columbia River.

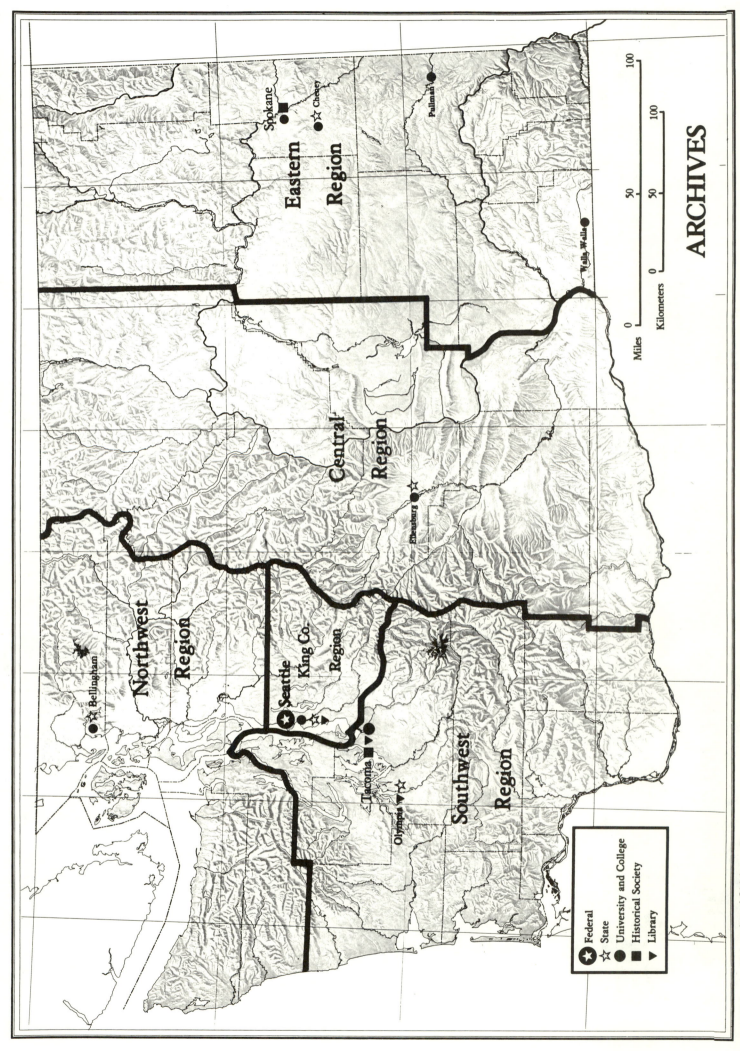

ARCHIVES

Eastern Region

Spokane

Cheney

Pullman

Walla Walla

Central Region

Ellensburg

Northwest Region

Bellingham

Seattle

King Co. Region

Tacoma

Olympia

Southwest Region

Federal
State
University and College
Historical Society
Library

Miles
Kilometers
0   50   100
0   50   100

Archives, both public and private, are found in every state in the union, but in few states, if any, have the links between the public and the private collections been more effectively made than in the state of Washington. Shown on the map are the five existing regional divisions of the state archives, as well as the federal, state, and other major archival centers.

Since the earliest days of the republic the written and other records of government—documents, seals, maps, and more recently, photographs—have been the concern of statesmen, government officials, and interested members of the public, particularly historians and other scholars. It is only in the past half century, however, that effective efforts have been made to organize the vast archival collections that have accumulated in federal, state, and local government offices. Now the National Archives and Records Services (NARS) maintains nine regional offices across the country, each of them serving one or more states. One of the nine is the Seattle Federal Records Center, which houses many of the records of Washington, Oregon, and Alaska generated by federal agencies during the past century and a half.

The first statute regarding archives in the state of Washington was enacted in 1909 when an Archives Commission was set up consisting of the governor, the secretary of state, and the state auditor. The statute did little to control or to organize the growing collections of state documents, and it was not until the 1950s that a professional archival staff was authorized and appointed. In 1957 the current archives and records management act was signed into law, and six years later a

state archives building was constructed and opened in Olympia. In 1981 administration of the archives passed from the Department of General Administration to the Office of the Secretary of State.

During the 1970s the decision was made to decentralize the state archives and to create a number of regional centers. Of the five centers designated since then, three are located on the campuses of the state's regional universities: Northwest Regional Center at Western Washington University, Bellingham; the Central Regional Center at Central Washington University, Ellensburg; and the Eastern Regional Center at Eastern Washington University, Cheney. The Southwest Regional Center is housed at the State Archives in Olympia. The King County Regional Center is in Seattle. Each center except the last serves a number of counties: the Northwest Regional Center serves seven; the Southwest, ten; the Central, nine; and the Eastern, twelve. Developed to ease the growing pressure on facilities in Olympia and to ensure greater efficiency and increased public service, in particular to students and scholars, the regional centers house for the most part the archival and other nonactive records of counties and cities within their boundaries. Archival and other records generated at the state level by state agencies remain the prime responsibility of the State Archives.

The private repositories are much more complex, and their organizations and controls are extremely varied. Some, such as those maintained by companies, hospitals, churches, and other private organizations, are seldom open to the public. Others, such as those maintained by universities and colleges, historical so-

cieties, museums, and libraries, include a wide range of public and private documents, including institutional records (which are, in many cases, public records generated by publicly funded bodies), business records, political records, and private papers, photographs, and miscellaneous materials of all kinds.

The two most important and comprehensive collections of public and private documents are housed at the University of Washington in Seattle and Washington State University in Pullman. Established many decades ago, both have built up impressive archival collections that cover virtually every aspect of the state's life and history. Other university collections are generally more regional in character and less diverse, including those at the three regional universities and three private institutions—Gonzaga University (Spokane), Whitman College (Walla Walla), and the University of Puget Sound (Tacoma). Extensive collections are also housed at two historical societies—the Washington State Historical Society (Tacoma) and the Eastern Washington State Historical Society (Spokane)—and at three of the state's public libraries—the State Library in Olympia and the Seattle and Tacoma public libraries.

The holdings of each of the above-mentioned private repositories, as well as a host of others, are listed in the recently issued volume *Historical Records of Washington State: Records and Papers Held at Repositories*, while those of the state archives and its regional depositories are listed in a companion volume, *Guide to Records in the State Archives and Its Regional Depositories*.

NEWSPAPERS

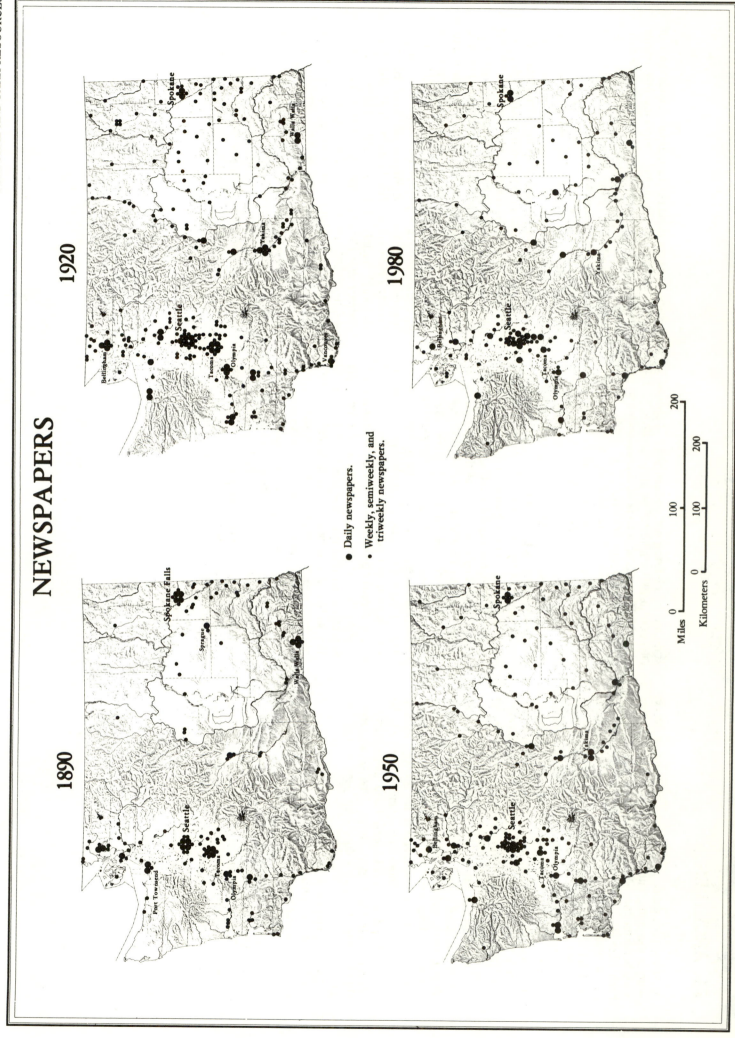

1890

1920

1950

1980

● Daily newspapers.

• Weekly, semiweekly, and
triweekly newspapers.

Miles

Kilometers

0   100   200

0   100   200

Since the earliest days of the republic, newspapers have been a major index of social and political life in both state and community, and in the settlement of the American West during the nineteenth century the itinerant newspaper editor, accompanied by his portable press, was frequently among the first arrivals. Few of the newspapers started then amounted to much—they were usually no more than four small pages in size—and not many of them lasted for any length of time.

The earliest newspaper published north of the Columbia River was the *Columbian*, a weekly, the first issue of which appeared on September 11, 1852. In December 1853, when Washington had attained territorial status, the paper was renamed the *Washington Pioneer*, but it was published as such for only a few weeks, and in January 1854 the name was changed once more to the *Pioneer and Democrat*, publication of which continued until 1861.

A handful of other early newspapers were published in coastal settlements around Puget Sound from Port Townsend on the west, through Olympia and Steilacoom in the extreme south, to Seattle and Whatcom on the east. Among the papers were the *North-West* of Port Townsend (1860–62); the *Port Townsend Register* (1860–61); the long-lived *Washington Standard* of Olympia (1860–1921); the *Puget Sound Courier* (1855–56) and the *Puget Sound Herald* (1858–64), both of Steilacoom; the *Weekly Intelligencer* of Seattle (1867–81), which merged with the *Seattle Weekly Post* in 1881 to become the still extant *Seattle Post-Intelligencer*; and the *Northern Light* of Whatcom, of which only eleven weekly numbers were published in 1858 at the height of the Fraser gold rush.

Away from Puget sound, other early newspapers included the Vancouver *Register*, published from 1865 to 1876, and the Walla Walla *Washington Standard*, which was started in 1861 and after many changes of title ceased publication as the *Evening Statesman* in 1910. Early Tacoma newspapers included the *Tacoma Herald* (1877–80) and the *Tacoma Daily News* (1883–1918). Among those of Spokane were the *Spokane Independent* (1882) and the *Spokane Falls Evening Review*, which was begun in 1884 and, after numerous name changes, became the *Spokesman-Review* in 1894.

Four maps have been drafted to show the distribution of newspapers for the years 1890, 1920, 1950, and 1980. In all four the clustering of newspapers in the central Puget Sound region is the most notable feature.

In 1880 newspapers were published in fewer than half of Washington's counties—which then numbered twenty-five and in only sixteen cities or towns. Ten years later newspapers were being published in all but one of the new state's thirty-four counties—Ferry County alone had no newspaper at that time—and in ninety-two cities or towns. The 28 newspapers of 1880—3 dailies, 1 triweekly, and 24 weeklies—had mushroomed to 181 papers, including 23 dailies, 1 triweekly, 149 weeklies, 1 semimonthly, and 7 monthlies. Seattle alone had 17 newspapers, including 2 foreign-language papers (in Danish and Swedish). Spokane and Tacoma each had 16 newspapers, including 2 foreign-language papers in both. Twenty-four smaller towns had more than one newspaper, including Walla Walla with 7, Port Townsend with 5, and Dayton with 3.

By 1920 the number of newspapers had increased dramatically as various trade papers and other special-interest publications were added. Of the total, 38 were dailies and 249 were weeklies. All thirty-nine of the state's counties had at least one newspaper, and there were 189 different places of publication. Seattle with 64 papers, including 2 in Norwegian or Danish, 3 in Japanese, and 1 in Swedish, was far and away in the lead. Tacoma had 19 papers, including 3 in foreign languages, and Spokane had 16. Thirty-five other cities or towns had 2 or more papers.

During the years between 1920 and 1950 considerable changes occurred in the newspaper industry as mergers increased and as many foreign-language papers folded. In 1950 there were only 213 newspapers being published, 24 of them dailies. Nineteen of the dailies were evening papers, while 186 other papers were weeklies. Seattle's dominance in publishing continued to increase, its total of 85 papers including 3 in foreign languages. Spokane with 15 papers, and Tacoma with 7, were the only other publishing centers of any importance.

By 1980 the number of newspapers in the state had declined still further. A total of 152 newspapers were being issued, 115 of them weeklies and 27 dailies. The latter, however, represented a slight increase over the 1950 figure.

During the past few decades the areas served by major dailies—in particular the *Seattle Post-Intelligencer*, the *Seattle Times*, the *Spokesman-Review* of Spokane, and in southwest Washington, the Portland *Oregonian*—have greatly expanded. Today virtually the whole state is regularly served by one or more of four major regional newspapers. In turn, the remaining newspapers have tended to become increasingly more local in their coverage of news as well as in their appeal. One other phenomenon to be noted is the incursion of national newspaper chains, such as the Gannett Company, into local newspaper publishing.

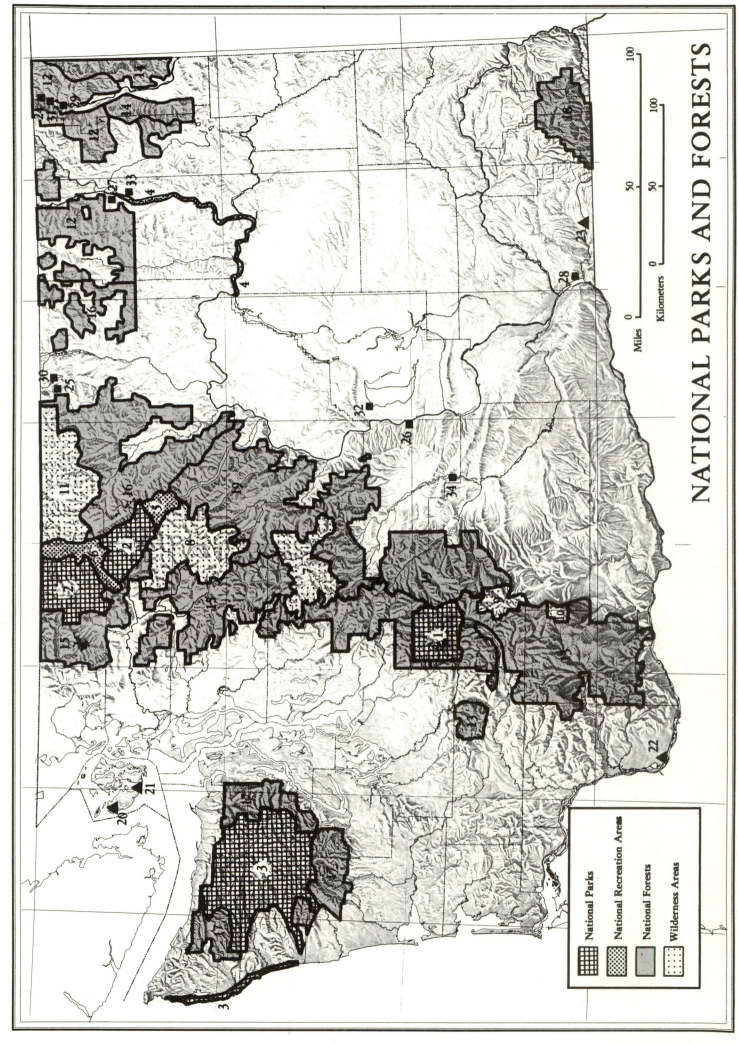

NATIONAL PARKS AND FORESTS

	National Parks		
	National Recreation Areas		
	National Forests		
	Wilderness Areas		

100

100

50   50

0
Kilometers

0
Miles

© 1988 by the University of Oklahoma Press

Today's extensive system of national parks and forests in Washington represents a hard-won compromise between the advocates of quick profit and full-but-short-run resource utilization, on the one hand, and increasingly powerful and well-organized efforts at preservation of natural beauty and significant sites and long-range resource management on the other.

The national parks movement in the United States may be traced to the mid-nineteenth-century advocacy of landscape architects Andrew Jackson Downing and Calvert Vaux. Along with Frederick Law Olmsted, these men argued for extensive parklands as an antidote for the conditions of industrial-urban life. The creation of Yellowstone National Park in 1872 and the subsequent establishment of three more national parks in 1890 may have been, in part, a response to the movement's growing influence, although a clear sense of momentum was not evident until early in this century.

The Antiquities Act of 1906 bestowed upon the president authority to establish national monuments. By 1916 national park lands totalled 4,750,000 acres, including, in Washington, Mount Rainier National Park, founded in March 1899, and Mount Olympus National Monument, established in 1909. The National Park Service had been formed in 1916, but many potential park sites remained outside that agency's control until the 1933 Reorganization Act, which consolidated federal parks under the Park Service.

Pressure for additional national parks increased also in the 1930s. In 1935, Congressman Mon C. Wallgren introduced a bill to create a park of 728,360 acres on the Olympic Peninsula, but despite support from Interior Secretary Harold Ickes, the measure stalled in Congress. In 1937, Representative Wallgren prepared a new park bill—this one setting aside 910,000 acres. On Ickes's advice, President Roosevelt negotiated a measure creating a park of 680,000 acres. The bill passed

in June 1938. Later Presidents Roosevelt and Truman both added acreage to the original park.

By the mid-1960s the National Park Service administered in Washington a total of 1,228,750 acres. In the 1960s the idea of a North Cascades park was revived and publicized by the Cascades Conservation Council. After extensive public hearings in 1967 and 1968, Senator Henry M. Jackson and Congressmen Lloyd Meeds, Thomas Pelley, and Tom Foley succeeded in steering a bill through the Congress. As finally approved, the measure established a North Cascades National Park, the Ross Lake National Recreation Area, and a Lake Chelan National Recreation Area.

National forest lands, which account for a large share of federal holdings in the state—occupy a grand total of 9,052,610 acres. The concept of a national forest was the outcome of a national movement that emerged in the 1860s, aimed at halting wholesale destruction of America's timber resources. In the fall of 1891, President Benjamin Harrison set aside 2,437,120 acres of such forest land in Wyoming and Colorado, and by the end of his presidency 13 million acres of national forest land had been designated. His successor, Grover Cleveland, added thirteen forest reserves totalling 25.5 million acres, including a Washington Forest Reserve (renamed Gifford Pinchot National Forest in 1949). By 1907 twenty-eight percent of Washington's land area was reserved forests, and when word of further planned additions reached the Pacific Northwest, the region's congressional delegation, with potent support from logging and mill interests, succeeded in getting legislation that required the approval of Congress for any new reserves in Washington and five other western states.

Meanwhile, however, the scope of authority and structure of the National Forest Service were being defined and strengthened. Chief Forester Gifford Pinchot fashioned an efficient organization, persuaded Presi-

dent Theodore Roosevelt to reserve another 148 million acres, and launched an eventually successful campaign to persuade the wood products industry that the national forests were an economic boom.

Cooperation between the National Forest Service, the state, and the private sector grew, especially after passage of the Clarke-McNary Act of 1928. The significant expansion of federal conservation programs in the 1930s and 1940s also had a noticeable impact. Forest Service responsibilities grew further with the passage of the Wilderness Act of 1964, which established a wilderness system comprising more than 9 million acres of the national forest.

National Parks, Forests, and Other Federal Reserves

1. Mount Rainier National Park
2. North Cascades National Park
3. Olympic National Park
4. Coulee Dam National Recreation Area
5. Lake Chelan National Recreation Area
6. Ross Lake National Recreation Area
7. Alpine Lakes Wilderness
8. Glacier Peak Wilderness
9. Goat Rocks Wilderness
10. Mount Adams Wilderness
11. Paysaten Wilderness
12. Colville National Forest
13. Gifford Pinchot National Forest
14. Kaniksu National Forest
15. Mount Baker National Forest
16. Okanogan National Forest
17. Olympic National Forest
18. Umatilla National Forest
19. Snoqualmie National Forest
20. English Camp National Historic Site
21. American Camp National Historic Site
22. Fort Vancouver National Historic Site
23. Whitman Mission National Historic Site
24–34. Other federal areas, including national wilderness areas.

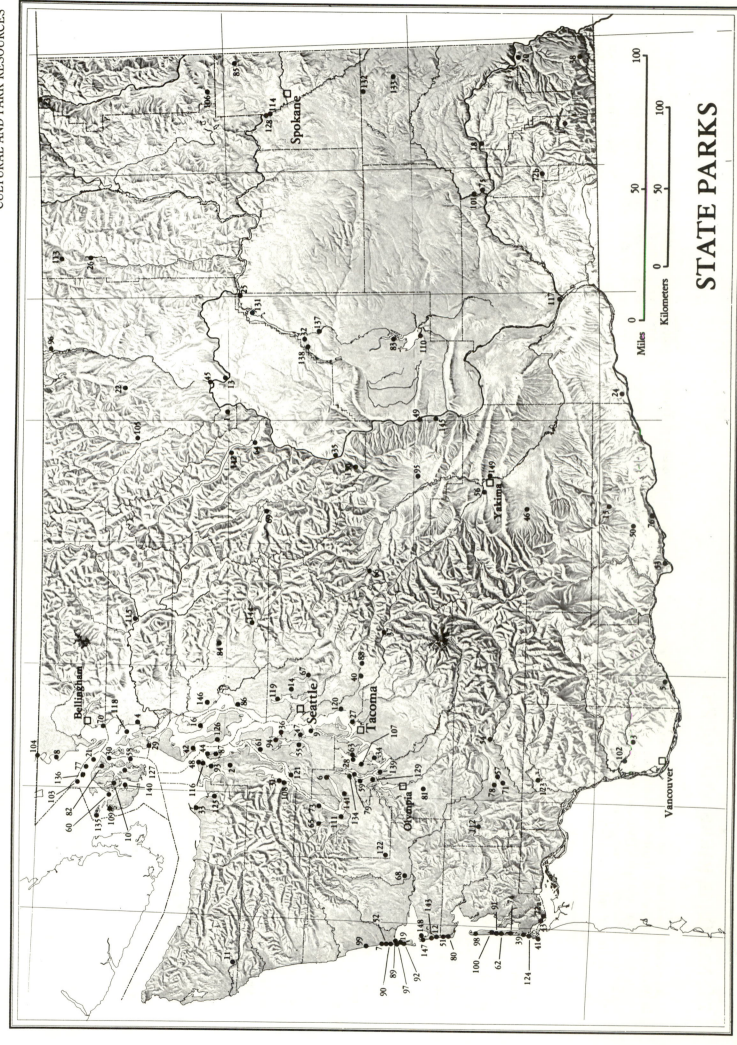

STATE PARKS

Miles

Kilometers

0   50   100

0   50   100

Washington's state park system, like those in most far western states, came late, attendant upon large-scale automobile travel, development of an interstate and state road network, and a rising public interest in preserving parts of the public domain for recreational purposes. The first State Park Board was established in 1912 by Governor Marion Hay, a fervent supporter of state control of natural resources, who wanted to make Washington a model of what could be accomplished without federal interference. As formalized by the legislature in March 1913, the Board of Park Commissioners was an ex officio body composed of the governor, secretary of state, land commissioner, treasurer, auditor, and one lay member appointed by the governor. Neither staff nor budget nor parks existed until, in 1915, executors for the estate of Charles Larrabee of Bellingham donated a twenty-acre site overlooking Chuckanut Bay. Two more gifts of land—five acres of virgin timber near Chehalis in 1917 and 2,900 acres (subsequently increased to 5,000 acres) on Orcas Island—were accepted before, in 1921, pressure from the Seattle-based Natural Parks Association led the legislature to strengthen the system by reconstituting its board as a State Parks Committee made up of the secretary of state, land commissioner, and state treasurer, and empowering it to employ an executive secretary. By 1923 the Parks Committee had authority to hire supervisory and maintenance staff for the parks and a modest budget for which annual appropriations averaged $8,000 until 1933.

Park acquisitions continued to come mainly from private donations of land, although some additions were made by the state land commissioner, who had the power to reserve from sale up to five acres of any tract of state land adjoining or near a public highway. The Parks Committee also could arrange land swaps with private individuals or firms. Outright purchase of park land was limited in the years through 1939 to a mere two hundred acres. Nonetheless, by the close of the 1930s, Washington's park system embraced 45,000 acres.

During the Depression years the state park system benefited from government efforts directed at reducing unemployment through public works projects. State officials tapped the Parks and Parkway Fund for $60,000 to employee laborers in state parks in the spring of 1933, but this was dwarfed by federal efforts. From June 1933 until the close of 1938, Civilian Conservation Corps workers were utilized in developing fourteen state park sites, and eight others were improved or developed by personnel assigned by the Federal Emergency Relief Administration and the Works Progress Administration. These workers constructed park buildings, roads, and trails, carved new camping and picnic grounds from undeveloped park lands, and instituted litter-control programs. Major park developments were undertaken at the Beacon Rock, Deception Pass, Gingko, Lewis and Clark, Millersylvania, Moran, and Riverside state parks.

Meanwhile, pressure grew for an expanded and more efficient park administration. A study group representing the National Park Service and the State Planning Council prepared a report on Washington's park needs at the behest of Governor Clarence Martin in 1938 which recommended a strengthened and enlarged park system—a recommendation that was finally acted on in 1947. A seven-member Parks and Recreation Commission was created. Each commissioner was to be appointed by the governor and confirmed by the Senate and would serve a six-year term. Under the commission and a parks director appointed by it, the system grew rapidly. By 1960 an estimated 7 million visitors utilized 119 sites. Five years later 124 parks served over 13 million persons, and by 1970, 179 sites, which included an additional 20,000 acres, were used by 20 million visitors. An estimated 30 million persons used Washington's parks by 1975. Funds for park acquisition and maintenance, drawn from drivers' license and other fees, revenue from the enforcement of state highway laws, concessions and leases, and legislative appropriations, were bolstered by special bond issues such as Referendum 28, passed in 1972, which made available

$40 million for the planning, purchase, preservation, and improvement of recreational areas and facilities. Still, the pressure of increased numbers of park visitors mounts yearly.

STATE PARKS

1. Alta Lake
2. Anderson Lake
3. Battle Ground Lake
4. Bay View
5. Beacon Rock
6. Belfair
7. Benner Gap
8. Birch Bay
9. Blake Island
10. Blind Island
11. Bogachiel
12. Bonge
13. Bridgeport
14. Bridle Trails
15. Brooks Memorial
16. Camano Island
17. Camp Wooten
18. Central Ferry
19. Chance à la Mer
20. Chief Timothy
21. Clark Island
22. Conconully
23. Crawford
24. Crow Butte
25. Crown Point
26. Curlew Lake
27. Dash Point
28. Cutt's Island
29. Deception Pass
30. Doe Island
31. Dosewallips
32. Dry Falls
33. Dungeness
34. Eagle Island
35. Lincoln Rock
36. Fay Bainbridge
37. Federation Forest
38. Field's Spring
39. First Street
40. Flaming Geiser
41. Fort Canby
42. Fort Casey
43. Fort Columbia
44. Fort Flagler
45. Fort Okanogan
46. Fort Simcoe
47. Fort Ward
48. Fort Worden
49. Gingko
50. Goldendale
51. Grayland Beach
52. Heath Gap Road
53. Horsethief Lake
54. Ike Kinswa
55. Illahee
56. Indian Painted Rocks–Yakima
57. Jackson House
58. James Island
59. Jarrell Cove
60. Jones Island
61. Kitsap Memorial
62. Klipsan
63. Kopachuck
64. Lake Chelan
65. Lake Cushman
66. Lake Easton
67. Lake Sammamish

68. Lake Sylvia
69. Lake Wenatchee
70. Larrabee
71. Lewis and Clark
72. Lewis and Clark Trail
73. Lilliwaup Tidelands
74. Loomis Lake
75. Lyon's Ferry
76. Maryhill
77. Matia Island
78. Matilda Jackson
79. McMicken Island
80. Midway
81. Millersylvania
82. Moran
83. Moses Lake
84. Mount Pilchuck
85. Mt. Spokane
86. Mukilteo
87. Mystery Bay
88. Nolte
89. Ocean City
90. Ocean City
91. Ocean Park
92. Ocean Shores Catala.
93. Old Fort Townsend
94. Old Man House
95. Olmstead Place
96. Osoyoos Lake State Veterans' Memorial Park

97. Oyhut
98. Oysterville
99. Pacific Beach II
100. Pacific Pines
101. Palouse Falls
102. Paradise Point
103. Patos Island
104. Peach Arch
105. Pearrygin Lake
106. Pend Oreille
107. Penrose Point
108. Pleasant Harbor
109. Posey Island
110. Pot Holes
111. Potlatch
112. Rainbow Falls
113. Ranold MacDonald's Grave
114. Riverside
115. Rockport
116. Rothschild House
117. Saca Jawea
118. Saddlebag Island
119. Saint Edward
120. Saltwater
121. Scenic Beach
122. Schafer
123. Sea Quest
124. Seaview
125. Sequim Bay

126. South Whidbey
127. Mulkilteo
128. Spokane House
129. Squaxin Island
130. Squilchuck
131. Steamboat Rock
132. Steptoe Battlefield Memorial
133. Steptoe Butte
134. Stretch Point
135. Stuart Island
136. Sucia Island
137. Summer Falls
138. Sun Lake
139. Tolmie
140. Turn Island
141. Twanoh
142. Twenty-five Mile Creek
143. Twin Harbors
144. Wallace Falls
145. Wanapum
146. Wenberg
147. Westhaven
148. Westport Light
149. Yakima Sportsman

REFERENCES

GENERAL

American Heritage Magazine. *The American Heritage Pictorial Atlas of United States History.* New York: American Heritage Publishing Co., 1966.

Avery, Mary W. *Washington: A History of the Evergreen State.* Seattle: University of Washington Press, 1965.

Freeman, Otis W., and Howard Martin. *The Pacific Northwest: An Overall Appreciation.* 2d ed. New York: John Wiley & Sons, 1954.

Fuller, George W. *A History of the Pacific Northwest.* New York: Alfred A. Knopf, 1949.

Johansen, Dorothy O. *Empire of the Columbia.* 2d rev. ed. New York: Harper, 1967.

Lavender, David. *Land of Giants: The Drive to the Pacific Northwest, 1750–1950.* Lincoln: University of Nebraska Press, 1979.

Meinig, Donald W. *The Great Columbia Plain: A Historical Geography, 1805–1910.* Seattle: University of Washington Press, 1968.

Miles, Charles, and O. B. Sperlin, eds. *Building a State: Washington, 1889–1939.* Tacoma: Washington State Historical Society, 1940.

Office of Financial Management. *Washington State Data Book.* Olympia: State Printer, annually.

Office of Program Planning and Fiscal Management. *State of Washington, 1970 Census Data Book.* Olympia: State Printer, 1972.

Pryor, Nancy, ed. *Washington: A Dissertation Bibliography.* Ann Arbor, Mich.: University Microfilms International, 1980.

Winthur, Oscar O. *The Great Northwest: A History.* New York: Alfred A. Knopf, 1950.

———. *The Old Oregon Country: A History of Frontier Trade, Transportation and Travel.* Lincoln: University of Nebraska Press, 1969.

MAP 1. LOCATION

United States Bureau of the Census. *Statistical Abstract of the United States.* Washington, D.C.: Government Printing Office, annually.

MAP 2. TOPOGRAPHY

Easterbrook, Don J., and David A. Rahm. *Landforms of Washington.* Bellingham: Western Washington State College, 1970.

Atwood, Wallace W. *The Physiographic Provinces of North America.* Boston and New York: Ginn & Co., 1940.

McKee, Bates. *Cascadia: The Geologic Evolution of the Pacific Northwest.* New York: McGraw Hill & Co., 1972.

MAP 3. LANDFORMS

Atwood, Wallace W. *The Physiographic Provinces of North America.* Boston and New York: Ginn & Co., 1940.

Easterbrook, Don J., and David A. Rahm. *Landforms of Washington.* Bellingham: Western Washington State College, 1970.

Fenneman, Nevin M. *Physiography of the Western United States.* New York: McGraw Hill & Co., 1931.

McKee, Bates. *Cascadia: The Geologic Evolution of the Pacific Northwest.* New York: McGraw Hill & Co., 1972.

MAP 4. SURFACE WATERS

Pacific Northwest River Basins Commission. *Water Today and Tomorrow.* Vol. 3, *The States.* Vancouver, Wash., 1979.

Wolcott, Ernest E. *Lakes of Washington.* 2 vols. Olympia: Washington State Department of Ecology, 1973.

MAP 5. MEAN ANNUAL PRECIPITATION

Climatological Handbook Task Force. *Climatological Handbook: Columbia Basin States.* Vol. 2, *Precipitation.* Vancouver, Wash.: Pacific Northwest River Basins Commission, 1969.

National Climatic Center. *Climate of Washington.* Climatology of the United States, no. 60. Asheville, N.C.: National Climatic Center, NOAA, 1978.

MAP 6. CLIMATE

National Climatic Center. *Climate of Washington.* Climatology of the United States, no. 60. Asheville, N.C.: National Climatic Center, NOAA, 1978.

MAP 7. VEGETATION

Franklin, Jerry F., and C. T. Dyrness. *Natural Vegetation of Oregon and Washington.* General Technical Report, PNW, no. 8. Portland, Ore.: Pacific Northwest Forest and Range Experiment Station, United States Forest Service, 1973.

Kuchler, A. W. *Manual to Accompany the Map of Potential Natural Vegetation of the Coterminous United States.* Special Publication, no. 36. New York: American Geographical Society, 1964.

MAP 8. LAND USE

Pacific Northwest River Basins Commission. *Water Today and Tomorrow.* Vol. 3, *The States.* Vancouver, Wash., 1979.

Washington State Planning and Community Affairs Agency. *Land Use Planning in the State of Washington.* Olympia: State Printer, 1976.

MAP 9. INDIAN MIGRATION

Driver, Harold E. *Indians of North America.* 2d ed. Chicago: University of Chicago Press, 1972.

Kirk, Ruth, with Richard D. Daughterty. *Exploring Washington Archeology.* Seattle: University of Washington Press, 1978.

MacGowan, Kenneth, and Joseph A. Hester. *Early Man in the New World.* Garden City, N.Y.: Doubleday & Co., 1962.

MAP 10. ARCHAEOLOGICAL SITES

Grabert, Garland, professor of anthropology, Western Washington University. Personal communication.

Kirk, Ruth, with Richard D. Daughterty. *Exploring Washington Archaeology.* Seattle: University of Washington Press, 1978.

MAP 11. INDIAN TRIBES CIRCA 1790–1820

Anastasio, Angelo. "The Southern Plateau: An Ecological Analysis of Intergroup Relations." *Northwest Anthropological Research Notes* 6 (2) (Fall, 1972): 109–229.

Driver, Harold E. *Indians of North America.* 2d ed. Chicago: University of Chicago Press, 1972.

Ray, Verne F. "Native Villages and Groups of the Columbia Basin." *Pacific Northwest Quarterly* 27 (1936): 99–152.

Spier, Leslie. *Tribal Distributions in Washington.* Menasha: Wis.: George Banta Publishing Company, 1936.

Swanton, John R. *The Indian Tribes of North America.* Bureau of American Ethnology Bulletin 145. Washington, D.C.: Government Printing Office, 1952.

Taylor, Herbert C., Jr., professor of anthropology, Western Washington University. Personal communication.

MAP 12. INDIAN POPULATION, CIRCA 1820

Anastasio, Angelo. "The Southern Plateau: An Ecological Analysis of Intergroup Relations." *Northwest Anthropological Research Notes* 62 (Fall 1972): 109–229.

Driver, Harold E. *Indians of North America.* 2d ed. Chicago: University of Chicago Press, 1969.

Kroeber, Alfred L. *Cultural and Natural Areas of Native North America.* University of California Publications in American Archaeology and Ethnology, no. 37. Berkeley: University of California Press, 1939.

Mooney, James. "The Aboriginal Population of America North of Mexico." *Smithsonian Miscellaneous Collections* 80 (1928), no. 7.

Swan, James G. *The Northwest Coast, or Three Years Residence in Washington Territory.* 1857. Reprint, Seattle: University of Washington Press, 1972.

Taylor, Herbert C., Jr. "The Utilization of Archeological and Ethnohistorical Data in Estimating Aboriginal Populations." *Bulletin of the Texas Archeological Society* 32 (1962): 121–40.

MAP 13. INDIAN LINGUISTIC GROUPS

Driver, Harold E. *Indians of North America.* 2d ed. Chicago: University of Chicago Press, 1969.

Drucker, Philip. *Cultures of the North Pacific Coast.* New York: Thomas Y. Crowell and Harper & Row, 1965.

Taylor, Herbert C., Jr. Personal communication.

Voegelin, C. F., and F. M. Voegelin. *Map of North American Languages.* Washington, D.C.: American Ethnological Society, 1966.

MAP 14. INDIAN RESERVATIONS

Hilliard, Sam B. "Map of Indian Land Cessions," *Annals of the Association of American Geographers* 62 (1972), map supplement no. 16.

Taylor, Herbert C., Jr. Personal communication.

Yonce, Frederick Jay. *Public Land Disposal in Washington.* Ann Arbor, Mich.: University Microfilms, Ph.D. diss., University of Washington, 1969.

MAP 15. EXPLORATION OF THE NORTHWEST COAST OF AMERICA

Baker, J. N. L. *A History of Geographical Discovery and Exploration.* London: George C. Harrap, 1948.

Cook, Warren L. *Flood Tide of Empire: Spain and the Pacific Northwest, 1543–1819.* New Haven: Yale University Press, 1973.

Wagner, Henry. *The Cartography of the Northwest Coast of America to the Year 1800.* Berkeley: University of California Press, 1937.

Whitebrook, Robert B. *Coastal Exploration of Washington.* Palo Alto: Pacific Books, 1959.

MAP 16. THE VANCOUVER EXPEDITION, 1792

Meany, Edmond S. *Vancouver's Discovery of Puget Sound.* Portland, Ore.: Binfords & Mort, 1957.

Morgan, Murray. *Puget's Sound: A Narrative of Early Tacoma and the Southern Sound.* Seattle: University of Washington Press, 1979.

Whitebrook, Robert B. "Vancouver's Anchorages on Puget Sound," *Pacific Northwest Quarterly* 44 (July, 1953): 115–28.

MAP 17. OVERLAND EXPLORATION OF THE OREGON COUNTRY, 1792–1844

Baker, J. N. L. *A History of Geographical Discovery and Exploration.* London: George C. Harrap, 1948.

Brebner, J. B. *The Explorers of North America, 1492–1806.* London: Adam & Charles Black, 1933.

Gilbert, E. W. *The Exploration of Western America, 1800–1850: An Historical Geography.* New York: Cooper Square Publishers, Inc., 1966.

Goetzmann, William H. *Exploration and Empire.* New York: Alfred A. Knopf, 1967.

Thompson, David. *Travels in Western North America, 1784–1812.* Edited by Victor G. Hopwood. Toronto: Macmillan of Canada, 1971.

MAP 18. THE WILKES EXPEDITION

Stanton, William. *The Great United States Exploring Expedition of 1838–1842.* Berkeley: University of California Press, 1975.

Tyler, David B. "The Wilkes Expedition: The First United States Exploring Expedition, 1838–1842." *American Philosophical Society Memoirs* 73 (1968).

Wilkes, Charles. *Narrative of the United States Exploring Expedition During the Years 1838, 1839, 1840, 1841, and 1842.* 5 vols. and atlas vol. Philadelphia: Lea & Blanchard, 1845.

MAP 19. INTERNATIONAL RIVALRIES

Allen, H. C. *Great Britain and the United States: A History of Anglo-American Relations, 1783–1952.* New York: St. Martin's Press, 1955.

Cook, Warren L. *Flood Tide of Empire: Spain and the Pacific Northwest, 1543–1819.* New Haven, Conn.: Yale University Press, 1973.

Gough, Barry M. *Distant Dominion: Britain and the Northwest Coast of North America, 1579–1809.* Vancouver: University of British Columbia Press, 1980.

———. *The Royal Navy and the Northwest Coast of North America, 1810–1914.* Vancouver: University of British Columbia Press, 1971.

Manning, William R. *The Nootka Sound Controversy.* Washington, D.C.: American Historical Association, 1905.

Scholefield, E. O. S., and F. W. Howay. *British Columbia from the Earliest Times to the Present.* 4 vols. Vancouver: S. & J. Clarke, 1914.

MAP 20. THE SAN JUAN ISLANDS INTERNATIONAL BOUNDARY DISPUTE

Bemis, Samuel Flagg. *A Diplomatic History of the United States*. 3d ed. New York: Henry Holt, 1950.

Hutchinson, Bruce. *The Struggle for the Border*. New York: Longmans, Green, 1953.

McCabe, James O. *The San Juan Water Boundary Question*. Toronto, Canada: University of Toronto Press, 1965.

Murray, Keith A. *The Pig War*. Tacoma: Washington State Historical Society, 1968.

MAP EVOLUTION OF TERRITORIAL BOUNDARIES

Baker, Marcus. *Survey of the Northwestern Boundary of the United States, 1857–1861, Under the Direction of the U.S. Geological Survey*. Washington, D.C.: Government Printing Office, 1900.

Deutsch, Herman J. "The Evolution of Territorial and State Boundaries in the Inland Empire of the Pacific Northwest," *Pacific Northwest Quarterly* 51 (July, 1960): 115–31.

Gannett, Henry. *Boundaries of the United States and of the Several States and Territories, with an Outline of the History of All Important Changes of Territory*. Washington, D.C.: Government Printing Office, 1900.

International Boundary Commission. *Joint Report upon the Survey and Demarcation of the Boundary Between the United States and Canada from the Gulf of Georgia to the Northwesternmost Point of Lake of the Woods*. Washington, D.C.: Government Printing Office, 1937.

Lay, George C. *The Boundary Dispute Between Washington and Oregon*. New York, 1913.

Marshall, Robert B. *Retracement of the Boundary Line Between Idaho and Washington. . . .* Washington, D.C.: Government Printing Office, 1911.

Van Zandt, Franklin K. *Boundaries of the United States and the Several States*. Geological Survey Professional Paper 909. Washington, D.C.: Government Printing Office, 1976.

MAP 22. THE EARLY FUR TRADE, 1790–1820

Davidson, Gordon C. *The North West Company*. Berkeley: University of California Press, 1918.

Franchère, Gabriel. *Adventure at Astoria, 1810–1814*. Norman: University of Oklahoma Press, 1967.

Lavender, David. *The Fist in the Wilderness*. Albuquerque: University of New Mexico Press, 1979.

Meinig, Donald W. *The Great Columbia Plain: A Historical Geography, 1805–1910*. Seattle: University of Washington Press, 1968.

Ross, Alexander. *Adventures of the First Settlers on the Oregon or Columbia River*. New York: Citadel Press, 1969.

Wallace, W. Stewart, ed. *Documents Relating to the North West Company*. Toronto, Canada: Champlain Society, 1934.

MAP 23. THE LATER FUR TRADE, 1821–1850

Galbraith, John S. *The Hudson's Bay Company as an Imperial Factor, 1821–1869*. Toronto, Canada: University of Toronto Press, 1957.

Rich, E. E. *The Hudson's Bay Company, 1670–1870*. Vol. 2, *1763–1870*. London: Hudson's Bay Record Society, 1959.

———, ed. *Letters of John McLoughlin*. 3 vols. London: Hudson's Bay Record Society, 1943.

MAP 24. FORT VANCOUVER, 1846.

Hussey, John A. *The History of Fort Vancouver*. Portland, Ore.: Abbott, Kerns & Bell, 1957.

Rich, E. E. *Letters of John McLoughlin*. 3 vols. London: Hudson's Bay Record Society, 1943.

MAP PROTESTANT MISSIONS, 1834–1847

Drury, Clifford. *Marcus and Narcissa Whitman and the Opening of Old Oregon*. 2 vols. Glendale, Calif.: Arthur H. Clark, 1973.

———. *Nine Years Among the Spokanes: The Diary of Elkanah Walker, 1838–1848*. Glendale, Calif.: Arthur H. Clark, 1976.

Howell, Erle. *Methodism in the Northwest*. Nashville: Pantheon Press, 1966.

Loewenberg, Robert J. *Equality on the Oregon Frontier: Jason Lee and the Methodist Mission, 1834–43*. Seattle: University of Washington Press, 1976.

MAP 26. CATHOLIC MISSIONS, 1838–1850

Rauffer, Maria Ilma. *Black Robes and Indians on the Last Frontier*. Milwaukee, Wis.: Bruce Publishing Company, 1966.

Schoenberg, Wilfred P. *A Chronicle of Catholic History of the Pacific Northwest, 1743–1960*. Spokane, Wash.: Gonzaga Preparatory School, 1962.

———. *Paths to the Northwest: A Jesuit History of the Oregon Province*. Chicago: Loyola Press, 1983.

MAP 27. FORTS, CAMPS AND MILITARY ROADS, 1849–1882

Chance, David H. *Sentinal of Silence: A Brief History of Fort Spokane*. Coulee Dam, Wash.: Pacific Northwest National Parks Association, 1981.

Jackson, W. Turrentine. *Wagon Roads West*. Berkeley: University of California Press, 1952.

Whiting, Joseph S. *Forts of the State of Washington*. Seattle: privately printed, 1951.

Winthur, Oscar O. *The Transportation Frontier: Trans-Mississippi West, 1865–1890*. New York: Holt, Rinehart & Winston, 1964.

———. *The Old Oregon Country: A History of Frontier Trade, Transportation, and Travel*. Lincoln: University of Nebraska Press, 1970.

Goetzmann, William H. *Army Exploration in the American West, 1803–1863*. New Haven: Yale University Press, 1959.

MAP 28. INDIAN WARS

Beal, Merrill D. *"I Will Fight No More Forever": Chief*

Joseph and the Nez Perce War. Seattle: University of Washington Press, 1963.

Fuller, George W. *A History of the Pacific Northwest.* New York: Alfred A. Knopf, 1949.

Haines, Francis. *The Nez Percés: Tribesmen of the Columbia Plateau.* Norman: University of Oklahoma Press, 1955.

Ruby, Robert H., and John A. Brown. *The Cayuse Indians: Imperial Tribesmen of Old Oregon.* Norman: University of Oklahoma Press, 1972.

Utley, Robert M., and Wilcomb E. Washburn. *The American Heritage History of the Indian Wars.* New York: American Heritage Publishing Company, 1977.

MAP 29. PIONEER TRAILS, 1840–1860

Clackamas County History Society and Wasco County Historical Society. *The Barlow Road.* Portland, Ore.: J. J. Hollingsworth Company, 1979.

Dicken, Samuel N. *Pioneer Trails of the Oregon Coast.* Portland: Oregon Historical Society, 1972.

Haines, Francis D., and Marjorie O'Harra. *The Applegate Trail: Southern Emigrant Route, 1846.* Ashland: Southern Oregon State College, 1976.

Lavender, David. *Westward Vision: The Story of the Oregon Trail.* New York: McGraw-Hill, 1963.

Winther, Oscar O. "Inland Transportation and Communications in Washington, 1844–1859," *Pacific Northwest Quarterly* 30 (1939): 371–77.

———. *The Old Oregon Country: A History of Frontier Trade, Transportation and Travel.* Lincoln: University of Nebraska Press, 1969.

MAP 30. DONATION LAND CLAIMS

Johansen, Dorothy O., and Charles M. Gates. *Empire of the Columbia.* New York: Harper and Row, 1957.

Seattle Genealogical Society. *Washington Territory Donation Land Claims.* Seattle: Seattle Genealogical Society, 1980.

Shackleford, Charlotte. "Donation Land Claims." In Charles Miles and O. B. Sperlin, eds., *Building a State, 1889–1939,* pp. 403–52. Tacoma: Washington State Historical Society, 1940.

Yonce, Frederick Jay. *Public Land Disposal in Washington.* Ph.D. diss., University of Washington, 1969. Ann Arbor, Mich.: University Microfilms.

MAP 31. HOMESTEAD CLAIMS

Hibbard, Benjamin H. *A History of the Public Land Policies.* Madison: University of Wisconsin Press, 1965.

Robbins, Roy M. *Our Landed Heritage: The Public Domain, 1776–1936.* Lincoln: University of Nebraska Press, 1962.

Yonce, Frederick Jay. *Public Land Disposal in Washington.* Ph.D. diss., University of Washington, 1969. Ann Arbor, Mich.: University Microfilms.

MAP 32. TOWNSHIP/RANGE SYSTEM

Thrower, Norman J. W. *Original Survey and Land Subdivision: A Comparative Study of the Form and Effect of Contrasting Cadastral Surveys.* Monograph Series, no. 4. Chicago: Rand McNally, for the Association of American Geographers, 1966.

Yonce, Fred. "The Public Land Surveys in Washington," *Pacific Northwest Quarterly* 63 (1972): 129–41.

MAP 33. THE PIONEER ECONOMY TO 1880

Coman, Edwin T., and Helen M. Gibbs. *Time, Tide and Timber: A Century of Pope and Talbot.* Stanford, Calif.: Stanford University Press, 1949.

Cox, Thomas R. *Mills and Markets: A History of the Pacific Coast Lumber Industry to 1900.* Seattle: University of Washington Press, 1974.

Galbraith, John S. *The Hudson's Bay Company as an Imperial Factor.* Toronto, Canada: University of Toronto Press, 1957.

Meinig, Donald W. *The Great Columbia Plain: A Historical Geography, 1805–1910.* Seattle: University of Washington Press, 1968.

Oliphant, J. Orin. *On the Cattle Ranges of the Oregon Country.* Seattle: University of Washington Press, 1968.

Rich, Edwin E. *The Hudson's Bay Company, 1670–1870.* 2 vols. Vol. 2, *1763–1870.* London: Hudson's Bay Company Records Society, 1959.

MAP 34. POPULATION DISTRIBUTION AND DENSITY

1970 Census of Population. Vol. 1, *Characteristics of the Population,* chap. A, "Number of Inhabitants," pt. 49, Washington—PC70-1-A49. Washington, D.C.: Bureau of the Census, 1982.

1980 Census of Population. Vol. 1, *Characteristics of the Population,* chap. A, "Number of Inhabitants," pt. 49, Washington—PC80-1-A49. Washington, D.C.: Bureau of the Census, 1982.

MAP 35. POPULATION CHANGE

Morrill, Richard L. *Population Change in Washington: Redistribution and Forecasts.* Seattle: University of Washington, Department of Geography, 1982.

Washington State Office of Financial Management. *1981 Population Trends for Washington State*

———. *1982 Population Trends for Washington State*

———. *1983 Population Trends for Washington State*

MAP 36. URBAN AND INCORPORATED POPULATION

Schmid, Calvin, and Stanton E. Schmid. *Growth of Cities and Towns, State of Washington.* Olympia: Washington State Planning and Community Affairs Agency, 1969.

MAP 37. MIGRATION, 1970–1980

Morrill, Richard L. *Population Change in Washington: Redistribution and Forecasts.* Seattle: University of Washington, Department of Geography, 1982.

MAP 38. POPULATION GROUPS, 1980

1980 Census of Population. Vol. 1, *Characteristics of the Population,* chap. B, "General Population Characteristics," pt. 49, Washington—PC80-1-B49. Washington, D.C.: Bureau of the Census, 1982.

Schmid, Calvin F., Charles E. Nobbe, and Arlene E. Mitchell. *Non-White Races, State of Washington.* Olympia: Washington State Planning and Community Affairs Agency, 1968.

MAPS 39. AND 40. EVOLUTION OF COUNTIES, 1850–1860 AND 1870–1900

Abbott, Newton Carl, and Fred E. Carver. *The Evolution of Washington Counties.* Yakima, Wash.: Yakima Valley Genealogical Society of Klickitat County Historical Society, 1979.

MAP 41. COUNTIES OF WASHINGTON

Washington State Office of Financial Management.

Washington State Data Book. Olympia: State Printer, annually.

MAP 42. LEGISLATIVE DISTRICTS
Washington State Office of Secretary of State. "Maps of Current Legislature Districts." Olympia: Office of Secretary of State, 1981.

MAP 43. PRESIDENTIAL ELECTIONS
Murray, Keith A. "Issues and Personalities of Pacific Northwest Politics, 1889–1950." *Pacific Northwest Quarterly* 41 (1950): 213–33.
Peterson, Svend. *A Statistical History of the American Presidential Elections.* New York: Ungar Press, 1963.

MAPS 44. AND 45. NATIVE AMERICAN PLACE-NAMES AND SPANISH PLACE-NAMES
Cook, Warren L. *Flood Tide of Empire: Spain and the Pacific Northwest.* New Haven, Conn.: Yale University Press, 1973.
Hitchman, Robert. *Place Names of Washington.* Tacoma: Washington State Historical Society, 1985.
Meany, Edmond S. *Indian Place Names of Washington.* Seattle: Hyatt-Fowells School, 1908.
Meany, Edmond S. *The Origin of Washington's Geographic Names.* 1923. Reprint, Seattle: University of Washington Press, 1971.
Phillips, James W. *Washington State Place-names.* Seattle: University of Washington Press, 1971.
Stewart, George R. *Names on the Land.* New York: Oxford University Press, 1985.

MAP 46. RAILROAD LAND GRANTS
United States Bureau of Land Management, Oregon State Office, Portland. "Master Title Plats and Historical Indices."
Map Showing Land Grants of the Northern Pacific Railroad Company. Buffalo, N.Y.: Matthews, Northrup & Co., 1888.

Map of Central and Eastern Washington and Northern Idaho. St. Paul: Northern Pacific Railroad Company, n.d.

MAP 47. RAILROADS: 1890
Cheever, Bruce Bissell. *The Development of Railroads in the State of Washington, 1860–1948.* Bellingham: Western Washington College of Education, 1949.
Poor's Manual of Railroads, 1890.
Turbeville, Daniel E. *The Electric Railway Era in Northwest Washington, 1890–1930.* Occasional paper 12. Bellingham: Western Washington University, Center for Pacific Northwest Studies, 1978.

MAP 48. RAILROADS: 1980
Burlington Northern Railroad Company. Statistical information, 1979.
1979 Commercial Atlas and Marketing Guide. 110th ed. Chicago: Rand, McNally, 1979.
Transportation Map of Washington. Washington, D.C.: U.S. Geological Survey, for the Office of Policy and Program Development, Federal Railroad Administration, United States Department of Transportation, 1975.
Union Pacific Railroad Company. Statistical information, 1979.

MAP 49. INTERSTATE AND STATE HIGHWAYS
Scott, James W., ed. *Transportation in the Puget Sound Region: Past, Present and Future.* Occasional Paper 6. Bellingham: Western Washington University, Center for Northwest Studies, 1977.

MAP 50. EVOLUTION OF WASHINGTON PORTS
Hitchman, James H. *Waterborne Commerce of British Columbia and Washington, 1850–1970.* Occasional Paper 7. Bellingham: Western Washington University, Center for Pacific Northwest Studies, 1976.
Newell, Gordon R., ed. *The H. W. McCurdy Marine History of the Pacific Northwest.* Seattle: Superior Publishing Company, 1965.

Wright, E. W., ed. *Lewis and Dryden's Marine History of the Pacific Northwest.* Portland, Ore.: Lewis & Dryden Printing Company, 1895.

MAP 51. FERRIES
Grant, Patrick S. "The Evolution of Ferry Service in the San Juan Islands: An Historical Geography." M.S. thesis, Western Washington University, 1981.
Newell, Gordon R. *Ships of the Inland Sea: The Story of the Puget Sound Steamboats.* Portland, Ore.: Binfords & Mort, 1960.

MAP 52. AIRPORTS AND COMMUTER AIRLINES
Washington State Department of Transportation. *Washington State Airport System Plan.* Pt. 3, *Implementation Program.* Olympia: Washington State Department of Transportation, 1980.

MAP 53. OIL AND GAS PIPELINES
Washington Utilities and Transportation Commission. *Gas Service Areas Map.* Olympia, Wash.: 1978.

MAP 54. FARMS AND FARM ACREAGE
Brandt, Theodore R. "Agricultural Land Retention in the Puget Sound Region, Washington," M.S. thesis, Western Washington University, 1982.
State of Washington Crop and Livestock Reporting Service. *Washington Agricultural Statistics.* Olympia: Washington State Department of Agriculture and United States Department of Agriculture, annual.

MAP 55. MAJOR AGRICULTURAL PRODUCTS
State of Washington Crop and Livestock Reporting Service. *Washington Agricultural Statistics.* Olympia: Washington State Department of Agriculture and United States Department of Agriculture, annual.
Atlas of Washington Agriculture. Olympia: Washington State Department of Agriculture and United States Department of Agriculture, 1963.

xvi. REFERENCES

MAP 56. SPECIALTY CROPS

State of Washington Crop and Livestock Reporting Service. *Washington Agricultural Statistics.* Olympia: Washington State Department of Agriculture and United States Department of Agriculture, annual.

Washington State Department of Agriculture. *Atlas of Washington Agriculture.* Olympia: 1963.

MAP 57. COMMERCIAL FORESTS AND FOREST PRODUCTS

Cox, Thomas R. *Mills and Markets: A History of the Pacific Coast Lumber Industry to 1900.* Seattle: University of Washington Press, 1974.

Larsen, David N., Robert K. Wadsworth. *Washington Forest Productivity Study.* Phase 3, pt. 2, *Timber Harvest Projections for the 1980s and Future Decade in the State of Washington.* Olympia: Washington State Department of Natural Resources, for the Pacific Northwest Regional Commission, 1982.

Washington State Department of Natural Resources, Division of Technical Services. *Washington Mill Survey: Wood Consumption and Mill Characteristics.* Olympia: Washington State Department of Natural Resources, biannually.

————, Operations Research Section. *Washington Forest Productivity Study.* Olympia: Washington State Department of Natural Resources, for the Pacific Northwest Regional Commission, 1975.

MAP 58. FOREST PRODUCTS

Cox, Thomas R. *Mills and Markets: A History of the Pacific Coast Lumber Industry to 1900.* Seattle: University of Washington Press, 1974.

Washington State Department of Natural Resources, Division of Technical Services. *Washington Mill Survey: Wood Consumption and Mill Characteristics.* Olympia: Washington State Department of Natural Resources, biannually.

MAP 59. THE FISHING INDUSTRY

Andrews, Ralph W., and A. K. Andrews. *Fish and Ships.* Seattle: Superior, 1959.

Carstensen, Vernon. "The Fisherman's Frontier on the Pacific Coast: The Rise of the Salmon Canning Indus-

try." In John G. Clark, ed., *The Frontier Challenge: Responses to the Trans-Mississippi West.* Lawrence: University of Kansas Press, 1971.

Cobb, John N. *The Salmon Fisheries of the Pacific Coast.* Washington, D.C.: United States Bureau of Fisheries, 1911. (Later editions of 1917, 1921, and 1930 published under the title *Pacific Salmon Fisheries.*)

————. "History of Fisheries in the State of Washington." *Washington Historical Quarterly* 20 (1929): 3–11.

MAP 60. MANUFACTURING INDUSTRIES

Freeman, Otis W., and Howard Martin. *The Pacific Northwest: An Overall Appreciation.* 2d ed. New York: John Wiley, 1954.

Lewis, Howard T., and Stephen I. Miller. *The Economic Resources of the Pacific Northwest.* Seattle: Lowman & Hanford, 1923.

Seattle-First National Bank Economic Research Department. *Quarterly Summary of Pacific Northwest Industries.*

MAP 61. MINERAL RESOURCES

Melder, F. E. "History of the Discoveries and Physical Development of the Coal Industry in the State of Washington." *Pacific Northwest Quarterly* 29 (1938): 151–65.

Moen, Wayne S. *Mineral Resource Maps of Washington.* Olympia: Washington State Department of Natural Resources, Division of Geology and Earth Resources, 1978.

Pridgeon, Rodney. "The Coal Mining Industry of Washington: A Study in Historical and Economic Geography." M.A. thesis, Department of Geography, Western Washington University, 1978.

MAP 62. ENERGY PRODUCTION, 1980

Elrick and Lavidge, Inc. *Pacific Northwest Residential Energy Survey: Report for Bonneville Power Administration and Pacific Northwest Utilities Conference Committee.* Portland, Ore.: Bonneville Power Administration, 1980.

Power Planning Committee. *Review of Power Planning*

in the Pacific Northwest. Vancouver, Wash.: Pacific Northwest River Basins Commission, annually.

Holbrook, Stewart. *The Columbia.* New York: Holt, Rinehart & Winston, 1956.

Krutilla, John V. *The Columbia River Treaty: The Economics of an International River Basin Development.* Baltimore, Md.: Johns Hopkins University Press, for Resources for the Future, 1967.

Morgan, Murray. *The Columbia: Powerhouse of the West.* Seattle: Superior, 1940.

United States Water and Power Resources Service. *1979 Annual Report.* Washington, D.C.: United States Department of the Interior, 1980.

Washington State University Environmental Research Center. *Washington State: Energy Use Profile, 1960–1978.* Olympia: Washington State Energy Office, 1979.

MAP 63. IRRIGATION

Power Planning Committee. *Seasonality of River Use: Columbia and Lower Snake Rivers.* Vancouver, Wash.: Pacific Northwest River Basins Commission, 1975.

Pacific Northwest River Basins Commission. *Water Today and Tomorrow: A Pacific Northwest Regional Program for Water and Related Resources.* 4 vols. Vancouver, Wash.: Pacific Northwest River Basins Commission, 1979–80.

EROS Data Center. *The Columbia River and Tributaries Irrigation Withdrawals Analysis Project Executive Summary.* Sioux Falls, S.D.: Earth Resources Observation Systems Data Center, 1981.

MAP 64. URBANIZATION OF MAJOR WASHINGTON CITIES

City of Spokane, City Plan Commission. *Map of Annexations, Spokane, Washington.* 1980.

Planning Department, City of Seattle. Various maps, lists of annexations, etc.

Planning Department, City of Tacoma. Various maps.

Planning Department, City of Yakima. Various Maps.

Reps, John W. *Cities of the American West: A History of Frontier Urban Planning.* Princeton, N.J.: Princeton University Press, 1979.

Schmid, Calvin F., and Stanton E. Schmid. *Growth of Cities and Towns, State of Washington*. Olympia: Washington State Planning and Community Affairs Agency, 1969.

MAP 65. STANDARD METROPOLITAN STATISTICAL AREAS, 1981

1980 Census of Population. Vol. 1, *Characteristics of the Population*, chap. A, "Number of Inhabitants," pt. 49, Washington—PC80-1-A49. Washington, D.C.: Bureau of the Census, 1982.

MAP 66. THE PUGET SOUND REGION: URBAN AND SUBURBAN AREAS

Bish, Robert L. *Governing Puget Sound*. Seattle: University of Washington Press, for the Washington Sea Grant Program, 1982.

1980 Census of Population. Vol. 1, *Characteristics of the Population*, chap. A, "Number of Inhabitants," pt. 49, Washington—PC80-1-A49. Washington, D.C.: Bureau of the Census, 1982.

MAPS

67–69. PANORAMIC MAPS

Hibbert, John R. *Panoramic Maps of Anglo-American Cities: A Checklist of Maps in the Collections of the Library of Congress: Geography and Map Division*. Washington, D.C.: Library of Congress, 1974.

MAP 70. UNIVERSITIES AND COLLEGES

Washington State Office of Financial Management. *Washington State Data Book*. Olympia: State Printer, annually.

Watts, Susan, ed. *The College Handbook*. 16th ed. New York: College Entrance Examination Board, 1977.

MAP 71. COMMUNITY COLLEGES

Washington State Office of Financial Management. *Washington State Data Book*. Olympia: State Printer, annually.

Watts, Susan, ed. *The College Handbook*. 16th ed. New York: College Entrance Examination Board, 1977.

MAP 72. LIBRARIES

American Library Directory. 34th ed. New York and London: R. R. Bowker, 1979.

MAP 73. MUSEUMS AND ART GALLERIES

Alexander, Edward P. *Museums in Motion*. Nashville, Tenn.: American Association for State and Local History, 1979.

Washington State Library. *Museums of the State of Washington*. Olympia: State Library, 1971.

MAP 74. ARCHIVES

National Historical Publications and Records Commission. *Directory of Archives and Manuscript Reposito-*

ries. Washington, D.C.: National Archives and Record Service, 1978.

Washington State Historical Records Advisory Board. *Historical Records of Washington State: Records and Papers Held in Repositories*. 2 vols. Olympia, 1981.

MAP 75. NEWSPAPERS

Ayer's Directory of Publications. Philadelphia: Ayer Press, 1890, 1920, 1950, 1980.

Hamilton, Kathryn S. *Newspapers on Microfilm in the Washington State Library*. Olympia: Washington State Library, 1980.

MAP 76. NATIONAL PARKS AND NATIONAL FORESTS

Butcher, Devereux. *Exploring Our National Parks and Monuments*. 7th ed. Boston: Gambit Press, 1976.

Kirk, Ruth. *Washington State: National Parks, Historic Sites, Recreation Areas and National Landmarks*. Seattle: University of Washington Press, 1974.

MAP 77. STATE PARKS

Washington State Parks and Recreation Commission. *Washington State Outdoor Recreation Guide*. Olympia: State Printer, annually.

INDEX